The Proletarian Moment

JAMES F.
MURPHY

The
Proletarian
Moment

The Controversy
over Leftism in
Literature

UNIVERSITY OF ILLINOIS PRESS
Urbana & Chicago

Library of Congress Cataloging-in-Publication Data

Murphy, James, 1945-
    The proletarian moment : the controversy over leftism in
literature / James Murphy.
        p. cm.
    Includes bibliographical references and index.
    ISBN 0-252-01788-9 (alk. paper)
    1. American literature—20th century—History and criticism—
Theory, etc. 2. Communism and literature—United States—
History—20th century. 3. Politics and literature—United States—
History—20th century. 4. Working class writings, American—
History and criticism. 5. Right and left (Political science) in
literature. 6. Criticism—United States—History—20th century.
7. United States—Intellectual life—20th century.
8. Depressions—1929—United States. 9. Marxist criticism—United
States. 10. Proletariat in literature. I. Title.
PS288.C6M87 1991
810.9'358—dc20   90-47966
                                                       CIP

Contents

Abbreviations

ARTEF	Arbeter Theater Ferband
BPRS	Bund proletarisch-revolutionärer Schriftsteller
CPUSA	Communist Party of the United States of America
FOSP	Federation of Organizations of Soviet Writers
IBRL	International Bureau of Revolutionary Literature
IURT	International Union of Revolutionary Theaters
IURW	International Union of Revolutionary Writers
IWDU	International Workers' Dramatic Union
IWW	International Workers of the World
KPD	Kommunistische Partei Deutschlands
LEF	Left Front of Art
NCDPP	National Committee for the Defense of Political Prisoners
RAPP	Russian Association of Proletarian Writers
VAPP	All-Russian Association of Proletarian Writers

Foreword

WITH THE COLLAPSE of Eastern Europe's communist governments and with the Soviet Union itself undergoing a period of radical change, it may seem quixotic now to recover the proletarian moment of American culture. What more proof do we need, some will argue, that the revolutionary art and criticism of the 1920s and 1930s read the imperatives of history incorrectly? Of course the resurgence of Marxist criticism in the 1970s and 1980s depended in part on drawing a distinction between Marxist cultural analysis and the development of existing communist governments. As a result, many in the humanities and social sciences have learned again what politically aware people already knew decades ago: that Marxism is especially adept at foregrounding and explaining social injustice and conflict, and at understanding the social, political, and economic roots and effects of all forms of cultural production. Long before communism began to disintegrate in Eastern Europe, many on the left realized it was sufficiently revolutionary to pressure Western societies into living up to their own democratic principles.

The distinction between Marxist cultural theory and efforts to promote radical political change is more difficult to maintain in the period James Murphy discusses, for many writers and artists thought nothing less than the overthrow of capitalism could relieve the misery of the Great Depression. This revolutionary fervor, plus the distortions of subsequent historiography, especially during the Cold War fifties have led many of us to believe that the criticism and literature of the 1920s and 1930s was much more uniform than in fact it was. People have consequently assumed that there is no need to read widely in this period, that it has nothing to teach us. What we have lost as a result is not only our memory of the uniquely American inflection of a revolutionary moment—from its radical readings of the meaning of democracy to its adaptations of modernist style to its synthesis of a long tradition of cultural critique—but also a literature powerfully engaged with issues like the dangers of the workplace, the dynamics of race relations, and the experience of poverty, all issues no less relevant now than they were sixty years ago. We have lost as well an extensive body of informed debate on the relations between politics and literature.

It is on that second group of texts—the critical debates of the 1920s and 1930s—that Murphy concentrates in his book. The myth that has dominated American historiography for fifty years is that subtle analysis of the relations between art and politics only began with the editors of the original *Partisan Review*'s criticism of "leftism" between 1934 and 1936, before the magazine's editors left the Communist party for an "independent," "anti-Stalinist" Marxism, and finally abandoned Marxism entirely to become fervid anticommunists. The Party's contributions to the debates of the period, so we have been repeatedly told, were simplistic, unreflective, and uniform. Yet the Party in America actually often lacked a clear policy in regard to art and literature. For a time, the Party expected writers to show a definite revolutionary commitment but left open the decision about what form and style that commitment should take. This left considerable room for differences about the aims, methods, and intended audiences for a revolutionary art.

By taking the trouble to read *The Daily Worker, New Masses, International Literature,* and other now largely ignored publications, Murphy demonstrates that the positions taken up both in Party publications and in journals aligned with the Communist party were in fact quite varied and sometimes quite sophisticated. There were stirring and sometimes crude polemics; there were detailed efforts at historical recovery; and there were careful reflections on the paradoxes of an art simultaneously private and collective. The arguments of those who broke with the Party thus added little to the wide range of positions already articulated in Party publications both here and abroad. Available here, to those who choose to seek it out, is a rich cultural resource: a series of impassioned essays on politics and culture written by people who believed these relations mattered.

Murphy's book not only corrects the false and self-interested narratives of some of those who broke with the Party—narratives that later scholarship has too often taken at face value—but also gives clear and accurate summaries of the international discussions about art and politics that dominated a large part of the critical writing of those decades. Much of this will be unfamiliar to contemporary readers. As a result, we learn that the supposedly "vulgar" Marxism of the 1930s was often not so vulgar at all. Indeed, it often lays out arguments we have since had to reinvent because of widespread ignorance about the history and achievements of the American left. Perhaps, now that the Cold War has receded into the background, we can begin to recover this suppressed part of our cultural heritage. The result will be not only a considerably altered image of American culture but also a much fuller understanding of the sociology of art. James Murphy's book should be an integral part of that process.

Cary Nelson

Introduction

WITH THE COLLAPSE of the stock market in 1929 and the subsequent spread of unemployment, homelessness, and hunger throughout the United States in the early thirties, large numbers of writers and other intellectuals moved toward the left and sought radical solutions to the country's social and economic problems.[1] Some of them joined worker-writers in creating a school of fiction, poetry, and drama, which, in different ways and with varying degrees of explicitness, called for the abolition of capitalism and the creation of a new socialist order under the revolutionary leadership of the Communist party. While social conditions contributed to the growth of this literature, it was not, however, simply a spontaneous response to the Depression. In fact, most of the writers involved were associated in one way or another with a conscious movement to create "proletarian literature" that was international in scope and had its own organizations and periodicals, as well as a history extending into the preceding decade and beyond.

Among the most prominent organs of the movement in the United States were the magazines *New Masses* and the original *Partisan Review*. In addition to featuring short fiction, poetry, and reportage, both publications engaged in literary criticism and formulated aesthetic principles for writers and critics. In the mid-thirties, in the two magazines and in the American proletarian literature movement as a whole, the term *leftism* was employed as an epithet characterizing certain attitudes and practices that were considered unacceptable. Among these was sectarianism in relations with non-Communist writers, and the view that proletarian writers had nothing to learn from bourgeois writers of the past or present. In addition, leftism referred to the disregard for aesthetic values, the limitation of literary criticism to sociological analysis, and the demand that proletarian literature be narrowly agitational in character, addressing events of the moment. In criticism of individual works the term was directed against tendentiousness, which included the stereotyped portrayal of workers and capitalists as heroes and villains, the insertion of abstract propaganda into fiction, poetry, and drama, and the general distortion or coloring of reality for political ends.

Since the 1930s a particular interpretation of the discussion over these attitudes and practices has become firmly established among American literary historians. In numerous books and articles the criticism of leftism is described as a dissident position that first emerged in the original *Partisan Review,* and was directed against views that dominated the proletarian literature movement and were propagated by the *New Masses.* The first formulations of this interpretation can be found in articles written by members of the original *Partisan Review*'s staff—including Philip Rahv, William Phillips, Alan Calmer, and James T. Farrell—after the magazine had ceased publication in 1936, and they had severed their connections with the Communist party. As they moved toward Trotskyism in the last years of the decade, their criticism of leftism and the cultural politics of the Communist party were incorporated into a general attack on Stalinism.

In 1942 Phillips and Rahv's interpretation of the discussion over leftism reappeared in *On Native Grounds,* by Alfred Kazin, and was in evidence five years later in Leo Gurko's *The Angry Decade.* By the time the Cold War reached its peak in the mid-fifties, it had become an integral part of the general ideological assault on communism and the "red decade." The tone that marked much of the writing on the subject during this period can be found in Murray Kempton's 1955 book, *Part of Our Time.* Though far better informed and less polemical, Walter Rideout presented basically the same interpretation as Kempton a year later in *The Radical Novel in the United States.* During the McCarthy period and afterward, the *Partisan Review*'s version of the debate over leftism received further endorsement from writers and critics who had been involved in the proletarian literature movement in the thirties, and were now anxious to disown their radical past. Writings of Malcolm Cowley might be mentioned here, including his 1964 book, *Dream of the Golden Mountains.*

While the sixties and seventies witnessed a general questioning of Cold War assumptions by so-called revisionist historians, this process did not extend to the debate over leftism in the thirties. Daniel Aaron's 1961 book, *Writers on the Left,* contains a wealth of documentary information on the proletarian literature movement and various writers who were associated with it. He does not, however, deal with the discussion over leftism in any detail. James B. Gilbert's *Writers and Partisans,* which appeared in 1968 and contains the most extensive account of the alleged dispute between the original *Partisan Review* and the *New Masses,* adopts uncritically the former magazine's own interpretation. Not surprisingly,

William Phillips described it in his 1983 autobiography as the "only study I know of the early history of *Partisan Review* that is faithful to the facts and the spirit of the epoch . . . " (*A Partisan View* 290). The majority of the contributors to David Madden's 1968 anthology of essays, *Proletarian Writers of the Thirties*, share Gilbert's assumptions about the debate over leftism, as does Richard Pells in his 1973 book, *Radical Visions and American Dreams.*

Up to the present, the interpretation formulated in the late thirties by former members of the original *Partisan Review*'s staff remains basically unchallenged. It has reemerged most recently in historical studies of the "New York Intellectuals," including Terry Cooney's 1986 book, *The Rise of the New York Intellectuals: Partisan Review and its Circle, 1934–1945,* and Alan Wald's *The New York Intellectuals: the Rise and Decline of the Anti-Stalinist Left from the 1930s to the 1980s,* which was published in 1987. Here, as in his two previous books,[2] Wald simply repeats the *Partisan Review*'s version of the discussion over leftism.

This discussion remains relevant and merits reexamination for several reasons. First of all, it revolved around several questions that are no less important today: the specific nature and function of creative literature; and the relation between art and politics, literature and propaganda, and fiction and journalism. The arguments and positions formulated on these questions in the *New Masses* and other organs of the proletarian literature movement were by no means as simple and crude as has often been suggested, and deserve review for their own sake.

Second, the discussion accompanied a literary movement, the effect of which was pervasive in the cultural life of the thirties, and involved directly or indirectly some of its best-known writers. Among these were Sherwood Anderson, Richard Wright, Langston Hughes, John Dos Passos, James T. Farrell, and Clifford Odets. Its influence was discernible in novels such as John Steinbeck's *In Dubious Battle* and *Grapes of Wrath,* and in Hemingway's *To Have and Have Not.* In addition, a number of Hollywood screenwriters, including Albert Maltz and Dalton Trumbo, began their literary careers in the movement, as did many people who were active in the Federal Theater and Federal Writers Projects. Reconstructing the discussion over aesthetics in the proletarian literature and theater movement can thus contribute to an understanding of cultural developments in the thirties as a whole.

Third, the debate over leftism has to do with the early history of a magazine, the *Partisan Review,* which has occupied an established position in American intellectual life since its refounding in 1937. In his 1984 book, *The Intellectual Follies,* Lionel Abel goes as far as to call it "the leading journal" in the United States in the forties and fifties (50). While this can be taken as the exaggeration of a member of the magazine's circle, the *Partisan Review* was certainly one of the country's most influential cultural publications in the postwar period and the early fifties. Although it no longer enjoys this position, its history and development have been discussed in a flurry of books in recent years. Some of these centered around former and present editors. Phillips's own autobiography has already been mentioned. In addition there was *The Letters of Delmore Schwartz* (1984), edited by Robert Phillips; Stephen J. Whitfield's *A Critical American: The Politics of Dwight Macdonald* (1984), and Mark Krupknick's *Lionel Trilling: The Fate of Cultural Criticism* (1986). Mary McCarthy, who was drama critic for the revised *Partisan Review* in the late thirties, published her memoirs in 1987, and in the following year Carol Gelderman's *Mary McCarthy: A Life* appeared.

The *Partisan Review* has also figured large in books about the New York Intellectuals, a group that includes Irving Howe, Alfred Kazin, Sidney Hook, Norman Podhoretz, Meyer Shapiro and Daniel Bell, as well as the above-mentioned members of the *Partisan Review* staff. Almost all started out in left-wing politics in the thirties, went through a period of Trotskyism, and eventually became established in university posts in the forties and fifties. They have been commonly associated with the magazines *Dissent, Commentary,* and the *New York Times Book Review,* in addition to the *Partisan Review.* Recent books on this group include Abel's *The Intellectual Follies,* Irving Howe's *A Margin of Hope* (1982), William Barrett's *The Truants* (1982), Terry Cooney's *The Rise of the New York Intellectuals* (1986), Alexander Bloom's *Prodigal Sons* (1986) and Alan Wald's *The New York Intellectuals* (1987).

Throughout the fifty years since the magazine's refounding, it has repeatedly referred to the disputes of its early years in justifying its positions on current political issues. During the McCarthy period the editors' anticommunist stance found expression in attacks on liberals who were "soft on communism," with William Phillips supporting the American Committee for Cultural Freedom (Webster 220). This same organization, a subsidiary of the European-based, CIA-financed Congress for Cultural Freedom, endorsed the *Partisan Review* in the sixties (Lasch 80).

More recently Phillips, who continues as editor, alluded to the early history of the *Partisan Review* in connection with the magazine's position in regard to the peace movement of the mid-eighties. Defending the arms buildup and the policies of the Reagan administration in Central America in a 1985 editorial, he saw "the ideology of pacifism and neutralism" reaching "staggering proportions," and specifically mentioned the rise of the Greens and the "campaign against armament in Germany." The *Partisan Review* position, he explained, was that "this new ideological tide should be combatted, just as the fellow-travelling of the thirties had to be countered by those intellectuals who did not jump on bandwagons" ("Stalinism" 167–68).

The final reason why the discussion over leftism in the thirties remains relevant involves the way it has been approached up to now. The readiness with which literary historians have adopted the *Partisan Review*'s interpretation provides a classic example of how politics affects the writing of history. The distortion and misrepresentation that have resulted can only be described as an indictment of much of the American scholarship in this area. To the extent that a reexamination of the actual discussion succeeds in refuting the prevailing interpretation, it might help foster a more open, inquisitive attitude toward the proletarian literature and theater movement of the thirties, and the works that emerged from it.

In the July 1937 issue of the *Saturday Review of Literature* Alan Calmer, one of the former editors of the original *Partisan Review*, settled accounts with the proletarian literature movement and the staff of the *New Masses*. Coming a few months before the reestablishment of the *Partisan Review* on a new political basis, independent of the Communist party and sympathetic to Trotskyism, the article reads less like a balanced account of the proletarian literature movement and the role of one of its principal organs than an accusation of opponents and an exercise in self-justification. Nevertheless, the views that Calmer put forth here helped lay the groundwork for what was to become the standard interpretation of the alleged dispute between the original *Partisan Review* and the *New Masses* over leftism.

Describing the situation within the movement in the early thirties, he attributes certain shortcomings in proletarian literature to the influence of the *New Masses*. The "strident appeals of the *New Masses* for a pugnacious culture," he explains, "harmfully affected the literary striving of the period" ("Portrait" 3). Encouraged to comprehend artistic values "chiefly in terms of an immediate utility," writers produced poetry that consisted of "external depersonalized composition" and formula short stories that

customarily ended with the sudden conversion of the hero to Communism ("Portrait" 3–4). Calmer depicts the rejection of tendentiousness
and the development of proletarian literature beyond short-term political
agitation as a protest of younger writers against demands and restrictions
imposed by members of the *New Masses'* staff:

> ... gradually, in the vaguest way, he [the young writer] began to
> sense the limitations of this sort of writing. Almost imperceptibly
> a change took place, and was reflected in a mounting fatigue, and
> later distrust, for wooden action and platitudinous sermonizing, for
> twisted wish-fulfillment masquerading as literature.... Before long
> this became a conscious direction and was defined as a movement
> away from "leftism": by this was meant the zealous effort to squeeze
> imaginative writing into the lean compartment of an immediate
> political program....
>
> This new tendency, reflected in poetry, fiction, and criticism, con-
> stituted a reaction to what had become recognized as the official
> brand of proletarian literature. Soon the protest was directed not only
> against old practices but old practitioners. (4)

Specifically, Calmer mentions Joseph Freeman and Michael Gold, who
were later joined by other members of the *New Masses'* staff such as
Granville Hicks and Isidore Schneider. This group, he points out, "com-
manded the strategic avenues of literary opinion on the left" (4), castigat-
ing writers who insisted on aesthetic values and the development of a
native literary tradition:

> The young proletarian moved toward a discipline which endeavoured
> to affirm and extend accepted literary values and, moreover, to assert
> and deepen the native quality of modern American writing. It was
> finally apparent to him that mature literature could not be created
> solely out of the immediate plans and activities of a party but must be
> cut out of the whole grain and fibre of national existence. Although
> he was denounced by his "leftist" comrades, who insisted that he
> was relapsing into an art-for-art's sake position, he was not trying to
> sever the tree of literature from its social roots but from the obstruc-
> tions which would not allow it to spread its branches. (14)

Writing at about the same time as Calmer, William Phillips and Philip
Rahv described the criticism of leftism in similar terms, as a protest
against the demand for tendentious, agitational literature that allegedly

issued from the *New Masses.* Referring to "the strike novel," "agitational drama," and "sloganized poetry," they wrote:

> The very restrictions of these utilitarian genres placed in an insecure political role the more conscious craftsmen in fiction and poetry, who would not surrender themselves to the new aesthetic code promulgated by critics of the type of Granville Hicks and Michael Gold. . . . As the novelty of this literature wore off, rifts and contradictions developed within Marxist criticism itself, and the younger writers stigmatized as "Leftism" the passion for uniformity, the pious utilitarianism, and the contempt for tradition that, despite all protestations to the contrary, determined the mentality of the sectarian Marxists. ("Literature in" 172)

In 1939 Rahv went a step further, claiming that tendentiousness was actively promoted, not only by members of the *New Masses'* staff but by Communist literary critics in general. In the first half of the thirties, he asserted, writers had been "persuaded by the party-critics to turn out sentimental idealizations of the worker-types they were describing in their stories and plays" ("Proletarian Literature" 624).

Calmer maintained that the insistence on tendentious, agitational literature and the disregard for aesthetic values and the bourgeois literary heritage persisted until 1935. In that year, he contended, Communist literary critics opportunistically joined the campaign against leftism in an effort to forge a broad antifascist alliance embracing all classes. "Carping reprimands for the slightest deviations were now replaced by affable acceptance of all comers," Calmer wrote. "It was a relief to see the old 'leftist' excesses routed, but these excessive emphases were wiped out so thoroughly that there remained no (Marxist) emphasis at all" ("Portrait" 14).

Adopting the interpretation formulated in the late thirties by the former editors of the original *Partisan Review,* Walter Rideout refers to the magazine as "the base of operations for one side in a literary civil war," which reflected "a basic division of attitude toward the creative process" and revolved around the relative importance of form and content (228–29). The *Partisan Review,* Rideout explains, opposed "the 'placard' or 'slogan' method in fiction," and insisted that proletarian writers learn technique from bourgeois writers (231). The *New Masses,* on the other hand, encouraged tendentiousness and downplayed form. Referring to Hicks and Gold, he writes: " . . . the pressure of two leading shapers of *New*

Masses' literary policy was generally toward persuading the proletarian novelists ... that they should deal with the more obvious aspects of the class struggle, melodramatize their characters into good workers versus evil *bourgeoisie,* and end on a carefully affirmative note whether the internal logic of the novel demanded such a conclusion or its opposite" (227–28).

James Gilbert sees Phillips and Rahv's repudiation of leftism "in part an attack on the *New Masses* and on the older established proletarian critics" (127). The *Partisan Review* and the other proletarian "little magazines," he states, "proved to be subversive to the established party organ, the *New Masses*" (89), which disregarded the literary heritage and demanded that literature express transitory Party policies. Referring to Phillips and Rahv, he states: "Both editors felt that it was wrong to make literature the vehicle for ideas that were politically expedient at the moment. ... Second, they argued that literary history must be preserved, even if it was largely the history of middle-class authors writing for middle-class audiences" (122). Like Gilbert, Terry Cooney claims that the original *Partisan Review*'s insistence on "the importance of high artistic standards" (79) and its attacks on leftism were directed at "the writing most vigorously encouraged by the Communist Party" and at the literary criticism practiced by "the most prominent leaders of proletarian literature, the editors of the *New Masses* ... " (78).

In his book, *The Dream of the Golden Mountains,* Malcolm Cowley sees modernism as the central issue in the controversy over leftism. The discussion in the mid-thirties, he explains, revolved around "whether proletarian writers could profit from the technical experiments of bourgeois writers such as Joyce and Eliot, for instance, and even Henry James, or whether they should confine themselves to straightforward narrative, clear political messages, folksong, mass chants, and other forms of writing that would stir the workers to action" (245–46). Like Gilbert, he claims: "There was a continued bitter argument between *Partisan Review,* founded in 1934 as an organ of the John Reed Club, and *The New Masses,* which was more directly controlled by the Communist Party. *Partisan Review* advised its readers to study the new bourgeois writers as examples of technique. *The New Masses* spoke in several voices, but usually it said, in effect, "Down with technique and hurrah for writing that follows the party line" (246).

More recently this view was presented by Alan Wald in the introduction to his 1983 book, *The Revolutionary Imagination.* Starting in the late twenties, he claims, antimodernism was "official Communist dogma" (3), and was propagated thereafter by "leading Party critics" (13). The original *Partisan Review*, on the other hand, "achieved distinction largely through its willingness to openly ratify modernism as a movement for Marxists to study and from which to learn new techniques" (15). He describes the situation that existed on the literary left in the mid-thirties as "internecine warfare on the issues of style and technique" between the Communist party and "its most talented literary allies" (14). Drawing a parallel to the Brecht-Lukacs debate among German writers in exile in the late thirties, he places the *Partisan Review* and James T. Farrell in the Brecht camp (16).

Common to all of the above authors is the assumption that the campaign against leftism originated in the *Partisan Review*, and gained momentum primarily through its influence. Gilbert states that Phillips and Rahv, in arguing for the preservation of the literary heritage and calling for the expansion of proletarian literature beyond short-term political agitation, fired "the first shots" in the controversy over leftism (122). Gilbert, Rideout, and Cooney repeat the claim, originally made in the *Partisan Review* in 1934, that the denunciation of leftism at the Second National Congress of the John Reed Clubs—a gathering of proletarian writers from all over the United States in that year—was due to its influence. Commenting on the congress, Cooney writes: "The *Partisan* side in this war, insisting on the importance of high artistic standards for radical literature, had gained enough ground against 'leftism' to claim a major victory at the national meeting of the John Reed Clubs in September 1934" (79).

In an article in the *Journal of Human Relations* Jack Salzman maintained: " . . . it was only with the formation in 1934 of *Partisan Review* (which, unlike the New Masses, believed that the Left could learn from bourgeois writers), and the publication in 1936 of James T. Farrell's *A Note on Literary Criticism*, that the literary Left began seriously to question such contentions as that of Michael Gold, that 'Technique has made cowards of us all' " (41).

Throughout the literature on leftism, *A Note on Literary Criticism*, which was written while Farrell was theater critic for the *Partisan Review*, is assigned a key role. Usually it is described as a summary of the dissident attack on the leftism of the *New Masses* staff and Communist party critics in general. Cooney writes: "Launching his own barrage against 'leftism,' Farrell combined the arguments of Phillips and Rahv, the complaints of other writers, and his own perceptions in a sustained assault on the leading lights of the *New Masses* . . . " (83). Rideout states that Farrell's criticism was directed primarily against "both 'revolutionary sentimentalism,' as represented by Gold, and 'mechanical Marxism,' as represented by Hicks" (232). Commenting on the reaction from the left to Farrell's book, he repeats the claim that the controversy over leftism pitted younger writers and critics against the *New Masses'* old guard. "The most important point which the controversy emphasized was that a sizable number of radical novelists and younger left-wing critics approved Farrell's attitude toward the creative process . . . " (234). In his 1983 book, *The Heyday of American Communism,* Harvey Klehr describes Farrell's antileftist positions simply as an attack on "the Communist Party's cultural stance" (357). In *Literature at the Barricades* Donald Pizer states: " . . . Farrell in the 1930s had been a vigorous opponent of a reductive Marxist literary creed. His *A Note on Literary Criticism* (1936) had angered such writers as Granville Hicks and Mike Gold because of his attack on formula notions of the collectivist and proletarian novel and because of his defense of fiction as 'a branch of the fine arts' " (71). In a 1983 article in *Radical America,* Paul Berman stated: "Gold and his comrade critics did of course substitute political for aesthetic judgement . . . " (47). Farrell, on the other hand, "had advocated a purer Marxism against Gold's 'revolutionary sentimentalism' " (48). In an anthology entitled *Marxistische Literaturkritik in Amerika,* which appeared in West Germany in 1982, editors Olaf Hansen and Martin Christadler described Farrell's book as a criticism of leftist dogmatic literary theory (513), which they associate with *New Masses* editors.

Using *A Note on Literary Criticism* as his main source of information on the discussion in the mid-thirties, a contributor to the *CLA Journal,*[3] Alvin Starr, claimed that Party critics discouraged writers from learning from the bourgeois literature of the past and present, and promoted tendentiousness. Farrell, in contrast, insisted that the proletarian writer could not "ignore the influences of contemporary non-Communist writers, as well as such writers of the past" (46), and demanded that authors "integrate their revolutionary message into their stories" (44) and avoid political sloganizing. By a process of association Starr argues that novelist Richard Wright's advocacy of these same principles was due to Farrell's influence.

In "Blueprint for Negro Writing," Wright holds that reading both non-Communist and Communist authors is an important part of the background of the proletarian writer. . . . Obviously, Wright is agreeing with Farrell that a Communist writer's craft need not be learned only from Communist writers. (46–47)

Rather than tacking a message onto a piece of fiction, Wright felt a black writer should make that message an integral part of his work. . . . Once again, Wright's position paralleled those he heard Farrell take in 1935. (44–45)

Since the *Partisan Review* is seen as the source of the attack on leftism, the publication of articles in the *New Masses* criticizing tendentiousness and the disregard for aesthetic values is depicted as capitulation to an enemy, an abandonment of old positions and practices for purposes of political expedience. Two articles that have been discussed in these terms appeared in 1935. One was a summary by Alan Calmer of the most common shortcomings he observed in proletarian novels that had been submitted in an amateur contest. The other was an attack by Edwin Seaver on the hasty dismissal of Henry Roth's novel, *Call It Sleep,* in a short *New Masses* review. Referring to these two articles, Rideout states that "the 'Centrists' [the writers and critics supporting the *Partisan Review*] carried the fight into the strongest enemy position . . . " (231). "Speaking as a 'Centrist' literary critic," he explains, "Calmer attacked the 'Leftist' tendencies to 'sloganize' and to end with an unprepared-for conversion . . . and he objected to the lack of concern shown for literary technique" (238). Richard Pells similarly describes Calmer's attack as a rejection of "edicts" that had been propagated by the *New Masses*. He interprets its publication in the magazine as an admission that "proletarian literature was not fulfilling its promise" (180). Commenting on the *New Masses'* criticism of leftism, Murray Kempton writes that the *Partisan Review* was "in the vanguard of that literary counterrevolution which in 1936 saw a number of *New Masses'* contributors resolve the dilemma between art and propaganda by leaping most of the way to art with *Partisan Review*" (122).

The reason most commonly given for the *New Masses'* capitulation is the Popular Front. Noting that "arguments against leftism even began to appear there after 1935," Gilbert explains: "Rahv and Phillips had actually won their argument about sectarian literature, but to the Communist literati this was a dead issue by the end of 1936" (152). Alan Wald asserts: " . . . the party's cultural orientation shifted in accordance with zigzags in the political line, moving from an ultraleft 'proletarian' cultural perspective to a liberal 'people's' outlook with the advent of the popular front in

1935" (*The Revolutionary* 14). Referring to the discussion over Farrell's book, Rideout states: " . . . the most curious point about the controversy was that, like Andrew Jackson's Battle of New Orleans, a decisive fight occurred after the enemy had, for reasons of its own capitulated. . . . 'Leftism' had been for some time found wanting in the Party's own orientation" (234). The better writers, who opposed leftism, Rideout continues, "should have rejoiced in their victory . . . but with the introduction of the People's Front policy they found that the very premises of a revolutionary literature had been officially rejected" (245).

As these remarks indicate, Rideout does not equate the *Partisan Review*'s stand on leftism with a repudiation of the concept of proletarian literature. Other writers, in contrast, describe tendentiousness as a defining quality of proletarian literature, and portray the campaign against leftism as a rejection of the movement as a whole. Characterizing proletarian writers as a group, Leo Gurko states in David Madden's anthology, *Proletarian Writers of the Thirties:* "As a rule the proletarian writers relentlessly pumped their messages into their work" (58). He goes on to say that "straight, quasi-Marxist statements, baldly injected into the narrative flow, was standard proletarian procedure" (59). Likewise characteristic was the disregard for aesthetics. "Jamesian preoccupations with fiction as an art form were so much decadent nonsense. Concern with aesthetics as such was empty, frivolous, or irrelevant" (47). Gurko contrasts the proletarian writer with John Dos Passos, who, he explains, "never equated art and propaganda" (47).

In the same anthology Chester E. Eisinger describes "tendentious simplicity" as the hallmark of the "orthodox Marxist novel" (165), while another writer, Lee Baxandall, sees the "moralizing propaganda novel or play" as the "typical product of the 'proletarian' school" (213).

The claim that the *Partisan Review*'s insistence on aesthetic values and the heritage was an affront to basic premises of the proletarian literature movement is explicitly stated by Gilbert. The character of the *Partisan Review,* he writes, reflected Phillips and Rahv's "criticisms of the existing Communist movement" (110). He describes as "a major premise of proletarian art" the idea that the proletarian writer "must go beyond and even reject the literary accomplishments of the bourgeoisie" (141). In reference to an article by Phillips in the magazine *Dynamo* in 1934, he states: " . . . he raised two interrelated questions that could have been interpreted as a challenge to the fundamentals of proletarian art. The first related to the place of aesthetics in the new literary movement and the role of traditional critical standards" (112). The movement "seemed to suggest," Gilbert claims, that the latter be "cast aside" (112). Finally, he asserts, Phillips and Rahv's position on these questions "eventually became the rationale for rejecting the whole movement" (122).

In addition to sharing many of the same assumptions, American literary historians of leftism have approached the subject in similar ways. In describing the opposition between orthodox and dissident they have tended to focus attention almost exclusively on the *Partisan Review* and the *New Masses*. In the chapter, "The First Partisan Review," in which Gilbert deals with the discussion over leftism, he quotes the magazine itself more than any other source. The same is true of Terry Cooney's treatment of the discussion. Rideout gives almost equal coverage to the *New Masses* but also concentrates heavily on the two magazines. In regard to the "orthodox" Communist approach to literature and criticism, nowhere is there any serious analysis of the *Daily Worker,* which, unlike the *New Masses,* was an official organ of the Communist party. Furthermore, generalizations about the *New Masses'* position on proletarian literature and literary criticism are based on a relatively small number of articles and reviews that actually appeared in the magazine during the period in question. Often statements are quoted that were either made earlier or were published elsewhere. Rideout (229), Cowley (246) and Salzman (41), for example, all describe remarks made by Michael Gold in 1930 in a dispute over Thornton Wilder as typical of his and the *New Masses'* approach to literature. Richard Pells likewise cites essays of Gold's from 1929 and 1930 to demonstrate his "dogmatic" views on proletarian literature (176–77). On the other hand, numerous articles and reviews that Gold wrote after this are completely ignored. As for Granville Hicks, the source most frequently mentioned to demonstrate his positions is his book *The Great Tradition,* a review of American literature since the Civil War. Leo Gurko writes of Hicks's study: "Its tone was doctrinaire, its arguments pretentious, its conclusions naive and dogmatic..." (*The Angry Decade* 69–70). Pells calls it a "classic example of how Communist critics frequently treated art and ideas during the 1930s" (174).

Another common characteristic of the literature on leftism is that, although Soviet influence is commonly assumed to be behind these attitudes and practices, the actual discussion in the United States is examined in isolation from the proletarian literature movement as an international whole. Generalizations as to what views were orthodox are made with no reference to *International Literature,* the organ of the

Soviet-based International Union of Revolutionary Writers (IURW), with which the *New Masses* and John Reed Clubs were affiliated. Nor is there any consideration of the discussion in other centers of the proletarian literature movement, such as pre-Hitler Germany.

While little attention is paid to the actual development of literary theory within the movement as a whole, the very use of the term *orthodox* to describe the supporters of leftism implies that their views were more in keeping with those of the central organization. Several writers, in fact, explicitly connect the IURW with leftism. The IURW assumed, Deming Brown writes, that

> ... an autonomous proletarian culture, based upon the dominance of a new social class and largely independent of the cultural heritage of the past, could be built quickly for the purpose of performing specific revolutionary tasks.... Problems of literary creation were considered subordinate to the task of organizing the new movement and disciplining it ideologically .... Utilitarian literature of immediate political relevance was prized above all else. (57–58)

Only as sentiment grew for a popular front against fascism did the IURW abandon "its insistence on purely proletarian themes of immediate agitational import" (58).

James Gilbert maintains that the IURW encouraged sectarianism toward non-Communist writers at the International Conference of Proletarian-Revolutionary Writers at Charkov in the Ukraine in 1930. Upton Sinclair, he claims, was excluded from the John Reed Clubs in accordance with Soviet policy. "Whatever indigenous distrust of intellectuals already existed in the American movement," he explains, "was thus reinforced by similar attitudes coming from the Soviet Union" (104).

In his 1986 book, *American Writers and Radical Politics, 1900–39,* Eric Homberger is ambiguous on the connection between the IURW and leftism. On the one hand he disagrees with Gilbert on the Charkov Conference, pointing to the "constant reference to the need to win over fellow travellers" and the implicit denunciation of "leftist exclusiveness" (136). On the other hand he repeats the assertion that the IURW only abandoned leftism with the approach of the Popular Front. He describes the criticism of sectarianism and tendentiousness at the John Reed Clubs convention in 1934, not as the expression of established policies, but rather as the harbinger of a new Party line: " ... there was a perceptible move towards the right by the party leadership. A resolution condemning 'sloganized tracts disguised as poetry and fiction' was passed. Alexander Trachtenberg, director of the party's publishing house and the link between the Central Committee and the JRCs [John Reed Clubs], spoke at length against sectarianism" (139). Homberger explains: "Between 1930 and 1934 the IURW, following the left turn of the Comintern, emphasized a policy which wholly integrated literature within the class struggle. . . . From 1935 the party's attempt to create a people's front was accompanied by a substantial move to the right. Leftist and sectarian attitudes were to be avoided" (139–40).

Other writers who see Soviet influence behind various aspects of leftism are Richard Pells and Max Eastman. Pells argues that "pressure from Moscow" led Communist literary critics to set up "edicts" and to judge books on their "ability to elicit a militant response from the reader" (179–80). Soviet influence, he contends, caused Americans to "simplify and vulgarize what might otherwise have been an interesting cultural experiment" (179). Eastman, who was probably the first American writer to connect the RAPP with leftism, stated in his 1934 book, *Artists in Uniform,* that, although it was occasionally admitted "that the proletariat has to learn 'technique,' or has to learn about 'form,' from the artists of the class enemy" (206), in general "loyal revolutionists dared not even discuss whether a work of art possessed talent or not, or so much as mention the question of form above a whisper . . . " (144). He quotes another writer, Louis Fischer, who had stated: "RAPP critics never cared about artistic quality. They scarcely ever appreciated ability. Their only criterion was politics . . . " (qtd. in Eastman 159). Accordingly, Eastman claims, there was no discussion of aesthetics at Charkov, and the question of the specific nature of art as a weapon—the relationship between literature and propaganda—remained unanswered (14–15).

A final characteristic of the literature on leftism is the tendency to draw a simple, direct connection between political developments and literary theory when discussing the Soviet Union or the proletarian literature movement in the United States. In both cases political expedience is seen as the cause of sudden turns and about-faces in the approach to literature. In reference to American Communists, James Gilbert explains: "Literature was always viewed in relation to politics and never particularly prized for itself" (103). Discussing the approach to literature in the Soviet Union, he connects Stalin's defeat of Bukharin in 1928 with the propagation of proletarian literature after that year (103–4).

Occasionally a connection is seen between the RAPP's concept of proletarian literature and the First Five-Year Plan. Between 1928 and 1932 writers in the Soviet Union were called upon to depict the process of industrialization and collectivization in factory and farm. To this end, writers groups visited the areas of development in order to gather information for later works. "Shock brigades" of workers and farmers who had displayed writing talent did the same, compiling long works of reportage describing what they had witnessed. The RAPP's promotion of this activity has led some writers to assume that the politically immediate, "utilitarian," largely journalistic literature that emerged was the fulfillment of the RAPP's aesthetic theory. The concept of proletarian art, Deming Brown writes, had been "tested in practice in the drive for a Five Year Plan literature in the Soviet Union" (57). Walter Rideout states: " . . . while the Russian Association of Proletarian Writers (RAPP) was 'mobilizing' authors during the First Five-Year Plan from 1928 to 1932, 'proletarian literature' was in effect the official literary strategy of the Soviet Fatherland" (166).

Just as in the United States, where leftism was reputedly abandoned only with the introduction of the Popular Front, the formulation of socialist realism in the Soviet Union is described as a break with the past, a rejection of RAPP's concepts, undertaken for political reasons. In a 1980 book entitled *Marxism and Culture: The CPUSA and Aesthetics in the 1930s,* Lawrence Schwartz writes: " . . . socialist realism must be seen as a liberalizing tendency which was part of a larger and more general plan to gain cooperation from the intelligentsia and the skilled 'specialists'. Primarily, socialist realism was an organizing tool and not an aesthetic . . . " (32). Having examined neither the RAPP's concept of proletarian literature nor the theory of socialist realism, he emphasizes the discontinuity in the official adoption of the latter. Malcolm Cowley uses similar terms in discussing the connection between the two theories. Referring to developments in the United States, he writes: "Proletarian literature as a whole was to be pushed aside after a change in the party line; the new model was 'socialist realism'" (259). Commenting on the RAPP's literary theory, Max Eastman states that in 1932 "the dialectical method for creating a new and ultimate epoch in the cultural history of man was revoked, rescinded and annulled" (18).

In view of the serious gaps and inaccuracies in the literature on leftism, the purpose of this study will be to reconstruct the discussion that took place in the American proletarian literature movement in the thirties, and to reevaluate the established interpretation. Since a primary source of misunderstanding up to now has been the failure to examine this discussion as part of an international whole, attention will focus on the aesthetic theory propagated by the IURW in the mid-thirties and on theoretical developments that preceeded it, starting in the early twenties.

The first part, which covers the period ending in 1932, deals separately with the Soviet Union, Germany, and the United States—the countries singled out at Charkov as the three most important centers of the movement ("The Charkov Conference" 7). The section on the Soviet Union examines the concept of proletarian literature formulated by the RAPP in disputes with various rival groups in the twenties. Here American, English, and German sources have been consulted, including translations from the Russian of original documents.

In regard to Germany, the discussion within the Bund proletarisch-revolutionärer Schriftsteller (BPRS) is reviewed. This organization, founded in 1928, was the equivalent of the John Reed Clubs in the United States, and was specifically praised at Charkov for its contribution to the development of aesthetic theory.[4] Here, primarily German sources were used, including the *Linkskurve,* the organ of the BPRS.[5] It was in this magazine that Georg Lukacs published some of his most important essays of the early thirties, including one that appeared later in the *Partisan Review* and influenced that magazine's stand on the relation between literature and propaganda. This section, as well as the one on the Soviet Union, is intended as background to the discussion in the United States, and does not claim to add anything new to research already done by others.

The second part of the study deals with the period between 1933 and the end of 1935. The magazine *International Literature* is examined to establish the IURW's position on leftism. The disregard of this publication represents the single most serious flaw in the literature on leftism in the United States. In effect, a debate has been described, with one of the main participants missing. Of particular relevance were writings of Marx, Engels, and Lenin on literature and aesthetics, many of which appeared for the first time in English here and were cited in key articles by members of the *Partisan Review* staff and others attacking various manifestations of leftism.

The development of the antileftist position in the American movement in the mid-thirties is then retraced against this background. Here the magazines *New Theatre* and *New Masses* are reviewed, as well as the Communist party newspaper *Daily Worker,* which contained a cultural page and a regular column by Michael Gold. Finally, the original *Partisan*

Review's statements on leftism are analyzed, in order to demonstrate that they coincided with mainstream views within the movement and were in no way new or dissident.

Notes

1. Daniel Aaron describes and analyzes this process in his book *Writers on the Left*.

2. The books referred to here are *James T. Farrell: the Revolutionary Years* and *The Revolutionary Imagination: The Poetry and Politics of John Wheelwright and Sherry Mangan*.

3. This is a quarterly publication issued by the College Language Association.

4. In the April 1930 edition of the *Linkskurve* (p. 15) the editors noted that a series of articles on aesthetics by BPRS member Karl A. Wittvogel received special praise at Charkov.

5. The *Linkskurve* is available in a 1971 reprint, published in Frankfurt am Main by the Druck Verlags Vertriebs Kooperative.

Part One

Background and Development
of the Antileftist Position
from the Twenties to
the Early Thirties

1

RAPP's Concept
of Proletarian Literature

The Proletcult Controversy

THE SOVIET UNION in the twenties was the scene of heated rivalry among a plethora of literary groups, including the Proletcult and its various split-off groups, the circle of "fellow travellers" around Alexander Voronsky, and the former futurists organized in the Left Front of Art (LEF). Undertaken here is not a general assessment of the literary controversies that raged during this period, but rather the retracing of a particular line of development that led from the Proletcult debate of the early twenties to the aesthetic theory propagated by the Russian Association of Proletarian Writers (RAPP) toward the end of the decade.

An examination of the origins of the RAPP's concept of proletarian literature reveals that there was more continuity in the cultural politics of the Soviet Communist party than suggested by writers such as Deming Brown and James Gilbert. In drawing a close connection between the promotion of proletarian literature after 1928 and the First Five-Year Plan they downplay the fact that the Central Committee had already declared the hegemony of proletarian literature as its goal in 1925. The statement it issued at that time was an expansion on an earlier one, which had been based on views put forth by Lenin in the course of a dispute with the Proletcult in 1920.

The Proletcult had its origin in a group called *Vpered,* or "Forward," which split off from the Bolshevik wing of the Russian Social-Democratic Workers party after the defeat of the 1905 revolution. Among its leaders was Alexander Bogdanov, who for some years had been constructing a philosophical system in which he borrowed Marx's idea that the ideological superstructure of a society—including its laws, philosophy, and art—ultimately reflected the economic base, the prevailing forms of production and exchange. In discussing contemporary advanced capitalist society, Bogdanov reduced Marx's concept of the economic base to the actual machinery and technology of the mass production industry, and postulated a simple, direct connection between production conditions and ideology. The division of labor in the large factory, he argued, necessitated cooperation, which in turn gave rise to collectivism. The latter was the real ideology of industrial society as opposed to bourgeois individualism which, though still dominant, no longer reflected actual conditions. The political struggle for socialism was to be accompanied by a cultural one, conducted by organizations that were to be separate and independent of parties and labor unions. Their goal would be to make proletarian culture dominant, thus bringing the ideological superstructure in line with the economic base. This was to be accomplished by helping workers lend literary and artistic form to the collective consciousness that had been spontaneously generated in the factory.[1]

While rejecting Bogdanov's conceptual system, the group around Lenin promoted the development of working-class literature in practice through their newspaper, *Pravda*. Worker-writers occupied an important place in *Pravda* from the beginning, contributing poems and short fictional sketches in addition to purely journalistic material. Between 1912 and 1914 the newspaper assisted in the publication of two anthologies of worker-poems (one of which was compiled by Maxim Gorky) and initiated the establishment of a Society of the Proletarian Arts in May 1917.[2]

The latter was one of many groups dedicated to the development of proletarian culture, *Proletcult* for short, which sprouted up all over Russia in 1917. In order to coordinate their work, a conference of proletarian cultural and educational organizations was called in Petrograd just before the October Revolution (Gorzka 20; Gorbunow 43). Among those who initiated the conference was Anatole Lunacharsky, a former Vpered member who had gone over to the Bolsheviks and was soon to be appointed People's Commissar of Education (Gorbunow 43). In the course of the proceedings, a central committee of the Petrograd Proletcult organizations was formed, to which Lunacharsky and Krupskaya—Lenin's wife—were elected (Gorbunow 46; Gorsen et al. 154).

While the new government aided the Proletcult groups after the revolution, conflicts soon arose over positions held by Bogdanov and his supporters. In a country where the overwhelming majority of the population were peasants and where the skills of bourgeois professionals were indispensable, the Proletcult tended to view the industrial proletariat as the sole source of the future culture of Soviet society, in accordance with the idea that only through work in the factory could the requisite consciousness be acquired. In an attempt to simulate the collective production of the large factory, "laboratories" were set up in which workers were to cooperate with each other in creating art and literature. The average stay would be about a year, after which the worker was expected to return to his or her job at the factory (Gorsen et al. 72). Middle-class writers, including those who had supported the revolution, were to be limited to the role of instructors, imparting technical skills. While most of the leaders, including Bogdanov, insisted on knowledge of the bourgeois cultural heritage, the emphasis was more often placed on newness rather than continuity, and the laboratory arrangement itself, with the relatively short period of training it provided for, implied that the new culture of socialist society could be created without the long process of assimilating the culture of the past.

Another problem, in the eyes of the Party, was the relationship of the Proletcult to the government. The Proletcult, as centralized organization, was established before the formation of the People's Commissariat of Education—the government body responsible for cultural affairs—and attempted for two years to remain independent of it. As the influence of the former Vpered group increased, the possibility arose of the Proletcult's becoming a center of opposition. Against this background, the Party leadership turned its attention to cultural questions as the civil war came to an end in 1920.

The initiative was taken by Lenin, who addressed a resolution to the Central Committee in October calling for the subordination of the Proletcult to the People's Commissariat of Education. The position on proletarian culture that Lenin presented here, and elsewhere during this period, has sometimes been interpreted as a rejection of the concept as such. Eric Homberger maintains: "Proletarian literature or culture occupies an uncertain place in socialist thought. . . . Lenin was opposed to it . . . " (Homberger 120–21). However, while Trotsky rejected the term completely,[3] Lenin combined his criticism of the theory and practice of the Proletcult with the formulation of an alternative definition of proletarian culture, in which he emphasized the ideological viewpoint, the role of the Party, and the heritage. In Soviet society, he wrote, art and literature should be "imbued with the spirit of the class struggle being waged by the proletariat for the successful achievement of the aims of its dictatorship . . . " ("On Proletarian Culture" 112). As in all other areas of public education, the proletariat, "through its vanguard—the Communist Party—and through the many types of proletarian organizations in general, should display the utmost activity and play the leading part" ("On Proletarian Culture" 112). While, in Bogdanov's view, a spirit of collectivism, spontaneously generated, constituted the essence of working-class consciousness and culture, Lenin states that "the Marxist world outlook is the only true expression of . . . the culture of the revolutionary proletariat." Just as Marxism built on the accumulated knowledge of the past, so too must "a genuine proletarian culture" be based on a critical assimilation of the cultural heritage ("On Proletarian Culture" 112).

In other statements Lenin pointed out that the first prerequisite in this process was a generally high level of education and literacy—a goal that, he insisted, should have priority in the Proletcult. Although he approved of the idea of workers' cultural circles developing the literary and artistic abilities of their members,[4] he considered it an illusion to believe that the proletariat, alone, could already create a broad socialist literature and art in the Soviet Union, and characterized as artificial the attempt to accomplish this in "laboratories."

The discussion within the Central Committee following Lenin's resolution resulted in the Party's first major pronouncement on culture, a long article in *Pravda* entitled "On the Proletcults." While denouncing the leadership of the Proletcult for imbuing workers with "semi-bourgeois philosophical 'systems,' " the Central Committee declares its support, in principle, for organizational attempts to develop the artistic and literary talents of workers ("On the Proletcults" 114–15). The Proletcult was consequently not to be dissolved, but rather subordinated to the People's Commissariat of Education, which had already been directed "to create and maintain conditions that will guarantee the proletarians the possibility of free creative work in their establishments" ("On the Proletcults" 113). The statement continues: "Not only does the Central Committee not wish to restrict the initiative of the worker intelligentsia in the field of artistic creativity, it wants, on the contrary, to create the most healthy and normal conditions for it . . . " (114–15). As in Lenin's resolution, a distinction is made between "genuine" and "contrived proletarian culture" (115), with the Central Committee expressing its support for the former.

The October Group and the Central Committee's 1925 Resolution on Literature

Those who would later form the leadership of the RAPP emerged in 1922 as the October Group, setting themselves off from the Proletcult on two issues that had been stressed by Lenin: the leading role of the Party and the definition of proletarian culture according to its Marxist orientation. It was in addressing the latter point that the RAPP developed its concepts of dialectical materialism and the living person toward the end of the twenties.

Despite the government's conditional support, the Proletcult was already in decline as an organization by 1922, after having reached a peak membership of about 400,000 (Gorzka 27). Gradually it was superseded by other groups propagating proletarian literature, such as the *Kúznitsa*, or "Smithy," which broke off from the Proletcult in 1920. In the same year the Kúznitsa organized the first All-Russian Congress of Proletarian Writers in Moscow, at which the All-Russian Association of Proletarian Writers (VAPP) was established (Brown, *The Proletarian Episode* 10–12).

Not long after its founding, the Kúznitsa itself split in disagreement over the New Economic Policy, according to which the government relaxed restrictions on private business. In December 1922 a number of those who supported the Party in these measures joined with members of the Communist Youth League and founded the October Group. Among its leaders were Yuri Libedinsky and Leopold Auerbach, both of whom were later to head the RAPP (Brown, *The Proletarian Episode* 12–14). In 1923 they started publishing a weekly magazine, called *Na Postu,* or "On Guard," in which they announced their intention to "stand firmly *on guard over a strong and clear Communist ideology in proletarian literature*" (qtd. in Brown, *The Proletarian Episode* 20).

Following the introduction of the New Economic Policy, private publishing companies flourished, and various new literary groups were established. Toward the middle of the twenties rivalry among the latter became increasingly vociferous, with the October Group engaging in vehement polemics against non-Communist writers (Slonim 46–49). When its members requested official recognition as the Party's representative in the field of literature, the Central Committee turned its attention to literary matters once again, issuing its second major statement in this area.

Some commentaries on this document have emphasized the Central Committee's call for free competition among literary groups and the fact that it rejected the October Group's request. Thus it is seen as a reflection of the liberalism of the NEP period, which was to terminate with the resurgence of Proletcult views and the promotion of proletarian literature during the First Five-Year Plan. Referring to the 1925 statement of the Central Committee, Eric Homberger writes: "The final resolution

... reflected the NEP spirit of reconciliation. ... The proletarians' aggressive attempt to dominate Soviet literature was rebuked. While the Party generally supported their aims, there could be no official support for the proletarians or any other literary group. The resolution called for open competition" (127).

What this account fails to convey is the general tone of the statement and the strong commitment to the promotion of proletarian literature that it contains. The resolution begins with comments on the class conflict taking place in the country. On the one hand there is a cultural revolution underway, one of the manifestations of which is a "new literature" that begins with "embryonic" forms, such as worker and rural correspondence and ends with "ideologically aware artistic-literary products." At the same time the NEP has led to the "consolidation of a new bourgeoisie." Since, in a class society, "there is not and cannot be neutral art," this consolidation has been reflected on the literary scene, contributing to intergroup rivalry. The Party, the resolution states, must take sides in this matter. Regretting that the proletariat, under capitalism, had not been able to "work out the problems of the natural sciences nor technical problems, nor ... could it elaborate its own literature," the Central Committee announces its intention to assist it in doing so in future ("On the Party's Policy" 116–17).

Echoing Lenin it asserts that in literature as well as in other fields the proletariat must continually pursue and consolidate its leadership. While proletarian writers do not as yet enjoy such hegemony, the Party "must assist those writers to earn their historic right of such hegemony." As in Lenin's remarks, the leadership of the proletariat in the arts refers primarily to ideology, to the "penetration of dialectical materialism" into the realm of literature. This entails, in the first place, winning over middleclass writers and peasants "to the side of communist ideology." Second, the proletariat is to work out its "own literature, its own special art form, its own style." In this connection certain proposals were put forth that were subsequently adopted by the October Group and set the stage for later discussions in Germany and the United States. Proletarian literature, the statement continues, must be "a broad encompassing of phenomena in all their complexity; not being confined within the framework of the factory alone." It must become "a literature that does not belong in a workshop but to the great fighting class that brings the millions of peasants in its train." In addition it is to be understandable to the masses and to draw upon the cultural heritage. Proletarian writers were to make use of "all the technical achievements of the old masters" in working out "an appropriate form intelligible *to the millions*" ("On the Party's Policy" 117–19).

It was in the area of form and style that the Central Committee refused to commit itself. Since the proletariat still had no "definite answers to all the questions concerning artistic form" (117), the resolution states, there is to be "free competition between the various groups and streams" in the search for the "style appropriate to the epoch" ("On the Party's Policy" 118). While pledged to assist proletarian writers in general, the Party was not prepared to grant a monopoly to any particular faction in the sphere of form.

While the document did not mention the October Group by name, its demand that "communist criticism . . . drop the tone of literary command" (118) and that a "tactful and considerate attitude" toward "fellow travellers" (117) be adopted was probably directed primarily at them. In keeping with the Central Committee's recommendations the group attempted to improve its relations with non-Communist writers, assisting in the formation of the Federation of Organizations of Soviet Writers (FOSP), which was to include the latter. In addition they changed the name of their weekly to *Na literaturnom Postu,* or "On Literary Guard," suggesting that they would pay more attention to literary matters, and tone down their political polemics (Brown, *The Proletarian Episode* 48).

Although the Party refused to recognize the October Group as its official representative on the literary scene, relations between the two improved, and Auerbach and Libedinsky, along with other October Group members, joined the executive council of the VAPP (Brown, *The Proletarian Episode* 53).

At the first All-Union Congress of Proletarian Writers, held in Moscow in May 1928, the VAPP was renamed RAPP (Russian instead of All-Russian). Throughout the four years of the RAPP's existence the Party maintained close relations with the organization, while continuing to abide by its 1925 decision not to recognize any group as its official representative. The importance of the RAPP stemmed from its position as the largest organization of proletarian writers and from the significant contribution it was making to the ongoing discussion over the development of Marxist aesthetics at a time when the Party had not yet formulated its own theory.

The Influence of Plekhanov

For the groundwork of their aesthetic theory the RAPP turned to Georgy Plekhanov, who had attempted to develop a Marxist approach to literary history and criticism in the decades preceding the revolution. Plekhanov had been active in the workers' movement beginning in the 1880s and was the official representative of the Russian Social-Democratic Workers party at the Second International (Fomina 109–10). After the party split in 1903, he became a leading Menshivik. Some of his theoretical writings, which dealt with history and philosophy as well as aesthetics, were nevertheless highly regarded by Lenin, who ordered the publication of his works after his death in 1918 (Fomina 8). Plekhanov's influence on the discussion over Marxist aesthetics in the Soviet Union in the twenties extended well beyond the RAPP, a fact reflected in Lunacharsky's reference to him in 1928 as the "founder of Marxist criticism" ("Thesen" 169).

Like Bogdanov, Plekhanov took as the starting point of his theory Marx's concept of base and superstructure. Assuming that in every society ideas, art, and morals ultimately reflect production relations, he asserted that the first task of materialist critics was to translate the idea that a work expressed *"from the language of art to the language of sociology"* ("Vorwort" 219), to place it in its historical and social context. Having accomplished this they were to proceed to critical evaluation, applying criteria derived from Hegel's notion of the unity of the good, the true and the beautiful. Aesthetic judgement of a work of literature, he insisted, had to include consideration of the ideas and values it propagated. In this connection he set up a hierarchy, at the bottom of which were false ideas and hypocritical morals, while the highest position was occupied by the progressive ideas of the time and ethical values that corresponded to the objective good of the society as a whole. In contemporary capitalist society the latter qualities were to be found in the workers' struggle for socialism and democracy.[5]

In judging a work of literature, the critic was to consider not only the presence of these ideas and values but also the manner in which they were expressed. Making a distinction that had become common in aesthetics since Kant and Hegel, he draws a line between the methods of science and journalism, and those of art and literature. While the one attempted to comprehend nature and society through abstract laws, the other operated with concrete images. Establishing a basic principle of his aesthetic theory, he states: "... when the writer operates with logical arguments instead of with images or when the images are invented in order to prove a certain thesis, he is not an artist but a journalist" ("Die Kunst und das gesellschaftliche Leben" 249).

The highest form of literature, in Plekhanov's view, expresses progressive ideas and values through the portrayal of individuals in the context of great social movements. The ability of the writer to achieve this kind of realism is partly determined by the historical position of the class to which he belongs. Most favorable are revolutionary periods, in which his class unites with the broad population against a common enemy. Such was the case, for example, when the bourgeoisie was overthrowing the feudal aristocracy. As long as it was fighting a dominant, oppressor class, its ideologues spoke for the whole nation. The subjective values they propagated—in this case brotherhood, liberty, and equality—corresponded to the objective good of the society, so that there was mutual sympathy between the writer and a large part of the population.

The writer's situation changes when his class itself assumes the role of oppressor. Here a cleavage develops between subjectivity and objectivity, in the sense that prevailing values are no longer directed toward the good of the society as a whole, but rather toward preserving the power of the dominant class. Plekhanov traces what he considers to be the weaknesses of nineteenth-century French literature to the inability of writers to overcome this dichotomy. Unwilling to propagate bourgeois values, and unconvinced of the possibility of an alternative social order, they attempted to separate art and morals, by striving for either "pure art," removed from the social struggle, or uninvolved pseudoscientific objectivity based on psychology and physiology. Isolated from the revolutionary workers' movement they were unable to grasp society as a large, developing whole shaped by human action. Consequently, in choosing characters for their novels, they overlooked "the most interesting examples with the richest inner life" ("Die Kunst" 257), namely those working to establish socialism.

Faced with a general loss of content, bourgeois writers increasingly resorted to formal experimentation in their search for newness—a tendency Plekhanov regards as typical of a declining class. This, coupled with extreme subjectivity and individualism, he finds to be particularly prevalent in contemporary literature. The only way for writers to overcome these limitations and resolve the dichotomy between subjectivity and objectivity, ethics and aesthetics, he maintains, is to ally themselves with the new revolutionary class, to commit themselves to the workers' struggle to establish socialism and to create fiction, poetry, and drama from this vantage point.

The RAPP's Theory of the Living Person and Dialectical Materialism

Contrary to the contention of Max Eastman that the RAPP ignored aesthetic values, the group developed and applied an elaborate aesthetic theory based on Plekhanov's ideas. Under the slogans of the "living person" and "dialectical materialism" they propagated the very criteria that would be employed years later in the United States in attacking various manifestations of leftism in proletarian literature.

The RAPP leaders regarded this theory, which they constructed in the second half of the twenties as the fulfillment of the Central Committee's call for "the penetration of dialectical materialism" into literature. As applied to characters, dialectical materialism meant for the RAPP, first of all, the portrayal of development and change in living persons. A long resolution in *Na literaturnom Postu* in 1928 called on proletarian writers to depict "the complicated human psyche, with all its contradictions, holdovers from the past, seeds of the new, with all its conscious and unconscious elements." The slogan of the living person, it was pointed out, was directed against stereotyping, schematicism and a crass placard-like style ("Die Kulturrevolution" 370).

The term was used as early as 1922 in the first issue of the October Group's monthly magazine, *Oktyabr'*, in criticizing the Kúznitsa and a tendency then prevalent in proletcult literature. The euphoria following the revolution had found expression in ebullient lyrics in which the class struggle took place on a cosmic level, with omnipotent, mythical workers overcoming all forces of oppression in the universe. Commenting on this, the October Group announced its intention to present " 'living people' . . . in their proper perspective" in place of " 'iron psalms' " and "resounding words about the 'cosmic' sweep of the revolution" (qtd. in Brown, *The Proletarian Episode* 15).

One reason why the term had assumed such importance in subsequent years was the continuing tendency toward schematicism in proletarian literature. "We are still at such a low artistic level," RAPP leader Alexander Fadeyev stated in 1928, "that we have not learned to portray flesh and blood human beings" ("Der Hauptweg" 8).

The significance of the term extended, however, far beyond its use as a tool of criticism in attacking schematicism. In an obvious allusion to the Central Committee's 1925 resolution, Fadeyev claims that the concept of the living person involves no less than "the question of the hegemony of proletarian literature, the question of a new method" ("Der Hauptweg" 13). Quoting Plekhanov on the need to portray characters as part of the social whole, he explains that in proletarian fiction and drama each individual conflict and contradiction was, in reality, intimately related to the class structure of the society and the process of historical development. The dialectical-materialist method consisted of revealing the complicated process of interaction between the individual and social, the subjective and objective ("Der Hauptweg" 12). Fadeyev contrasts this approach to character with the "psychologism" of certain bourgeois writers, who, under the influence of Freud and Bergson, examine the soul in isolation from the social milieu, regarding the subconscious as the main force determining human action. In his view their portrayal of the ego as the only reality in a chaotic world, in which all development and change is accidental, is an expression of idealism, reflecting the historical position of a class which is no longer the agent of social progress ("Der Hauptweg" 14–16).

The writers who had gone furthest in creating living persons were the nineteenth-century French and Russian realists, but they too were limited by their class-determined inability to adequately grasp the dynamics of historical development. Expanding on Plekhanov, Fadeyev maintains that in capitalist society only the proletariat can comprehend the relation between the subjective and objective forces effecting social change, since it is the only class whose subjective dreams and hopes for the future correspond with its "objective role and the objective course of social development" ("Der Hauptweg" 12–13). Unlike Proletcult theoreticians, he does not mean, however, an awareness or consciousness that is spontaneously generated in the factory, but rather the accumulated experience of the revolutionary workers' movement, as expressed in Marxism-Leninism. The proletarian quality of a work was, therefore, determined less by the class origin of the writer or his choice of subject matter than by the ideological viewpoint. Citing the Central Committee's resolution, Fadeyev states that what is needed is not a literature restricted to factory themes, but rather one that grasps life in all its variety and complexity ("Der Hauptweg" 40–42).

The Dispute with the Left Front of Art

The RAPP further defined the dialectical method in a dispute with a rival group called the Left Front of Art (LEF). Here, two issues were addressed which were to emerge later in the German and American proletarian literature movements: the relation between imaginative literature and journalism, and the nature of art as an instrument of social change, as praxis. Contrary to Deming Brown's contention, utilitarianism was propagated, not by the RAPP as such, but rather by an opposition faction within the RAPP, called the Litfront, which was formed in 1930 (Brown, *The Proletarian Episode* 152). The unity of reflection and praxis, which the RAPP insisted upon in its criticism of the LEF's concept of art and literature, was later propagated by critics of utilitarianism in Germany and the United States.

The LEF was founded by a group of former futurists who supported the revolution, seeing it as preparing the way for the ultrarational social order they had been calling for in their art. A basic tenet of their literary theory was that fictitious characters and plots affected the instincts, lulling readers and directing them away from reality. The literature of the future was, instead, to be totally rational and concentrate on facts. The writer was seen as an artisan, to be given assignments and create socially useful products, providing form to journalistic material, such as diaries, reports, and documentary sketches. Literature was not to reflect reality in the manner of the nineteenth-century realistic novel, but rather to transform it. Through the arrangement or montage of factual material readers were to be made aware of connections not ordinarily perceptible in everyday life. Enlightened to the workings of society, they would then be in a better position to change it. LEF, in its pronouncements at least, was more consistent than the Proletcult in rejecting the bourgeois heritage, regarding it as outmoded and of no use in socialist society. In the first years after the revolution, they were very active, and their circle included Vladimir Mayakovsky, Sergei Eisenstein, and Vsevolod Meyerhold. They received some support from the Commissariat of Education but their ideas were more often regarded within the Party as a manifestation of bourgeois decadence.[6]

The vehemence of the RAPP's criticism of the LEF suggests that it saw in its theories a serious threat to goals it had set for proletarian writers. From the beginning of the movement the connection between journalism, on the one hand, and imaginative literature, on the other, had been very close. In the Party's 1925 resolution, the reference to workers' and rural correspondence as "embryonic" forms implied that it was to be one source of the broad all-encompassing literature that was envisioned for the future. Without denying the value of the short journalistic sketch, it suggested that proletarian literature was not to be restricted to them. Learning from the bourgeois heritage was to assist writers in broadening out into other forms. In the eyes of the October Group and the RAPP, the LEF probably posed a threat to the fulfillment of this goal, in providing writers with arguments for disregarding the heritage and restricting themselves to journalism. Second, they undermined the RAPP's criticism of the abstractness that it considered a shortcoming of much proletarian literature.

Fadeyev sees in the opposition between fact and art, postulated by the LEF, the implication of a separation of fact and theory. Accordingly he begins his criticism of the LEF by discussing the relation between fact and theory in science and art. Both of these disciplines, he asserts, are means of comprehending reality, proceeding from the world of fact and appearance to the essence, the laws of cause and effect determining change and development. Borrowing from Plekhanov, he explains that while science presents these laws abstractly, art does it sensually and concretely, in a unique combination of essence and appearance. In neither case are facts rejected as such, but rather selected according to their importance or relevance. As the scientist, in selecting those facts he considers important, proceeds from a theory, so does the artist select according to his world view, which in a class society reflects the interests of one class or the other. In art, as in science, not every theory grasps the real laws of development. Fadeyev repeats the point once again that only the class whose historical task is to abolish all classes is in a position to understand society's real motive forces; only its world view, Marxism, can explain the laws of society's development. The reliance on facts alone, without a theory to illuminate them, cannot reveal the true nature of things in movement. Instead of penetrating to the essence, the LEF remains fixed at the level of the accidental and contingent.

Just as Marxism, in explaining the world, attempts to change it, so does proletarian literature. Fadeyev rejects the dichotomy drawn by the LEF between reflection and praxis, and attacks the notion that proletarian literature must be utilitarian, limited to the agitation of the day. He sees the effect of art and literature as more indirect: "The art of the proletariat, permeated with Marxism . . . , acts upon the whole psyche of the human being, transforming it in the direction of socialism" ("Der Hauptweg" 29). In doing so, it addresses both the rational and irrational in the reader. The LEF's idea of a completely rational, socialist person is as unrealistic as the other extreme, where only the subconscious exists. Their exaggerated objectivity and rationality, and the pure subjectivity and psychologism of bourgeois writers, he argues, are actually two sides of the same coin ("Der Hauptweg" 35).

At the end of his speech Fadeyev returned to a main bone of contention with the Proletcult, namely the importance of the literary heritage. "In our study of literature," he insisted, "we must turn primarily to the classic realists." Proletarian writers were not, however, to mechanically transfer the methods of bourgeois realists to their own writing, but rather develop new methods to express new content. Here "nonrealistic" schools of literature could, he indicated, provide important impulses ("Der Hauptweg" 43–44).

In setting itself off from the Proletcult and the LEF, the RAPP had thus formulated, by 1928, most of the principles that would be applied later by opponents of leftism in Germany and the United States as similar questions and problems presented themselves: the importance of the cultural heritage, the definition of proletarian literature according to its ideological orientation rather than the class origin of the writer, the necessity of portraying contradiction and process in characters that were both individual and representative, and, finally, the unity of reflection and praxis and the corollary demand for a broad literature that went beyond daily agitation and factory themes.

On the other hand, the sectarianism for which the RAPP was notorious would later be criticized as leftist within the proletarian literature movement. This consisted in the tendency to dismiss and attack writers who did not abide by its precepts, which included not only its rivals on the left, but of course contemporary non-Communist authors as well. This all-or-nothing attitude toward literature, which was also evident in the magazine *Literature of the World Revolution* in 1931 and 1932, would contribute to the RAPP's demise as the discovery and analysis of Marx, Engels, and Lenin's statements on various bourgeois writers of their own time fostered a more differentiated approach.

Notes

1. See Gorbunow 175–76; Lorenz 7–9; Gorsen et al. 147–48.

2. See Gorbunow 29–30; Goriely 110; Gorzka 18. Gorzka gives the title of the anthology compiled by Gorky as the *"First Almanac of Proletarian Writers."*

3. Trotsky's often-cited argument, presented in his book *Literature and Revolution,* was that in capitalism the proletariat did not have the material prerequisites for creating art and literature. Under the short period of dictatorship, the political struggle would have priority. The art and literature after that period would be classless and socialist, rather than proletarian.

4. As Education Commissar, Lunacharsky was in frequent contact with Lenin. He explained Lenin's position on workers cultural circles in "Lenin und die Kunst" 146.

5. Plekhanov formulated these ideas in his essay "Die Kunst und das gesell-schaftliche Leben."

6. See Brown, *Russian Literature Since the Revolution* 30–39; Ermolaev 72; Gallas 93; Lenzer 376–89.

2

The Discussion in
the German Bund
Proletarisch-Revolutionärer
Schriftsteller (BPRS)

The Internationalization of the Proletarian Literature
Movement and the Founding of the BPRS

WITH THE expansion of the proletarian literature movement, issues that had been debated in the Soviet Union from the early Proletcult controversy to the dispute between the RAPP and the LEF were addressed elsewhere. After its establishment in 1930, uniting national sections from all over the world, the IURW played an active role in these debates. While Deming Brown and James Gilbert identify the central organization with leftism, in fact the IURW sided with the antileftist faction in various controversies that arose in the German BPRS in the two years following the Charkov Conference.

The growth of proletarian literature and theater in the Soviet Union stimulated the revival of traditions that had been cultivated earlier in other countries. In Germany revolutionary literature and theater, committed to the political and social emancipation of the working class, had roots long before the October Revolution. Early examples could be found in some of the literature of the *Vormärz,* including poems of Heinrich Heine, and in the writings of Georg Weerth, Ferdinand Freiligrath, and Georg Herwegh. The nineteenth-century Social-Democratic press commonly published militant political poetry by worker-writers, some of which was collected in the 1900 anthology, *Stimmen der Freiheit. Bluthenlese der hervorragendsten Schöpfungen unserer Arbeiter- und Volksdichter* (Stieg and Witte 25).

In regard to the theater, Engels himself wrote a one-act play in 1847 for a workers' theater in Brussels (Knilli and Münchow 12). In the second half of the nineteenth century, agitprop theatrical performances were regularly featured at meetings and festivals of workers' political clubs, and in 1876 the first of a series of anthologies appeared under the title *Sozialistische*

Theaterstücke (Barth 16). After the turn of the century, the increasing reformism of the Social-Democratic party (SPD) was accompanied by a decline in this kind of militant, class-conscious theater and literature. In the postwar period the rise of the Proletcult in the Soviet Union helped spark a revival. In 1920 Erwin Piscator founded his Proletarisches Theater in Berlin (Fähnders and Rector 1:141), and by the mid-twenties there was a growing body of literature and drama supportive of the Communist party's revolutionary aims. The authors included radicalized writers of middle-class origin, such as the expressionist poet Johannes R. Becher and the dramatist Berta Lask, as well as worker-writers like Kurt Kläber. The amateur agitprop theater received a renewed impulse when the Soviet troupe, the Blue Blouses, visited Germany in 1927, and by the end of the twenties there were similar groups in cities throughout the country.[1]

The first attempt to coordinate international efforts to promote proletarian art and literature was made in August 1920 during the Second Comintern Congress. Representatives from nine countries, including the United States and Germany, established a Provisional International Proletcult Bureau, with Lunacharsky as chairman of the executive committee. The bureau called for the organization of conferences on proletarian culture, the formation of Proletcult groups, and the eventual convening of a world Proletcult congress. Although groups emerged in a few countries, the movement failed to get off the ground and the planned Proletcult congress did not take place (Botka 543; Jegorow 208–11).

Just as the promotion of proletarian literature continued in the Soviet Union after the decline of the Proletcult, so did efforts to establish an international organization of proletarian writers. In July 1924 delegates attending the Fifth Comintern Congress in Moscow met with Lunacharsky and members of the VAPP to discuss the question once more. The result was a resolution calling for the formation of proletarian-writers organizations in other countries, similar to those that existed in the Soviet Union. In keeping with the redefinition of proletarian culture after the Proletcult controversy, less emphasis was placed on class origin than in the 1920 appeal, so that all were to be included whose writings organized "the feelings and thoughts of the reader in the direction of communism" (qtd. in Albrecht and Kändler 21). A contact office was set up, with Lunacharsky once again as chairman. In September 1924 a statement was addressed "To the Proletarian and Revolutionary Writers of All Countries," urging them to assist in the foundation of a red literary international (Simons 156–57).

By 1926 the office was in communication with a hundred representatives from all over the world and plans were underway for an international conference. The First International Conference of Proletarian and Revolutionary Writers took place in November 1927, and was attended by writers and artists from fourteen countries who were in Moscow for the celebration of the tenth anniversary of the October Revolution. Both Lunacharsky and Auerbach gave speeches, and various writers reported on the situation in their respective countries.[2] Paraphrasing a resolution that was agreed upon at the conference, Soviet literary historian Oleg Jegorow writes: "Soviet literature and the proletarian literature in the capitalist countries develop under different conditions, and each one of them has its own distinct features. What is necessary is the struggle for the hegemony of revolutionary literature in every country. This struggle must be conducted in alliance with . . . fellow-travellers. It is necessary to proceed immediately with the organizing of associations of proletarian and revolutionary writers in the capitalist countries . . . " ("Die sozialistische" 217). To assist in this effort, an International Bureau for Revolutionary Literature (IBRL) was set up.

By the time the Second Conference of Proletarian and Revolutionary Writers took place, in November 1930 in Charkov, there were writers' organizations in Germany, Hungary, Austria, Poland, Czechoslovakia, Japan, and the United States. Altogether, over a hundred delegates from twenty-three countries participated. In the course of the conference, the IBRL was renamed the International Union of Revolutionary Writers (IURW), and a twenty-five-member executive council was elected (Jegorow 221–22). The new designation coincided with a change in character, in that the IURW would be henceforth not a union of individuals, but of writers' organizations. Its task would be to coordinate the movement in the various countries, exchanging information as well as literary and theoretical material. To this end the IURW established as its official organ the magazine *Literature of the World Revolution,* later called *International Literature,* which appeared bimonthly in separate German, English, and French and Russian editions.

At Charkov, Germany was described as the second most important center of proletarian culture alongside the Soviet Union.[3] The fact that Germany had the largest Communist party in a capitalist country, as well as a long tradition of revolutionary workers' literature and theater, no doubt contributed to the rapid expansion of the movement there. The first initiative toward the creation of a proletarian-revolutionary writers organization under Communist auspices came in 1927, when the Communist party (KPD) decided to create a "red cultural front" to counteract bourgeois ideology in the field of culture (Simons 122). Toward the end of the same year four German Communist writers, including Johannes R. Becher, attended the First International Conference of Proletarian and Revolutionary Writers in Moscow. Shortly after their return home they began organizing a revolutionary writers organization, and in October 1928 the BPRS was founded (Simons 161; Albrecht and Kändler 26–29).

The organizational statutes of the BPRS stated that it accepted professional or semiprofessional writers as well as worker-correspondents. Although membership in the KPD was not required, there was no doubt of the organization's allegiances. A Program of Action, drawn up by the founders, included among its points the defense of the Soviet Union, and, in keeping with the politics of the "Third Period," called on its members to use their literature as a weapon in preparing for the imminent collapse of capitalism and for the approaching revolution (Albrecht and Kändler 34, 38).

The Confrontation in the Early *Linkskurve* over Proletcult Views

The political situation that existed at the founding of the BPRS influenced the concept of proletarian-revolutionary literature that emerged in the first issues of the *Linkskurve*. With all indicators pointing to economic crisis in the capitalist countries, the Comintern decided in 1928 to intensify its opposition against reformism in the workers movement, with the goal of assuming leadership in the revolutionary situation that was anticipated. Against this background the newly founded BPRS, in the initial stage of defining itself as a group, rejected potential supporters among non-Communist, left-wing writers, and tended toward a concept of proletarian literature that recalled the early Russian Proletcult. This phase was soon followed by a period of dispute over the relation between art and politics, ethics and aesthetics, which found the *Linkskurve* editorial staff approaching the RAPP's position on the nature and function of proletarian literature. In formulating their views they turned initially to Franz Mehring, a contemporary of Plekhanov, who had likewise attempted to develop a Marxist approach to literary history and criticism. The similarities in the ideas of the two writers in addressing questions and problems that later arose in their respective countries no doubt contributed to the convergence of the aesthetic theory of the RAPP and the BPRS leadership in the period preceding the Charkov Conference.

In the first issues of the *Linkskurve,* differing views on proletarian literature appeared side by side, but, in general, positions corresponding to those of the Proletcult and the LEF predominated. Proletarian literature was thus defined according to the subject matter—which should be working-class life—and the class origin of the author, with professional writers relegated to the role of instructor.[4] The distinction between imaginative literature and journalism was blurred to the extent that worker-correspondence was considered a form of proletarian literature, and the direct agitatory effect elevated to the primary criterion in evaluating individual works.[5] The superiority of proletarian literature was proclaimed, with the implication that there was little to be learned from the bourgeois heritage.[6] The attitude toward contemporary, middle-class writers was, in general, one of undifferentiated opposition, and criticism was directed at Kurt Tucholsky, Upton Sinclair, and the novelist Alfred Döblin, among others.

Contrary to the claim, widely held by American literary historians, that leftism was only rejected as the Popular Front approached, criticism of the above positions and attitudes began in Germany in early 1930—in the middle of the Third Period—and was initiated by representatives of the Party. They received the immediate support of the IURW when it was set up eight months later.

In the February 1930 issue of the *Linkskurve* an article appeared entitled "Die Urzelle proletarischer Literatur." The editors' wish to disassociate themselves from the opinions of the author, Erich Steffen, was suggested by the introductory remark, "Wir stellen diesen Artikel zur Diskussion" (Steffen 649). Steffen's views were summarized in the sentence, "We do not need to construct a proletarian literature, we have it already" (651). In the factory and mine, wherever the class enemies confronted each other, this literature emerged spontaneously, he asserted (650). Only workers themselves had the creative power to produce it, he continued, explicitly excluding writers belonging to other classes from the cultural movement. Generalizing about bourgeois writers and literature, past and present, he placed them all in the same category, regarding them as irrelevant to proletarian writers. Since proletarian literature was first and foremost a weapon in the class struggle, he argued, the only criterion to be applied to it was its agitatory and propaganda value. The attempt should not be made to "look for it with bourgeois glasses" or to "form" it (651–52).

The response to Steffen's arguments came in the following issue in an article by "N. Kraus," whose real name was Joseph Winternitz, and who was head of the agitprop department of the KPD's Central Committee (Fähnders and Rector 2:216). In criticizing Steffen's positions, he defined proletarian literature according to ideology, rather than the subject matter or the class origin of the author, and called on writers to learn from the heritage in expanding beyond correspondence and factory themes toward a broad proletarian literature reflecting the whole society.

Focusing on the equation of worker-correspondence and proletarian literature, he declares Steffen's views to be "completely wrong." At dispute is not the value of correspondence as such. An unpolished report about a strike for a factory newspaper can be more useful to the class struggle than a masterpiece of proletarian literature, he explains. In Winternitz's view, Steffen's basic mistake is that he confuses with the finished product works that, in the case of a relatively small number of correspondents, might be regarded as the beginnings of proletarian literature. Behind the overvaluation of worker-correspondence Winternitz sees the condescending attempt to limit the proletariat to *"literature for workers,"* in the belief that they are not capable of producing or appreciating greater works of art (654–55). Not only the everyday events in the factory, but the "whole life of human society, the life of all classes" must be reflected "from the standpoint of the revolutionary proletariat," or Marxism-Leninism (653–654). This being the defining characteristic, professional middle-class writers who have broken with their class can also be a source of proletarian literature. The task of the BPRS is to aid these writers in ridding themselves of the remains of bourgeois influence, while at the same time helping the interested and talented worker-correspondent become "a real proletarian writer" by acquainting him with the best examples of revolutionary literature, including that of the bourgeoisie (654).

Winternitz's line of argument was continued in the April issue, a month later, in a commentary by the editorial staff on a long letter by Maxim Vallentin, a BPRS member who headed an agitprop theater group called *Das Rote Sprachrohr* (Gallas 107). Vallentin had maintained that the collective form of work in the agitprop theater constituted the essence of proletarian-revolutionary culture, as opposed to bourgeois, and that only the agitatory value should be considered in judging the products of that theater. In regard to the first point, the editors, echoing Winternitz's criticism of Steffen, accuse the author of confusing the beginnings—in this case, agitprop—with the finished product—the proletarian-revolutionary theater. Turning to his second argument, they see in the separation of the artistic and agitational value a negation of art. If one were to accept such a dichotomy, they assert, the logical thing would be to simply read editorials from the stage. In effect, Vallentin is calling for pure tendentiousness without art, and admitting by implication the opposite possibility—pure art without tendency, or art for art's sake. Raising the agitational effect to the sole criterion of literary criticism, he has unwittingly landed in the camp of bourgeois aestheticism (Die Redaktion der *Linkskurve* 16–17).

Franz Mehring's Literary Theory

In their answer to Vallentin the editors mentioned Mehring as the source of their observations on tendentiousness and the relation between propaganda and the aesthetic value of art. That this question should become central at this point is understandable. From the beginning of the organized proletarian-culture movement in the Soviet Union, one of the defining characteristics of the new art and literature had been its proposed social and political role, in helping to bring about and develop socialism. Its function as a weapon of agitation and propaganda was bound to be emphasized even more in a situation in which Communist parties were anticipating revolution, as was the case in Germany in the late twenties. At the same time the goal of the BPRS remained an art and literature that was to be as all-encompassing as its bourgeois predecessor: broad in theme, varied in form, and high in artistic quality.

Writing in the decade before World War I, Plekhanov had suggested one answer to the dilemma now posed by the political and artistic goals of the movement. The best art, he maintained in 1912, avoided abstraction and distortion while propagating ideas that were true, and morals that were to the good of the society as a whole. Addressing the question of art and morals in his writings on aesthetics, Mehring, in contrast, was strongly influenced by Kant's division of the good, the true, and the beautiful into separate qualities, each of which is perceived by different powers or faculties of the mind. Accordingly, he sometimes saw artistic appreciation as a disinterested pleasure in form, in which, ideally, knowledge and ethics play no role. While Plekhanov believed that revolutionary periods provided the best conditions for great art, Mehring states, "In all revolutionary periods, in all classes fighting for their liberation, taste will be abundantly sullied by logic and morals" ("Aesthetische Streifzüge" 76). Since this has always been the case anyway, he advises the modern proletariat not to be ashamed if it prefers in its literature "a moral tagged on at the end" ("Kunst und Proletariat I" 20).

In actual practice, however, Mehring departed from the position that class bias, as such, compromised the aesthetic value of a work, and developed a concept of realism close to Plekhanov's. Tendentiousness in itself is not reprehensible, he explains, but rather the use of "artistically inadequate means" in expressing one's political and social bias (qtd. in Koch 144). To be avoided are abstraction and distortion. He writes that "rhymed editorials are even more reprehensible than unrhymed ones" ("Der heutige Naturalismus" 14). Likewise unacceptable in art is the "distortion or coloring of a real occurrence for certain political purposes" (qtd. in Koch 140).

For Plekhanov the best art combined essence and appearance, avoiding photographic reproduction of an accidental reality, on the one hand, and abstractness, on the other. Mehring similarly sees art as a union of the individual and the species—two terms he borrows from Kant. Comparing Gerhard Hauptmann's *Vor Sonnenaufgang* with Tolstoy's depiction of peasants in *Power of Darkness,* he finds that Tolstoy presents "a typical portrayal of Russian peasant life," while, in Hauptmann's drama, only a single figure "embodies a whole species in a thoroughly living individual." Two other characters he considers, "abstrakte Schemen" ("Aesthetische Streifzüge" 92–93). Only in *Die Weber* does he succeed in creating "a panoply of characters that are seen truly artistically: full of gripping, stirring life . . . and still not a brutal copy of an accidental reality" ("Aesthetische Streifzüge" 95).

Mehring applies the term *typical* not only to characters but to the historical process as well, describing *Die Weber* as historically typical ("Aesthetische Streifzüge" 95). Like Plekhanov, he sees the main weakness of most naturalist writers in their tendency toward photograph-like reproduction and in their inability to perceive the socially new and developing and to dramatically portray great historical material. "They found the lumpenproletariat in the brothel and the corner bar," he writes "but they didn't know where the class-conscious proletariat is working and fighting" ("Kunst und Proletariat II" 26).

Mehring's advice to naturalist writers as to the direction they should follow corresponds with Plekhanov's. With Hauptmann's drama *Die Weber* in mind, he explains that, in works where naturalism succeeds in breaking through "the capitalist way of thinking" and grasps "the beginnings of a new world in its inner essence," it becomes "a new form of artistic representation, "the equal of earlier ones in greatness and power," called upon to surpass them one day in beauty and truth," and revolutionary in its effect ("Der heutige Naturalismus" 13).

The Wittvogel Series

Shortly after the dispute over Steffen's and Vallentin's views a series began, which, in examining Mehring's writings on literature and aesthetics, attempted to lay the theoretical groundwork for future literary criticism in the *Linkskurve*. Karl A. Wittvogel, the author, was a member of the editorial staff and one of the leading literary critics of the KPD daily, *Die Rote Fahne* (Gallas 41, 53). Wittvogel attributes the contradictions in Mehring's views to the dual influence of Kant and Hegel, and formulates his own position on art and politics around those elements of Mehring's theory that he traces to the latter philosopher. In doing so he arrives at an approximation of the RAPP's theory of dialectical materialism in literature.

Wittvogel begins with an examination of differences in Kant's and Hegel's views on the relationship between nature and art. For Kant, he explains, art involves disinterested pleasure in form, separate from ethical and cognitive considerations; it imitates nature, but the beauty it attains is inferior to natural beauty (10, 15). Hegel, in contrast, places art above nature, seeing it as a means of comprehending and revealing the spirit—a higher reality not immediately perceptible in nature or society (16). Interpreting the "spirit" to be the laws of development governing natural and social processes, Wittvogel quotes Hegel in explaining that a genuine work of art expresses the profoundest truths accessible in a given historical period (24). While science and philosophy convey these truths abstractly, art presents them to the senses (15). In every period, he adds, the ability to grasp society's laws of development is class determined. Applying this principle to bourgeois literature, he connects the decline of realism to the fact that a true representation of society's contradictions would be too much of a self-indictment (21, 24).

Like Mehring he argues that realism must reflect not only the decaying but the developing as well. Naturalism, although it did deal with some of these contradictions, was unrealistic to the extent that it ignored the heroism of the class struggle. Only proletarian literature, he maintains, is capable of combining that heroism with an accurate revelation of society's contradictions. In doing so, it automatically has the effect of an accusation, and becomes a weapon in the class struggle, expressing the proletariat's desire to overthrow the bourgeoisie. But only if one accepts Kant's view of art as a "beautiful, subjective-oriented genre" can the "seriousness of these proletarian intentions" be seen as imposed on a work "from without," as Mehring in some of his writings saw it (24). Defining tendentiousness as the class-determined intention to elicit a response, Wittvogel explains that, for the proletarian writer, this intention need not compromise the realism of his work. Therefore not tendentiousness as such was to be shunned, but rather abstraction, distortion and a schoolmasterly tone. He argues: "The proletarian work of art, in contrast to the bourgeois, need not be ashamed of its tendentiousness. On the contrary, only in expressing profound and essential class experiences and intentions . . . is it a genuine work of art, great and true" (25).

The Role of the IURW

The degree of RAPP influence on the BPRS during this period has been largely a matter of speculation. In regard to the German group's politics, David Pike sees the attacks on left-wing, non-Communist writers such as Kurt Tucholsky as the aftereffect of a trip taken by a BPRS delegation to the Soviet Union in the Fall of 1929, at the height of the RAPP's campaign against the writer Boris Pilnyak. Pike indicates, on the other hand, that in the area of creative method there was less influence (*German Writers* 33–34). Verification of this can be seen in the complaint of BPRS member Alfred Kurella at Charkov that there was a lack of information on theoretical developments in the Soviet proletarian literature movement (Kurella 261–63). One of the resolutions drawn up at the conference likewise confirmed that there had been insufficient communication in this area ("Resolution on Political and Creative Questions" 86).

This situation changed with the creation of the IURW as central organisation of the proletarian literature movement. Starting in 1931 the IURW played an active role in the German discussion, supporting the BPRS leadership in the direction it had taken in the *Linkskurve* since early 1930.

The first comment on the dispute that had taken place in the magazine appeared in September of that year, in a report announcing the upcoming international conference of proletarian writers. Noting that Soviet writers had not been in a position to supply individual groups in other countries with Marxist critical material, the author, Bela Illes, the Hungarian secretary of the IBRL, reports that one purpose of the conference will be to arrange for the exchange of such material in the future. The economic crisis had brought many middle-class writers close to the Communist parties, he explains, so that relations with sympathetic writers was to be another focus of the conference. In his connection he praises the BPRS for struggling against what he calls "ultra-leftist sectarian tendencies" ("Vor dem" 16).

At the conference itself, Illes again noted that the *Linkskurve* had "disregarded possible cooperation with progressive petty bourgeois writers, and even repelled them" ("Report" 16). Addressing the question of sectarianism, Serafina Gopner, the representative of the Comintern at Charkov, explained: "The organization of revolutionary writers must not erect a superfluous barrier between itself and those whose revolutionary instinct is greatly developed but who have not succeeded as yet to come to any definite standpoint, who have not yet acquired firm Marxist views" (24). In this connection she defines as leftism the position that "we must refuse to seek revolutionary writers elsewhere, than in the worker-correspondent movement . . . " (25). Citing John Dos Passos and the German writer Ernst Glaeser as examples, a "Resolution on Political and Creative Questions," which was adopted at the conference, noted that the movement of sympathetic writers toward Communism was "a most complicated and responsible task. . . . a problem of guidance, not of command" (90). This statement would be quoted two years later in the *New Masses* in criticizing leftist sectarianism in the American movement.

The criticism of sectarianism at Charkov did not, however, apply to liberal writers in general, or to Social-Democratic leaders, in contrast to Popular Front policy later on. In keeping with the ultramilitant line of the Third Period, reform-oriented workers' parties, as well as supporters of Trotsky, were denounced as "social-fascist," as various speakers warned of rightist deviation. In regard to culture this referred to the denial of the proletariat's ability to create its own literature within capitalism, and to the underestimation of the worker-correspondents' role in this process. In this connection it was emphasized that while the defining quality of proletarian literature was its ideological orientation, ideally workers should form the main contingent in the movement.

While leftism was discussed in regard to Germany, the issue of "rightism" arose in a conflict surrounding the magazine *Le Monde,* which had been set up by the writer Henri Barbusse in response to the First International Conference of Proletarian Writers in 1927. While the early *Linkskurve* had rejected potential, non-Communist supporters, the French magazine had declared its independence of all parties and invited leading Social-

Democrats as well as Trotsky himself to contribute to a questionnaire in *Le Monde* on the crisis of socialism (Illes,"Report" 16). This was criticized at Charkov, as well as the failure to promote worker-correspondents.

Taking Barbusse to task, Gopner, speaking for the Comintern, at the same time warned: " . . . in this struggle we must avoid all demogogical excess . . . when referring to such writers, whose revolutionism is above all doubt" (27). In fact, the IBRL had endorsed the removal of Andor Gabor from the editorial staff of the *Linkskurve* in early 1930 for his overly harsh criticism of Barbusse and German non-Communist writers (Friedrich 192).

While the delegates at Charkov were called upon to reject both rightism and leftism, the BPRS would increasingly focus on the latter in the two years following the conference, with the active support of the IURW.

The endorsement at Charkov of the *Linkskurve*'s move away from sectarianism was coupled with approval of its approach to the question of creative method. The Wittvogel series received special praise (Gallas 54), and a speech by Auerbach tended in the same general theoretical direction as the series. Contrary to Max Eastman's claim that aesthetic matters were ignored at Charkov, the *Linkskurve* related that Auerbach "formulated the most important basic questions of Marxist literary science, resulting from years of theoretical and political discussion" ("Durchbruch" 2). The closeness to their own views was immediately apparent, so that the report had the effect of an additional endorsement of the magazine's theoretical direction. Paraphrasing Auerbach's speech, the *Linkskurve* reported that he had defined proletarian literature according to the "world-view of the revolutionary proletariat," or "dialectical materialism," rather than the class origin of the writer ("Durchbruch" 2). The realism to be striven for was to avoid both the bourgeois pseudo-objectivity as well as the "petit-bourgeois subjectivity" of modern literature. The revolutionary writers' "proletarian subjectivity" was declared to be the prerequisite for the "highest degree of objectivity" ("Durchbruch" 3). "Pseudo-marxist theoreticians" were criticized, who undialectically separated literature into that which imparted knowledge and that which changed society, and who proclaimed certain literary forms to be the only ones suitable to proletarian literature. "In all real art," the report states, these functions are "inseparably bound together," as in Marxism itself ("Durchbruch" 3). Finally, the importance of the bourgeois cultural heritage was emphasized, along with the need to improve the quality of proletarian literature.

Starting in mid-1931 the IURW, through a number of emissaries, took an active part in the German discussion, thereby providing further information on the views of the central organization during this period.

Since the founding of the BPRS, continuing differences had prevented agreement on the formulation of a program for the group. In mid-1931 two members started drawing one up, and in September their proposal was sent out to the other members with the announcement of a discussion about it in October (Albrecht and Kändler 76). Again there was disagreement, with the leadership of the Communist faction in the BPRS objecting to what it considered ultraleftist positions. Specifically they cited the neglect of the question of the heritage, a general lack of self-criticism and the corollary assertion that proletarian literature was qualitatively superior to bourgeois literature (*Zur Tradition* 488). In October 1931 Bela Illes criticized the program while visiting Berlin (Gallas 60), as did Auerbach, who was there in the beginning of 1932 (Weiss 307). In response to a request by *Linkskurve* editor Johannes Becher, the Executive Council of the IURW sent a lengthy criticism of the proposed program, which closely corresponded to the criticism made by the leadership of the Communist faction in the BPRS.[7] Thus the IURW attacked what it saw as a glossing over of the shortcomings of German proletarian literature, and criticized the disregard for questions of artistic quality, large forms and the cultural heritage. In addition, it observed that too much value was being placed on the sole fact of the writer's social origin, rather than on ideology (Weiss 307).

This criticism was shared by Georg Lukacs, who had also been sent to Berlin by the IURW in the summer of 1931 to take part in the discussion over the program. Approximately two years earlier the Hungarian literary historian and theoretician had moved from Vienna to Moscow, where he took up a research post at the Marx-Engels Institute. Founded on Lenin's initiative in 1921, the institute collected and edited Marx's and Engels's, and later Lenin's, writings. Here Lukacs collaborated with the Soviet aesthetician and philosopher Mikhail Lifschitz in examining the material collected by the institute, for the purpose of formulating an aesthetic theory based on Marxism-Leninism (Fekete and Karádi 144–46).

Although he failed to achieve consensus within the BPRS on a program, during his stay in Germany he published several articles in the *Linkskurve* that are of particular importance in understanding the development of Marxist aesthetics from the RAPP's concept of proletarian literature to the theory of socialist realism. First of all, in addition to providing a summary of the approach to aesthetics that was becoming dominant in the

IURW and the BPRS, the articles illustrate what that approach meant in actual literary criticism. Second, insofar as they anticipate basic elements of the concept of socialist realism, they demonstrate the continuity of the discussion over aesthetics, thereby questioning oversimplified assumptions concerning the connection between literature and politics. The striking parallels between Lukacs's criticism of German proletarian literature and the campaign against leftism in the United States later on, undermine the view that the rejection of tendentiousness and utilitarianism was a dissident position that was only adopted by the movement's leadership in connection with the Popular Front. Finally, Lukacs's frequent references to writings of Marx and Engels point to a key factor in the modification of the RAPP's theory that was to culminate in the formulation of socialist realism.

Lukacs's Distinction between *Tendenz* and *Parteilichkeit*

The first article in the series was a critical analysis of the literary method of Willi Bredel, a BPRS member who had recently published two novels. Bredel, a metal worker, joined the KPD shortly after its founding and wrote correspondence for the Party press until being sentenced to prison in 1930. Prevented from taking an active part in the daily Party work, he turned to the novel as a kind of extended correspondence, with the purpose of winning support for the KPD's united front against fascism.[8] The novels, which he had published by the end of 1931, were, in short, what would be commonly categorized as propaganda literature.

Lukacs begins his criticism of Bredel by praising the broad structure of his novels, which he characterizes as "epic," that is, complete or "closed" but without beginning or end ("Willi Bredels Romane" 720). Turning to Bredel's shortcomings he finds that the basic problem is that the general framework remains just that. Bredel fails to combine the abstract political with the concrete: "That which could make it [the plot] living: living people and living, changing inter-character relations, are just about missing completely." Instead the protagonists are like actors in character parts, with "one set characteristic (several perhaps), which are repeated and underlined at every possible and impossible opportunity" ("Willi Bredels Romane" 722). Their language is equally abstract. Lukacs gives the example of a young Communist woman who remarks, while listening to the radio with some workers, "The radio is a mouthpiece of the ruling class and hour after hour millions of people are worked upon by it and made stupid" (qtd. in "Willi Bredels Romane" 723).

Lukacs insists that such shortcomings in characterization are not merely a "technical" matter, but reflect a general failure to grasp reality dialectically, as contradiction and process. He observes that Bredel presents not real development with all its setbacks and difficulties, but results, so that, in the end, he distorts reality: "The decent non-Party member becomes 'suddenly' a Communist; the poorly functioning cell 'suddenly' takes the leadership of the strike into its hands; at meetings the revolutionary line always wins out over the union bigwigs, etc." ("Willi Bredels Romane" 725).

The kind of abstractness and distortion that Lukacs attacks in his review of Bredel's novels had been criticized earlier by Plekhanov, Mehring, and the RAPP. Attempts in Germany to apply a single term to these qualities had so far proved problematic. The contradictions in Mehring's concept of tendentiousness have been pointed out. Wittvogel's redefinition of the term and his distinction between proletarian and bourgeois tendentiousness was futile since, in common usage, the term continued to connote distortion and manipulation for political ends.

The next attempt at clarification was made by Trude Richter, First Secretary of the BPRS, in the *Linkskurve* in March 1932. Here she restricts the term *tendency* to a distorted portrayal of reality, expressing a "false consciousness." Since "proletarian class interest demands precisely the unadorned reflection of real conditions," it has no need for distortion, she writes. In this case "partisanship" coincided with objectivity (Richter 28–29). A few months later Becher makes the same distinction, arguing that proletarian-revolutionary writers need not realize any ideals, but simply set free in their work "the elements of the new society that have already developed within the bosom of the collapsing bourgeois order" ("Kühnheit" 10).

Richter's and Becher's remarks on partisanship and tendentiousness stimulated a discussion in the BPRS,[9] and in June, Lukacs devoted an entire article to this distinction. This same article appeared in translation in the second issue of the *Partisan Review,* two years later, and played an obvious role in forming the editors' approach to the propaganda question. Lukacs begins by tracing the history of the term *tendency* back to the mid-nineteenth century, when it was used as an epithet against progressive bourgeois literature. Later on, he recounts, proletarian writers in Germany adopted it to describe the political bias of their own work.

Repeating the point made by the editorial staff in their criticism of Maxim Vallentin in April 1930, he argues that this was a mistake, since it implied the possibility of non-tendentious, "pure" art ("Tendenz" 14–15). Once this dichotomy is granted, he maintains, the writer is faced with two possibilities. The first is to abjure all aesthetic values and restrict themselves to day-to-day agitation, as Vallentin had proposed. The other possibility is to accept the primacy of form while attempting to weave a political message, in the form of sermon-like commentary, into literary works—the moral tagged on the end that Mehring had found acceptable ("Tendenz" 15–17).

Underlying the pure art–propaganda dichotomy Lukacs sees an undialectical conception of art and morals. Rejecting a rigid separation between these two categories, the revolutionary writer, he insists, must portray radical sociopolitical demands, not as expressions of some moral ideal imposed from without, but rather as part of the actual trends of development of reality. An accurate, dialectical portrayal of reality must include the social aspirations and demands that have evolved in the course of the class struggle, and depict the process of their development. When the subjective, moral factor is conceived thus, the problem connected with the dichotomy between ethics and aesthetics is resolved. The writer imposes no demands from without, in the form of moralistic exhortation, nor does he "distort, rearrange or 'tendentiously' color reality." The bias in his work corresponds with the tendency of reality itself; the sociopolitical demands that emerge from his writing appear as an integral part of the dynamics of objective reality ("Tendenz" 19).

Lukacs recommends that the term *Tendenz* be applied to the undialectical portrayal of the subjective factor. In addition to moralizing commentary on the part of the author and characters, this refers to the idealistic glorification of that which the writer supports, as well as the caricature of that which he does not ("Tendenz" 20). The term *Parteilichkeit* is to be used to describe the essential quality of revolutionary proletarian literature—the commitment to "the class that is the vehicle of historical progress in our time," and to the party that represents the interests of the class as a whole. Far from leading to a distortion of reality, it is the "necessary prerequisite for the correct, dialectical representation and artistic formation of reality" ("Tendenz" 19). Lukacs makes it clear that this is a goal to be striven for, and not a description of the German proletarian-literature movement as it is. "Our literature," he writes, "even in its best products, is still full of 'tendentiousness' " ("Tendenz" 20).

Literature versus Journalism

In his next series of articles Lukacs returns to questions that the RAPP had addressed in its dispute with the LEF: the relation between literature and journalism, and the nature of art as a weapon. The occasion was the appearance of a novel by Ernst Ottwalt exposing the class nature of the judicial system. Basing his analysis of the novel on the distinction between art and science, Lukacs criticizes the manipulation of character and plot to insert abstract editorial commentary and documentary information, and calls for the union of essence and appearance in typical characters and situations. Addressing the question of utilitarianism, he rejects the restriction of proletarian literature to political agitation, and anticipates the "great proletarian work of art" ("Aus der Not" 17), which, in providing an undistorted reflection of the basic developmental trends of society, contributes to its transformation. All of these positions would later be argued by opponents of leftism in the United States. On only one issue did Lukacs differ from his American counterparts: in discussing the heritage he took a strongly antimodernist stand.

Lukacs sees Ottwalt's novel as representative of a whole literary direction in which writers such as Upton Sinclair and Ilya Ehrenburg employ journalistic methods in trying to get away from what they consider the outmoded bourgeois methods of the invented plot and artistically formed characters. Repeating Fadeyev's observation on naturalism and the LEF, he regards the emergence of this kind of novel as a reaction against the psychologism of the recent bourgeois novel, with its emphasis on private life and emotion. Rejecting this form of subjectivity, writers such as Ottwalt strive for a "purely social content," and objectivity that is "true to fact" ("Reportage oder Gestaltung 1" 25).

Since exposure of the abuses of capitalist society is their main concern, the portrayal of character becomes secondary. In Ottwalt's novel, for example, the main character's progress from student to judge is little more than a pretext for dealing with the various levels of the judicial system. This being his principal function, he is, as an individual, interchangeable with any number of others. The various characters in the novel are like scientific specimens, "a series of examples masked as characters" ("Reportage oder Gestaltung 2" 28). Their interaction is not organic, but often serves merely as an opportunity to introduce documentary information and abstract commentary.

Lukacs sees the class basis of the journalistic novel in petit-bourgeois opposition to capitalism. Like Fadeyev, he attributes the emphasis on facts to the lack of theory. Ignorance of the laws governing social change and development prevents the writers in question from perceiving economic and social phenomena of capitalist society as relations between people. Capable of comprehending only individual isolated facts, they attempt to "depict the objective purely objectively," without the dialectical interaction with the subjective. In practice, subjectivity does appear in their novels, but either as the superimposed moralizing commentary of the author, or in the form of short excursions into the private sphere of the characters, that have no organic connection to the action ("Reportage oder Gestaltung 1" 25).

In distinguishing between the methods of literature and reportage, Lukacs insists that the superiority of the one over the other is not at issue. Reportage he regards as an indispensable form of journalism, which can, like fiction, draw the connection between the particular and the general, the necessary and accidental. The principal difference lies in the way in which this connection is made. In reportage the fact—the individual case—is only an example, an illustration of the general, and, as such, is exchangeable with others. It becomes connected with the general social context and emerges as typical only through abstract explanation and commentary. Like all journalism, reportage operates with the methods of science, addressing primarily reason and understanding.

In literature, on the other hand, the particular—the individual fate must itself appear typical, containing class characteristics as individual ones. The artistic whole must be rendered typical through the living interaction of the characters ("Reportage oder Gestaltung 1" 27).

In the final article of the series, which appeared in the last issue of the *Linkskurve* before the Nazi takeover, Lukacs responds to Ottwalt's argument that the traditional novel is outmoded as form, and is unsuited to the role of weapon that proletarian literature must play in the present political situation. Turning to the question of utilitarianism, Lukacs again expands on positions that had been presented earlier within the RAPP and the BPRS. Differentiating between propaganda and agitation, he accuses Ottwalt of wanting to confine proletarian writers to the latter, and of taking into account only the immediate situation. Precisely at present, he argues, there is a need for "the great proletarian work of art," which summarizes the basic developmental tendencies of the whole period, without neglecting the actual and immediate. The higher the theoretical and literary niveau of such a work, the more effective it will be, both as agitation and propaganda ("Aus der Not" 16–17).

Addressing the question of the heritage, Lukacs sees in Ottwalt's remarks on the traditional novel a rebirth of the Proletcult idea of a completely new art and literature. Believing that they are rejecting everything bourgeois, writers such as Ottwalt, he asserts, actually wind up adopting tendencies of bourgeois literature in its decadent phase. Lukacs defines decadence in literature as a split between the subjective and objective, which he traces to the second half of the nineteenth century in France when Flaubert and Goncourt "initiated the subjectivistic transformation of realism," while Zola anticipated the journalistic novel ("Aus der Not" 20).

The exclusion of modernist writers from the heritage, as implied in Lukacs's remarks, would be the source of heated debates in the Soviet Union and among German writers in exile later on in the thirties. In the American movement, in contrast, a flexible, nondogmatic approach to the question persisted throughout the decade.

Notes

1. The influence of the "Blue Blouses" is discussed in Stieg and Witte 111.
2. The conference is discussed in Weiss 293–95; Jegorow 214–17.
3. Bela Illes, the Hungarian head of the IBRL, made this evaluation in his "Report of the Sekretariat of the IBRL" 15.
4. Andor Gabor took this position in his article "Über proletarisch-revolutionäre Literatur."
5. See, for example, Kurt Kläber, "An die Leser der 'Literarischen Welt.' "
6. See Johannes R. Becher, "Einen Schritt Weiter."
7. Excerpts from the IURW's position paper have been reprinted in Friedrich 414–18.
8. The information on Bredel was obtained from a reprint of his novel *Rosenhofstrasse* (W. Berlin: Oberbaumverlag, 1974), Appendix 159–60.
9. This connection was indicated in a footnote to Lukacs's article "Tendenz oder Parteilichkeit" in the June 1932 issue of the *Linkskurve* 13.

3

The American Communist
Party Press and the *New Masses*

The *New Masses* and the John Reed Clubs

A s was the case in Germany, working-class literature, advocating socialism and revolution, had its own tradition in the United States,
long before the emergence of the Proletcult in the Soviet Union. The
majority of workers being of foreign origin in the latter half of the
nineteenth century, much of the radical political poetry, prose, and agitprop theater of the time was created by German immigrant socialists.
Although they continued to employ their native language, publishing
mostly in newspapers such as the New York *Volkszeitung* and the Chicago
Arbeiter-Zeitung, they frequently addressed American social conditions
and events, and were, therefore, not simply adherents of a movement in
exile.[1] During the same period, miners in the Pennsylvania coal fields—
primarily of Irish and English extraction—cultivated the militant labor
song,[2] a tradition continued by the IWW in the years preceding World
War I. Antecedents of the proletarian fiction created by professional
writers could be seen in some of the works of Upton Sinclair and Jack
London.

In 1901 the first magazine specifically devoted to socialist art and
literature, the *Comrade,* made its appearance. Connected with the Socialist party, it published a wide range of political views, and featured writings by Maxim Gorky, Sinclair, and London (Aaron 18–19). The magazine did not survive long, and in 1911 another one, the *Masses,* was
founded. Following changes in the editorial board, it became explicitly
pro-Socialist by 1913. The magazine combined bohemian opposition
to bourgeois standards of morality and "good taste" with support for
workers' struggles. Its unequivocal antiwar stand resulted in its being
banned from the mails, and its editors were tried for obstructing the
draft (Aaron 36).

A central link between prewar cultural developments and the proletarian literature movement of the twenties and thirties was the radical

reporter and poet John Reed. Anticipating the cooperation between professional writers and the left wing of the labor movement that was common in the thirties, Reed and a group of other writers and artists assisted striking textile workers from Paterson, New Jersey, in staging a pageant in New York's Madison Square Garden in 1913, illustrating their cause.[3] Reed also published articles in the *Masses* on the strike, and a year later he joined the staff of the magazine. Daniel Aaron relates that between 1915 and 1917 he made plans for a workers' theater "along the lines of the Paterson pageant" (Aaron 39). Prevented from publishing in the United States because of his antiwar stand, Reed traveled to the Soviet Union on the eve of the October Revolution. After returning home he compressed his impressions of the revolution in his famous book, *Ten Days that Shook the World.*

As American representative at the Proletcult meeting in Moscow in 1920 (Botka 561), he provided the first direct link to the proletarian-literature movement of the Soviet Union. He died of a fever later in the same year, and an American section of the Proletcult never materialized. Nevertheless, articles on the subject of proletarian literature appeared in various magazines, such as V. F. Calverton's *Modern Quarterly* and the *Liberator,* which succeeded the *Masses* in 1918 and included Joseph Freeman and Michael Gold among its editors.

Another attempt at organization was reported by Freeman in his semiautobiographical account of the left-wing literary scene in the twenties and early thirties, *An American Testament.* He related that, in 1925, a form letter was sent from the Soviet Union to various well-known American writers, encouraging them to form a proletarian writers group and to join the executive committee of an existing international group of proletarian writers (372–73). In all probability the source of the letter was the VAPP, which, starting in 1924, had renewed the Proletcult's call for the formation of revolutionary-writers organizations in other countries. Freeman reported that many writers responded favorably but were unclear about what the nature and function of an American Proletarian Writers and Artists League should be, so that this second attempt at organization also failed (373).

The year 1926 was nevertheless of special significance in that it saw the establishment of the magazine *New Masses,* which was to play an important part in initiating the proletarian-literature movement at the end of the twenties. The *Liberator* folded in 1924, and former editors Gold and Freeman joined a group of liberals in founding the new magazine, which proposed to combine literature and politics in a manner similar to the old *Masses*. While support for workers' struggles in the factory and the law courts was expressed in short stories, poetry, and journalistic sketches from the beginning of the *New Masses,* it was not until 1928 that the magazine explicitly declared itself an organ of proletarian literature. In that year Gold became sole editor after the magazine encountered financial difficulties and a large part of the liberal contingent had left. A year later, members of the *New Masses'* staff founded the first John Reed Club in order to develop the talents of worker-writers and artists.

It was mostly members of the first John Reed Club and the *New Masses* who comprised the American delegation to Charkov. Both the club and the magazine became recognized as the American section of the IURW, thereby receiving the same status as the BPRS and the *Linkskurve* in Germany. Over the next year and a half, John Reed Clubs arose in cities throughout the United States. At their first national conference, in May 1932, a program was adopted in which adherence to the points agreed upon at Charkov—primarily to fight against fascism and to defend the Soviet Union—were included in the membership rules. The newly founded clubs, independent of each other up to then, were organized into a loose federation with a National Executive Board in New York.[4]

Like the BPRS, the John Reed Clubs were not formally an organ of the Communist party, and only about twenty-five percent of the members were actually in the Party. The social structure of the German and American groups was also similar: white-collar workers and members of the lower middle class outnumbered blue-collar workers, and unemployment was high in all three categories (Alexandre 91–94).

In the first years of the clubs' existence they stood in approximately the same relationship to the *New Masses* as the BPRS to the *Linkskurve,* that is, the magazine publicized their events, published literature by club members, and provided information on the movement in other countries. On the other hand, reflecting the general neglect of literary theory in the United States at this time, the *New Masses* devoted far less attention to aesthetics than the *Linkskurve*—a difference that would later elicit criticism from the IURW. Nevertheless certain principles were formulated on the Communist left in the period preceding the Charkov Conference, which pointed in the same direction as those propagated by RAPP and the BPRS leadership.

The Influence of Upton Sinclair
and V. F. Calverton

The discussion over proletarian literature and aesthetics began in the *New Masses* and the Communist party press long before there was a literary movement to speak of. The starting point can be found in the efforts of certain Communist writers to define the relation between literature and politics in face of antiliterary attitudes and extreme proletcult views within the party.

For the fledgling American Communist party, in the process of consolidating itself after emerging from the underground, and struggling to gain a foothold in the labor unions, cultural activity was low on the list of priorities in the mid-twenties. A review of the *Daily Worker* in 1924 and 1925 reveals how far removed American Communists were from the discussion over proletarian culture taking place in the Soviet Union. The views of Robin Dunbar, a semiregular contributor to the newspaper at this time, can be taken as an example. In a letter to the editor in 1924 he argues that "literature has no proper place in the proletarian revolution." His esteem for Gorky, Shaw, Sinclair, and London, he declares, has disappeared and passed on to "the heroes of the Third International . . . all the realists of today, who write their novels and plays in acts, not in words" ("Maxim Gorky's" page number illegible). In a whole-page article some months later, he revises his position somewhat, now dismissing not literature as such, but all that which is not explicitly Marxist-Leninist and written by workers for workers. He declares Greek art to be "rotten" because it was based on slave society, and envisions Mark Twain, Upton Sinclair, and Jack London, with their "slobbering heroes and heroines," being "thrown out of the door by the scruff of their necks" while the "clean high-spirited men and women actors of the factory are invited in" ("Mammonart" page number illegible). In the article he cites Proletcult leader, Pletnev, as the source of his position on literature, apparently unaware that an extensive criticism of Pletnev had appeared in *Pravda* the year before, under Lenin's direction (C. Vaughan James 50).

Lacking an earlier Marxist theoretician of the stature of Plekhanov or Mehring, and out of touch with the current Soviet discussion, Communist writers such as Michael Gold and Joseph Freeman, who did not share Dunbar's contempt for literature, now turned to Upton Sinclair and V. F. Calverton in attempting to work out their own position on literature and politics. Both Sinclair and Calverton wrote books in the mid-twenties claiming to be interpretations of literature from the standpoint of economics.

Referring to Sinclair's *Mammonart*, Joseph Freeman recalled: "For all its errors, confusions and sentimentalism, this book had a profound effect on us ..." (*An American Testament* 369). In the April 1925 issue of the *Workers' Monthly*, forerunner of the current Communist party publication *Political Affairs*, an ad described it as "the most revolutionary criticism of literature and the arts ever penned" (279). A month later it received a favorable review in the same magazine (Dell 326).

Addressing the question of pure art and propaganda, in what is essentially a polemic for the kind of novel for which he himself had become famous, Sinclair argues, like Mehring, that all art "deals with moral questions" and implies a class-determined world view (9). This being the case, it is propaganda for one class or another. In contrast to Mehring and Plekhanov, however, he does not go on to connect the class viewpoint with the ability to perceive the laws governing social change. Not the truth of the propaganda, but rather its "vitality" and "importance" determine the greatness of a work (10). Whereas the other two writers consider whether the author illustrates his ideas through living people and concrete images or through stereotyped characters and abstract polemics, Sinclair reduces the aesthetic to questions of technique, a category that remains largely undefined. Accordingly, he declares Shakespeare to be the "greatest poet of all time" (96), though he was a "poet and propagandist of the enemy" (104), because he conveyed his propaganda in "golden, glowing, gorgeous words" (95). More often, however, he simply disregards "technique" and judges writers according to the class for which they wrote, and the kind of extra-literary political activities in which they engaged. In the case of two writers, abstract moralizing as such is commended. John Bunyan, author of the Christian allegory *Pilgrim's Progress*, receives his praise (112), as does Robert Burns, who was not afraid "to discuss moral problems" or "to use his art to preach and scold" (150).

Only as a kind of afterthought, in anticipation of the charge that he "does not know the difference between a tract or sermon and a work of art," does Sinclair state, again in vague terms, that the writer's "impulse to teach and to preach" must not run away with his or her "inspiration" (352). Nowhere do the categories of abstraction and distortion—central to Mehring's analysis of propaganda and art—enter into the picture.

V. F. Calverton, founder and editor of the left-wing cultural magazine *Modern Quarterly*, was the second author to whom Communist writers turned at this time in formulating their position on literature. In an ad for Calverton's book *The Newer Spirit,* Michael Gold wrote in the July 1925 issue of *Workers Monthly:* " . . . we have at last a real philosopher in our revolutionary ranks." The same ad described the book as "the most important work in literary and social criticism in many years" (431).

Calverton, unlike Sinclair, was familiar with some of Plekhanov's writings and cited him as the source of his own approach to literature, which he calls the "sociological method." The Russian writer, he notes, "elucidated the sociological method with more completeness and exactitude than any of his forerunners" (*The Newer Spirit* 55). Borrowing Plekhanov's idea of base and superstructure, he states that "the scientific critic . . . studies literature as the product of the material conditions that created the society . . . " (*The Newer Spirit* 31). Despite his homage to Plekhanov, however, Calverton's approach differs in several important respects from his. While the other writer takes care in drawing the connection between the economic base and the ideological superstructure, Calverton is prone to simplification. Discussing the aristocratic tragedy, for example, he writes: "As long as the nobility remained the ruling class . . . it would be a sociological solecism to expect ideas to be other than reflections of the aristocratic, courtly attitude" (*The Newer Spirit* 32). Similarly, he maintains that "Shakespeare did nothing more than represent the esthetic conceptions of his period" (*The Newer Spirit* 29–30).

For Plekhanov, placing a work in its socioeconomic and historical context was only the beginning of the critic's task, to be followed by an evaluation of the ideas and values it contained, as well as the manner in which they were presented. Calverton, in contrast, states that literature "can only be satisfactorily approached, studied and criticized by the sociological method" (*The Newer Spirit* 50). "There can be no judgment passed upon a work of art or science," he goes on, "except in strict sociological terms" (*The Newer Spirit* 123). Despite the peremptory tone employed here, he was aware of the limitations of such an approach to literature, and attempted to go beyond it in several of his writings. The result was the same eclecticism that marked Sinclair's theory: alongside the sociological analysis or a work, the critic was to separately consider "technique" and "craftsmanship," categories that Calverton, too, leaves largely undefined ("The Need for" 9).

Criticism of Extreme Proletcult Views
and of Calverton's Sociological Method

While the *Partisan Review* has commonly been seen as the source of the antileftist position in the United States, already in the second half of the twenties a number of Communist writers rejected extreme Proletcult attitudes toward non-proletarian literature, insisted on the need to go beyond sociological analysis in literary criticism, and called for the union of the abstract and concrete in living characters. Among them were Joseph Freeman and Moissaye Olgin.

Freeman joined the Communist party in the early twenties and was one of the editors of the *Liberator* and later the *New Masses*. He wrote poetry as well as literary criticism and was an active participant in the discussion over proletarian literature and Marxist aesthetics in the twenties and thirties. As a poet in the early twenties he found himself on the defensive among those fellow Communists, of whom Dunbar was the prototype, who either held all art and literature in contempt or restricted their recognition to revolutionary agitprop written by and for workers. In fact, he later recounted, he had actually given up creative writing for several years during this period "None of us," he wrote, "seemed to be able to resolve what appeared to be the irreconcilable contradictions between poetry and politics, between art and revolution."[5] Conclusions reached in the Soviet discussion were of little help at this time since, as Freeman pointed out, "...for those of us who did not read Russian, it was extremely difficult to find out what was happening in Soviet art and literature."[6]

In the Spring of 1926 he had the opportunity to do so when he left on a ten-month visit to the Soviet Union, during which he became acquainted with a broad spectrum of writers from various groups. As he related afterwards, he "gravitated toward the RAPP group" and "felt most at home" with one of its leaders, Sergei Dinamov, who introduced him to the staff of Na literaturnom Postu (*An American Testament* 511–12).

His general reaction after arriving in the Soviet Union was relief to find "an attitude toward art and letters much more profound and much more understanding than the one I had left behind me in our American movement."[7] In letters to Michael Gold he attacked the attitude toward bourgeois literature, past and present, among the "Red Puritans" and "ultra-left friends" in the American party, pointing to Engels's respect for Goethe, and Marx's "addiction to Shakespeare" (*An American Testament*

636). Ernest Hemingway's *In Our Time,* a copy of which he had brought with him, was "sneered at" as bourgeois by some of the Americans with him in Moscow. "But it did not take me five minutes," he related, "to induce *Our Path,* a magazine published in Moscow for students of English, to reprint sections of that book—the first time Hemingway ever appeared in Soviet Russia" (*An American Testament* 637).[8] He also recounted to Gold a discussion he had had in which another American attacked James Joyce's *Ulysses* as a "decadent book, full of smut." Freeman, in reply, defended it as "a marvelous mirror of the decay of capitalist civilization" and "a great book" (*An American Testament* 636).

In addition to rejecting extreme proletcult attitudes toward bourgeois literature, Freeman, over the next several years, continually insisted on the need to go beyond sociological analysis in literary criticism. He first article after returning to the United States, entitled "Bulgarian Literature, or the Perfect Critical Method," was a satire on Calverton's "sociological method." The basis of the satire is the fact that, in almost two pages, nothing is said about Bulgarian literature itself. In fact, the fictitious author, Vincent Chatterton, states in the beginning, "I am totally ignorant of Bulgarian literature ... " (9). The basic assumption of his method is that "Art depends upon economic conditions; it is related to social life" (9). He writes: "It is true that Marx ... said something a little like it; but he had one unfortunate habit. When he discussed Shakespeare he talked not only about the poet's social notions, but also about his observations of human nature, the characters he created, his glorious language, and so on. Whereas the only correct way to discuss Shakespeare is not to discuss Shakespeare at all, but write an elaborate political and economic history of Queen Elizabeth's reign" (9–10).

A year later he again addressed himself to the limitations of the sociological method. "American literature," he agrees, "can best be understood in the light of American economics; yet this would reveal only the anatomy of literature; its feeling would still be lacking ... " ("Notes on American Literature" 515). Elaborating on this point he suggests Plekhanov's and the RAPP's distinction between science and art. If one were to analyse literature simply in terms of economics, he explains, "the flavor of experience which literature gives us—as distinct from information, which is the business of science—would be lost altogether" ("Notes on American Literature" 515).

In June 1929 he warns of a simple equation of economic base and ideological superstructure: "Some of our younger critics ... have attempted to explain the evolution of literary patterns by the simple method of describing the economic conditions under which a book is written. There they stop, omitting all explanations of the tangled skein of intermediate forces which lead from economics to 'ideology' " ("Literary Patterns" 14).

Literary criteria that he himself applied, in going beyond sociological analysis, anticipated elements of the RAPP's theory. Commenting on Henri Barbusse's novel *Chains* in the *Workers' Monthly* in February 1926, he calls for contradiction and movement, and attacks the author's abstractness: "The story becomes an unending indictment of class rule. . . . Life has no up and down, only down. . . . almost no incident is related objectively. . . . Things do not happen, they are merely talked about. . . . long parliamentary debates take place between exponents of conflicting philosophies. . . . Instead of the dialectic world we know, we are presented a world in which the more things change the more they are the same" (188–89).

While in the Soviet Union Freeman sent back to the *New Masses* an article from *Pravda* by Bukharin, in which the call for contradiction was coupled with the demand for living characters. Attacking what he calls "bureaucratic ideological creative works," Bukharin insisted: "There must be a bigger variety of questions. . . . More attention to life with all its variegated colors, many-sidedness, its extreme complexity. . . . We do not want walking saints, even of the proletarianized type who think it is their duty to kiss machines. . . . We need a literature of vigorous people penetrating to the depths of life." (Poetry and Common Sense" 10)

The demand for living characters and the rejection of abstractness also appeared in the *Daily Worker* a few months later in articles by Moissaye Olgin. Olgin was one of the founders of the American Communist party, and was a member of its National Committee for years. In addition he edited the Yiddish Communist party daily, the *Morgen Frehet*, until his death in 1939 and was chairman of the Jewish Communist monthly, the *Hammer*. As a native of Kiev, where he had studied and been active in the underground before the revolution, he knew Russian and, like Freeman, was one of the few American Communist writers who were informed on Soviet literary discussions at this time. He immigrated to the United States in 1915 at the age of thirty-seven. In two articles that appeared in April 1927, Olgin dealt with the propaganda question in the context of plans to develop workers' theaters in the United States. He quotes Lunacharsky, who had stated, "God save us from a play which is a strike bulletin in five acts!" (qtd. in "For a Workers Theatre" 1:4). "We do not want a theatre," Olgin continues, "which makes direct propaganda for this or that 'cause' "

("For a Workers Theatre" 1:4). Expanding on this statement a week later, he envisions a form of realism which avoids abstractness at the one extreme and naturalism at the other: "We do not wish a theatre that preaches. We detest moralizing pieces. . . . We wish to see both suffering and joy, injustice and struggle, sweeping passions and life-giving ideas, wisdom and mirth . . . —all this not in the abstract, but incarnated in people, appearing in the actions of living men and women. . . . it is safe to say, negatively, that such theatre will not imitate life, mimic or photograph life . . . " ("For a Workers Theatre" 2:4).

The Views of Michael Gold

The American Communist writer who most closely approached the RAPP's theory of the living person in the period preceding the Charkov Conference was Michael Gold. Nevertheless in most of the literature on leftism he has been identified with extreme Proletcult views and positions commonly associated with the LEF. Thus it is claimed that he disregarded the heritage, placed no value on form or technique, judged literature solely on the basis of its propaganda value, called for journalistic forms as opposed to fiction, and insisted on worker authorship.[9] The explanation for this paradox is to be found in contradictions in Gold's own writing, as well as the fact that generalizations about his views have been based on a relatively small number of articles and statements, while others have been ignored.

Any attempt to summarize Gold's views is complicated by the fact that they were not presented methodically in theoretical essays in the manner of Wittvogel or Lukacs, but were rather scattered throughout various articles, many of which were addressed to events of the moment. Admittedly not a theoretician, Gold, as writer and journalist strongly committed to the development of proletarian literature, occasionally seemed more interested in provoking discussion and drawing attention to the fledgling movement than in maintaining theoretical consistency.

No name is more closely connected with the proletarian literature movement in the United States than Gold's. In his recent book on the left-wing theater, Ira Levine describes him as "the country's leading and most provocative proponent of proletarian art" (44). An article of Gold's, written in 1921, was possibly the first to appear in the United States on the subject of proletarian culture.[10] As sole editor of the *New Masses* between 1928 and 1930 he made proletarian literature the main focus of the magazine, encouraging workers to write and urging young writers to discover the world of revolutionary labor. His well-known book *Jews Without Money*, published in 1930, is generally regarded as the first American proletarian novel.

In working out his own critical method, Gold, like Freeman, rejected the limitation of the critic's task to sociological analysis. After initially acclaiming Calverton's *The Newer Spirit*, he found the author to be "undeveloped in esthetic insight" ("America Needs" 138). Going beyond sociology, Gold applied the same criteria as Olgin and Freeman, calling for living characters and contradiction. Commenting on Upton Sinclair's novels in 1928 he finds that, though he is the "great American pioneer in revolutionary fiction" and "the most important writer in America" ("In Foggy California" 171), he "prefers to overlook the dirt in life" and "makes his heroes too perfect, and his villains too villainous" ("In Foggy California" 168). Behind the "easy victories of virtue" in his novels Gold sees a "faint trace of the Protestant minister." Sinclair seems, he states, to be unaware that, while there is "nobility in the revolutionary camp; there is also gloom, dirt and disorder." "The worker," Gold points out, "is not a bright radiant legend like one of Walter Craine's Merne England peasants." Declaring his own preference for "the variety of life to abstraction," Gold urges: "Let us not rob the worker of his humanity in fiction. Not every worker is like Jesus" ("In Foggy California" 169).

Beyond rejection of melodramatic, black/white characterization in the novel, Gold further defined his concept of the living person in criticizing various tendencies that he found on contemporary, middle-class writers. In the famous Wilder-Gold controversy in 1930 he attacked the gentility and derivativeness of Thornton Wilder, whose novels he described as a "historic junkshop," peopled with "wan ghosts" undergoing "little lavender tragedies" ("Wilder: Prophet" 198–99). He likewise criticized what he considered the escapism of emigre writers such as Hemingway, who regarded personal, private problems as the only real ones, and took as their subject matter the "amours and drinking bouts of Americans of income who rot in European cafes" ("Hemingway" 157). Gold contrasted the "silly little agonies" of characters in some bourgeois literature with the "*real conflicts* of men and women who work for a living,"[11] and insisted that the individual and personal must be "merged in a large, objective pattern" ("A Letter from" 192). This pattern, he pointed out, was not the static world of naturalistic fiction and drama, in which the worker appeared as passive victim. Like Mehring in his remarks on naturalism, he saw the realism of writers such as Theodore Dreiser as limited by the fact that they did not perceive the "immense armies of workers who all over the world cooperate in the great task of creating a new scheme of things" ("American Intellectuals" 5). "Proletarian literature," he predicts, "will reflect the struggle of the workers in their fight for the world."[12]

Gold was more explicit than Freeman or Olgin in making truth the essential criterion in distinguishing between acceptable and unacceptable propaganda. He also went beyond the other two writers in connecting the author's class viewpoint with his ability to avoid distortion in portraying characters and society. "Art is truth or it is nothing"; he declared, "reaction has always been sentimental and romantic" ("O Californians" 124). Proletarian writers, on the other hand, did not have to "lie about our hero in order to win our case."[13] Like the RAPP, he rejected the dichotomy between literature that merely reflected and that which moved the reader to act, asserting that "truth in America leads to rebellion against the liars of Wall St. and Washington" ("A Barbaric" 26).

Despite the closeness to the RAPP's theory evident in many of his articles, Gold occasionally took positions that were more reminiscent of the Proletcult and LEF. This contradiction was particularly noticeable when he discussed the relation between proletarian and bourgeois culture. Gold's inclination toward the sweeping, provocative statement makes it relatively easy to find one quote or another to demonstrate his alleged rejection of everything bourgeois. Nevertheless, more often than not his approach to middle-class writers of the past and present was marked by differentiation. While criticizing Hemingway's choice of subject matter, for example, he valued the precision of his writing and predicted that revolutionary writers would learn from him ("Hemingway" 160; "Three Schools" 14). If he found shortcomings in Dreiser, Sherwood Anderson, Sinclair Lewis, and Carl Sandburg, he declared them to be "pioneers in a new realism" who "blazed clear trails for the proletarian writers of tomorrow to follow."[14] While describing modernist writers as "verbal acrobats,"[15] he extolled Dos Passos's efforts to go beyond the conventions of the nineteenth-century realistic novel ("A Barbaric" 26). In 1923 he included T. S. Eliot among those contemporary writers who, though pessimistic and unaware of the new world developing, were "nevertheless of vast usefulness," for they were "breaking down the hypocrisies and conventional lies in which American capitalism is founded" ("American Intellectuals and Communism" 5).

In regard to the bourgeois literary heritage, Gold frequently pointed to writers of the past as standards by which he measured current literature. Some Americans he mentioned were Whitman—whose influence on his own poetry was unmistakeable—Emerson and Thoreau ("O Californians" 124; "Wilder: Prophet" 201). Writers who were affected by the French revolutionary tradition, such as Wordsworth, Shelley, and Blake, received his praise, as did Tolstoy and Dickens, who worked "for a better world" ("America Needs" 130, 139). Distinguishing between the humanist writer who "shares the ideas and life of mankind" ("American Jungle Notes" 9) and the individualist who attempts to divorce literature from life, Gold predicted that in the future classless society there would be "more Shakespeares and Goethes and fewer Oscar Wildes" ("America Needs" 133). In the course of the dispute over Wilder, he praised Walter Scott as a writer who "had social passions, and used the past as a weapon to affect the present and future" ("Wilder: Prophet" 199).

In direct contrast to this approach to the heritage were statements in which he described proletarian culture as the spontaneous expression of a naturally acquired class-shared instinct or intuition, and envisioned it emerging completely new after the destruction of "the old culture." "Art," he wrote, "is the tenement pouring out its soul through us . . ." ("Towards Proletarian Art" 62, 65). Similarly, he described the proletarian writer at the end of the twenties as a "wild youth," whose communism was a matter of instinct rather than theory, and whose writing was the "natural flower of his environment" ("Go Left" 188).

Occasionally Gold reduced his demand for nativism and realism to the call for a narrow industrial literature, a kind of extended worker-correspondence. After converting the *New Masses* into an organ of proletarian literature in 1928, he advised young writers to find their material by "working as a wage slave around the cities and prairies of America" ("Go Left" 188). Two years later he went a step further, proposing that John Reed Club writers attach themselves to one industry and form "a staff of industrial correspondents, whose function will be to report each month in prose, poetry, plays, and satire, what is happening in each part of industrial America" ("A New Program" 21). This proposal was criticized in 1931 in *Literature of the World Revolution* by BPRS leader Otto Biha, who compared it to Erich Steffen's views in the *Linkskurve* ("On the Question" 91).

In demanding truth in literature Gold sometimes placed an emphasis on fact that was reminiscent of the LEF. Referring to proletarian writers around the world, he states: "They do not adorn, stylize or pose; they put down the facts. And it is literature; it is art; it is the new and creative thing in the world" ("A Letter from" 191). In another article he predicted: "The proletarian writer will cut away from the stale plots, love stories . . . of the fictionists of the past. He will work with facts."[16]

Of possible relevance in explaining the contradictions in Gold's views is his strong commitment to induce workers to write, and certain problems that accompanied this effort. The urgent tone of his calls for workers to write for the *New Masses* suggests that it was not easy to obtain material from this source. One factor was no doubt the intimidation that many felt before the word *culture* and the task of writing. In this case the advice to "forget the past" ("Let It Be" 26) and to simply relate the facts of one's own experience was, at the same time, an invitation to begin writing. The advice not to worry about style and to stick to facts was also possibly directed against a tendency that was later noted by Alan Calmer in proletarian novels written by amateurs. In some worker-writers the effort to assimilate the heritage resulted in the very kind of purple prose that Gold had attacked in certain middle-class writers. It was in this context that Gold made the frequently quoted statement that "Technique has made cowards of us all." When a fellow *New Masses'* editor, Joshua Kunitz, praised Thornton Wilder's "subtle use of words" and "splendidly organized prose" (J. Q. Neets 18), Gold interpreted his remarks as a recommendation that proletarian writers study and imitate Wilder's style. Replying to Kunitz, he wrote: "This whole business of style study is classroom nonsense. . . . There is no 'style'—there is only clarity, force, truth in writing. If a man has something to say, as all proletarian writers have, he will learn to say it clearly in time: if he writes long enough" (*New Masses,* June 1930: 22). Writers such as Jack Salzman and Malcolm Cowley, who cite these statements as evidence of Communist critics' disregard for form and technique, overlook the fact that in the course of this same dispute Gold held up other bourgeois writers as models. Thus he contrasts Wilder's "tailor-made rhetoric" with "the language of the intoxicated Emerson," the "clean, rugged Thoreau" and the "vast Whitman" ("Wilder: Prophet" 200–201).

Over the next few years Gold would include additional writers in the heritage, while placing increasing emphasis on formal excellence.

Literature of the World Revolution

The representatives of the *New Masses* and the John Reed Clubs who attended the Charkov Conference included Gold, A. B. Magil and artist William Gropper. All three were elected to the executive council of the IURW, along with several members of the BPRS. A report in the *New Masses* following the conference pointed out that "Germany and the United States were declared the two most important countries for the development of a proletarian-revolutionary literature" and that they were "the only two that gave reports on the work in their countries before the entire conference" ("The Charkov Conference" 7).

However, while the *Linkskurve* was commended for its theoretical work, the *New Masses* and groups from other countries were found wanting in this area. Questions that had been under discussion for years in the Soviet Union, it was stated, had not yet been dealt with by most of the foreign delegations. One speaker singled out the *New Masses* for being particularly negligent in this area (Epstein 181).

The "Program of Action" adopted by the representatives of the *New Masses* and the John Reed Clubs called for "The strengthening of the theoretical aspects of our work—which have been almost entirely neglected—by holding discussions and by taking steps to secure the translation into English of the classics of Marxist literary criticism such as Plekhanov, Franz Mehring, etc., as well as the writing of a book of Marxist criticism based on specific American conditions" ("The Charkov Conference" 7).

For a reader of the *Linkskurve* or *Na literaturnom Postu,* the *New Masses* no doubt conveyed an impression of theoretical disorientation during the period of Gold's editorship. Contributing to this were not only the contradictions in Gold's own writing, but in the literary criticism in general. If one article depicted Proust as the epitome of the art-for-art's sake decadent esthete,[17] a review of his novel *Swann's Way* praised its "fine delineation and careful artistry coupled with a boldness and realism that sends a thrill through the reader" (Flury 16). While Gold found much to criticize in Hemingway, Dos Passos declared his *Farewell to Arms* to be "the best written book that has seen the light of day in America for many a long day . . . a magnificent novel."[18]

While individual articles touched on one aspect or another of literary criticism and theory, there was no equivalent of the Wittvogel series in the *Linkskurve* during this period, nor was there any information on the discussion in progress in the Soviet Union or Germany. Whether or not it was advisable to present such material at a time when worker-writers were making their first halting literary efforts is another question. In any case it was not until the publication of *Literature of the World Revolution* that information became generally available on the literary theory that had been developing in Germany and the Soviet Union.

Publication of the magazine began in June 1931, and altogether five issues appeared by the end of the year. During these first months Plekhanov's essay "Art and Social Life" was published, along with a number of articles indicating the RAPP's insistence on aesthetic standards and touching on various aspects of their theory. In the second issue RAPP leader Leopold Auerbach wrote: " . . . the reconstruction of literature must not be achieved at the expense of aesthetic quality. A period of gigantic socialist offensive must have a great art, not hack-work, numerous and reddish, good for the day and let it go at that" ("The Speed" 103). In the same issue a report on various conferences called by the RAPP on the subject of creative method related that Auerbach "raised before the proletarian poets and proletarian literature as a whole, the slogan of struggle for improving the quality of artistic production" ("Proletarian Poetry" 107).

The group's position on the relation between the abstract and concrete, and on the living person, was suggested in an analysis of Eisenstein's early films. The reviewer criticized the film director's inability to "solve dialectically the problem of the general and the particular" (Anisimov 107). In *October,* the author states, Eisenstein "presents merely allegorical schemes" (109), while in *The General Line* his characters "are deprived of personality and presented in a scheme of 'non-psychological' characteristics" (112).

An example of Auerbach's approach to the heritage was provided in an article in 1932 in which he discusses those qualities of Goethe's writing that make them relevant to socialist society. Auerbach sees Faust's "discontent with his environment, his striving after great endeavor, his effort to change life," as the "reflection of the rise of the bourgeoisie" ("A Great Man" 127). These traits, he asserts, no longer characterize the modern bourgeoisie, but are rather "that legacy of Goethe which belongs to us alone—to the world proletariat in the country of victorious socialism . . . " (127).

Finally, the same article touches on the relation of subjectivity and objectivity, making the same distinction that Lukacs makes between tendentiousness and partisanship in the *Linkskurve.* The proletariat, Auerbach argues, "is the only class whose subjectivism is the historic tendency, the objective result, and the law of human evolution." He goes on to attack "that vaunted 'proletarian tendentiousness' which degrades and vulgarizes the world historic activity of the working class—ostentatiously 'red' and high-falutin' piffle which poses as the acme of genuine proletarian art" ("A Great Man" 129).

Information on the discussion in progress in the German BPRS was provided by Otto Biha, editor of the *Linkskurve*. He mentions two factors affecting the present direction of that discussion, one of which is the movement of middle-class writers toward the Party and the need to offer them guidance, while applying "serious Marxist analysis" to all the writing emerging from the proletarian-revolutionary literature movement. He credits Mehring and Plekhanov with having furnished valuable ground in this undertaking, although the latter writer's influence on the German discussion has been limited by the fact that his articles on literature were not available in translation. He also cites the Wittvogel series as having been of benefit ("On the Question" 93).

The second factor, related to the first, is the necessity of the cultural movement to proceed beyond the stage when "almost the sole claim to consideration in its literary products lies in their contents." The "question of the hour," he states, is "the problem of creative method" ("A Soldier" 138). He sees the views expressed by Erich Steffen in his *Linkskurve* article, "Die Urzelle proletarischer Literatur," as typical of past mistakes, among which he includes disregard of the bourgeois heritage, the defining of proletarian literature according to where the author worked, and the confusing of correspondence with literature. "Reports do not constitute literature," he writes. Factory newspapers, important as they were in the political struggle were not literary works ("On the Question" 91). Mistaking a proposal of Michael Gold's for an official position of the John Reed Clubs, he sees a corollary to Steffen's insistence on worker authorship in "one of the basic theses of the John Reed Club ... which bases the proletarianism of its literature on the fact that its members went to the factories, turning into worker-writers in this roundabout way." He calls it a "*Proletcult* delusion" to define proletarian literature according to the "starting point" rather than the "goal towards which it strives" ("On the Question" 91). Not the present occupation of the author determined the proletarian character of his or her writing, but the viewpoint, which must be that of the revolutionary working class ("On the Question" 90–91).

This was to be expressed in the creative method as well as in the general ideological trend. The method to be developed must combine the general and particular in such a way to avoid naturalism on the one hand, and abstract propaganda, on the other. Biha sees the latter as particularly prevalent in proletarian literature. In striving for proletarian relevance many writers, he states, overlook the subjective individual, and "fail to present the sentiments, ideas, and aspirations of our class, or a portion of our class, in their connection with the whole situation of society. Thus it happens that the political slogans are put into the mouths of the literary characters in cut-and-dry fashion . . . " ("On the Question" 104). While the "schematic, anti-psychological method" might be "quite efficient for immediate practical purposes" ("On the Question" 104), in the next stage of the movement's development writers must strive for more concreteness while taking care not to make psychology an aim in itself. Proletarian literature, Biha insists, must "draw living men and women with all their inner contradictions that they still possess as a hang-over from a past not yet overcome" ("A Soldier" 138).

Biha's articles, which contained the most elaborate exposition in *Literature of the World Revolution* of the theory of the living person and dialectical materialism, reflected the anti leftist struggle going on in the BPRS. In general, however, in 1931 and '32 the magazine maintained the ultraradical tone of the Third Period. As its title indicated, the emphasis was on revolution, and it was repeatedly stressed that proletarian literature should be a weapon in the anticipated final confrontation between labor and capital. Thus, while some attention was given to creative method and aesthetics, as often as not the demand for explicit class commitment and militance led to the simple dismissal of literature that did not fulfill this demand.

It was perhaps because of the ambiguity in *Literature of the World Revolution* in the approach to aesthetics that the theory of the living person and dialectical materialism, propagated by Biha, found no immediate resonance in the *New Masses*. In general the magazine showed little change in regard to literary theory in the year following the Charkov Conference. In early 1932 a long article in *Literature of the World Revolution* reviewing the previous year's issues of the *New Masses* found that the magazine was still failing to provide guidance to the American movement in this area. The reviewer states: "The backwardness of the *New Masses* (and also of the John Reed Club) on the front of literary theory which existed at the time of the Kharkov Conference . . . impels the IURW at this stage to check up this branch of the activity of *New Masses* with particular attention. It has to be confessed that this backwardness is still far from having been eliminated" (Elistratova 111).

The article is significant in that, first of all, it demonstrates once again that in the midst of the Third Period, with all its revolutionary rhetoric, the demand for establishing aesthetic criteria and defining the relation between literature and propaganda continued to proceed from within the movement. Second, it provides a good example of the tone of condescension and command that prevailed during the RAPP period in the Soviet Union. The zealous, twenty-year-old author, Anna Elistratova, found little good to say about the *New Masses* and took the magazine to task for a long list of political sins. On the one hand, it had failed to direct criticism at Max Eastman and V. F. Calverton (Elistratova 107). Eastman, a member of the old *Masses* staff, had become a supporter of Trotsky in the twenties and was soon to publish his famous polemic against the cultural politics of the Soviet Communist party, *Artists in Uniform*. V. F. Calverton had also become increasingly sympathetic to Trotsky in his magazine, *Modern Quarterly*. On the other hand, Elistratova complained that the *New Masses* had not given sufficient attention to "fellow travellers," noting that no article had appeared on Dos Passos in 1931 and that the "activity of Upton Sinclair remained outside the journal's field of vision during the whole year" (Elistratova 113). As at Charkov, criticism was thus directed at both rightist and leftist tendencies. However, as was the case in Germany between 1930 and '32, attention in the American movement was to focus increasingly on leftism over the next few years.

It was possibly in response to the charge of theoretical backwardness that a long essay by Lunacharsky was published in the *New Masses* toward the end of 1932.[19] Translated by Joseph Freeman, the essay occupied a central position in the development of aesthetic theory in the *New Masses,* in that it expressed views that had also been presented by Freeman, Gold, and others over the preceding years, and, at the same time, anticipated many of the issues that would be addressed in the campaign against leftism in the mid-thirties.

Lunacharsky begins by discussing art as part of the ideological superstructure. Like Freeman, he warns against mechanical materialism, or oversimplifying the connection with the material base:

> ... it [Marxian analysis] seeks to determine the relations between various legal theories, philosophical systems, religious teachings and schools of art and the various groups within the basic classes, or even intermediary classes in society. Often a given society is extremely complicated. It is a crime against true Marxism to take ideological

phenomena and explain them by the interests of only one of the important classes. The history of ideas is entirely rooted in the history of society, and as the evolution of society is varied and complex, ideologies are equally varied and complex. ("Marxism and Art" 12)

Like Gold, he views art as reflection and praxis, and asserts that the proletariat is the only class that has no need to distort reality. Art, along with other parts of the ideological superstructure, not only reflects reality, but acts upon it as well:

These reflections themselves become social forces: they become banners and slogans around which the social class gathers, with the aid of which it fights its enemies and recruits among them its agents and vassals. (12)

Marxism is the only ideology which does no violence to reality. This is due to the fact that the proletariat is the class of the future; it is to the interest of the proletariat to base itself on that science which points out what actually exists and indicates the tendencies of the future. (13)

Defining the specific nature of art, Lunacharsky explains how it differs from science: " . . . scientific knowledge is abstract; it says nothing to human emotion. In order to understand any aspect of reality thoroughly it is not enough to have merely an intellectual concept of it; it is also necessary to have an emotional attitude toward it" (12).

Turning to the literature of the past, he establishes humanism as a principle criterion in determining what is of value and relevance to the proletariat. Thus he includes in the heritage works that express the spirit "of man's faith in his own powers, of aspiration for knowledge and a just life," or that proclaim "the rights of the oppressed sections of mankind" (13). He contrasts these with works that "deliberately avoid all living content and resort to an empty play of intellect or vaporous dreams, in order to escape reality, to evade all responsibility for it" (13).

In regard to modernism, he argues that even works created by a class in its declining phase can be valuable "in so far as they are symptoms of certain social phenomena and increase our historical knowledge . . ." (14). In addition, he maintains, " . . . it is possible to find in a degenerate work of art something which is very useful from the technical point of view" (14). Summarizing his position on the heritage, he states: "The Marxist can thus learn something from every work of the past and transmit that knowledge to others" (14).

Lunacharsky's article would be quoted a month later in the *New Masses* in what was to be the first major confrontation in the magazine over leftism.

Charkov and the Criticism of Leftist Sectarianism in the John Reed Clubs

While the Charkov Conference had no immediate effect on the discussion over aesthetic theory, it did influence the literary politics of the American movement in establishing principles on relations with non-Communist writers friendly to the Party. In a report on the conference in the *New Masses* Gold related: "An interesting discussion was begun by the German delegation, and everyone participated in it. It was our familiar *New Masses* discussion . . . as to the place of the petty bourgeois intellectuals in the revolutionary movement. . . . The Congress declared that it was of vital importance to enlist all friendly intellectuals into the ranks of the revolution. Every door must be opened wide to the fellow travellers" ("Notes from Charkov" 5). Both Gold and A. B. Magil indicated that personal contacts were also established between BPRS members and the Americans. Gold spent a lot of time with novelist Ernst Glaeser ("Notes from Charkov" 6), and Magil shared a room with Ludwig Renn after the conference (Magil, "Red Front" 16). He later recalled that Renn "acted as a kind of chaperone to the American and English delegates," informing them of developments in the BPRS, particularly in regard to the struggle against leftist tendencies (Magil, "Red Front" 16).

Referring to a dispute within the American delegation Gold explained: "The general line taken by the Congress was not the one taken by our leftists" ("Notes from Charkov" 5). The majority of the Americans present had criticized the IBRL's policy of maintaining contacts with prominent individual writers such as Theodore Dreiser and Upton Sinclair, while no contacts had been established with the John Reed Club. Objection had also been raised to the admission of Sinclair to membership in the IBRL (Homberger 236). In the context of the discussion started by the Germans, the leadership of the IURW responded by attacking what it called ultraleftist sectarian tendencies that had earlier been observed in the BPRS and now had emerged in the American delegation (Sekretariat des IVRS 4). It also expressed regret that so few sympathetic, non-Communist writers were present. As Daniel Aaron indicates, Dos Passos had received an invitation but had not come (220). The Program of Action adopted by the *New Masses* and the John Reed Clubs stated that, in addition to "extending the proletarian base" of the cultural movement, they were to direct their efforts towards the "winning over of radicalized intellectuals" ("The Charkov Conference" 7).

As evidenced in his attack on Wilder, the tone of Gold's journalism was not always conducive to winning over non-Communist writers. A year after that controversy he also wrote a scathing article in the *New Masses* on the liberal writer Lincoln Steffens, referring to him as "the white-haired boy and Sir Galahad of a generation of reformers" ("Mr. Steffens" 5). Nevertheless Gold could claim a certain degree of continuity in the favorable approach to "fellow travellers" he was to promote within the John Reed Clubs. Already in 1924 his praise for Dreiser, Anderson and other writers had moved one *Daily Worker* reader to accuse him of courting bourgeois intellectuals (Wicks 5). The "familiar *New Masses* discussion" that Gold referred to in his report on Charkov involved Sinclair, whom he had defended against those who, in Gold's words, judged Sinclair "solely as a member of the Socialist Party." The function of a revolutionary writer, he argued in a letter in the *New Masses* in December 1929, was not "to suggest political platforms and theses, but to portray the life of the workers and inspire them with solidarity and revolt," something Sinclair had done "magnificently." "The only way to criticize Sinclair as a *writer,* not as a politician," Gold insisted, was for the Communist movement "to develope a few novelists and playwrights with his skill, social passion, appetite for hard work, and general incorruptibility" (23).

As John Reed Clubs proliferated in cities throughout the country, Gold and Freeman worked to overcome resistance to the admittance of middle-class writers. A conference of the clubs, which was held in the summer of 1932 in Chicago, found Freeman and Gold pitted against young club members on this question. A report on the conference indicated that a member of the Hollywood John Reed Club objected to "the conciliatory invitational attitude of Mike Gold toward middle-class intellectuals" (Oakley Johnson 14). Another participant objected to Sinclair's being on the editorial board of *Literature of the World Revolution* (Oakley Johnson 14). In arguing against these positions Gold cited the Charkov Conference, where any writer "who subscribed to the political platform was admitted" (qtd. in Oakley Johnson 14). Considering the difficult conditions under which proletarian writers lived, it would take a long time, he explained, before they would "attain the technique and polish of bourgeois writers," so that it was "a matter of life and death to attract and bring into the movement revolutionary writers of middle class origin" (qtd. in Aaron 227–28). Freeman likewise argued that the movement needed "fellow travellers," and warned, " . . . we must not underestimate the importance of sympathetic individuals . . . " (qtd. in Oakley Johnson 14). The document that was adopted by the clubs at the conference proposed to "develope organizational techniques for establishing and consolidating contacts of the Clubs with potentially sympathetic elements," in addition to assisting in developing worker-writers and artists (qtd. in Oakley Johnson 15).

The first major confrontation in the *New Masses* over the issue of the sympathetic, non-Communist writer took place toward the end of 1932. On the one side was A. B. Magil, while Philip Rahv was on the other. Earlier in the year Rahv had joined the staff of *The Rebel Poet*, a magazine that had emerged from the Sacco-Vanzetti protests of the twenties and was edited by Jack Conroy. As James Gilbert relates, Rahv fought against "a conciliatory policy toward liberal or socialist fellow travellers," while Conroy "wished to keep the magazine a publication open to a wider group of young poets" (113). Gilbert explains: "There was so much bickering and factionalism . . . that he [Conroy] dissolved the group in New York, and the magazine folded shortly thereafter" (113).

An article he published in the *Rebel Poet* in 1932 reveals Rahv to be among those in the left wing of the movement who continued to rigidly separate everything bourgeois and proletarian, and to dismiss contemporary middle-class writers. While such attitudes had also occasionally been expressed by contributors to *Literature of the World Revolution* and by Michael Gold, Rahv outdoes most of them in the vehemence of his rhetoric:

In the course of the last few years we have observed the rise of the proletarian movement in literature, comprising a drastic deviation from the "nice and waterish diet" of emasculated, unsocial writing, perennially engaged in futilitarian introspection. . . . Under the remorseless impact of economic reality, the autistic thinking of bourgeois ideology has been exposed in all its uselessness and debility. The antithesis of proletarian literary class-consciousness has succeeded in undermining the original condition of equilibrium, with the result that the conflict is growing ever sharper and sharper, gathering momentum for a complete irreconcilable separation between the two camps. Anyone who is at all aware knows that the bourgeois literati are now fighting a rear-guard action. . . . "There's nothing more up that street," someone recently remarked about lyrical poetry. The same sentence can be applied to all literature that pretends—or misguidedly endeavors —to rise above class interests, or to ignore this central issue by means of thematically immuring itself in what it falsely conceives to be neutral subjects—like love, for instance (Lawrence), expeditions into the unconscious (Joyce), superficial social satire (Huxley, Mencken), bestiality and crime (Faulkner). These subjects, when treated from the static standpoint of the bourgeois writer who considers states of mind and moral-emotional situations intrinsically determined by the psychological reflexes of the production-relations at a given stage of society, as unique, a-social phenomena, merely offer an oblique reflection of the doom of the dominating class class. Such literature is wholly negative as well as irrelevant to the historical process of development which society is now undergoing. . . .

Too long has literature been standing on its head, doped by the mephitic fumes of idealist opium. Dialectical materialism demands that we put it back on its feet. . . .

We must sever all ideological ties with this lunatic civilization known as capitalism. ("An Open Letter" 3–4)

Reviewing "Scottsboro Limited," four poems and a play by Langston Hughes, Rahv writes in the August 1932 issue of the *Rebel Poet:* " 'Scottsboro Limited' is a class-struggle pamphlet in the form of a play. There is no metaphysical religiosity, no futile psychologising about it; it is a genuine example of the new literature whose theme is the collective, not some mythical INDIVIDUALISTS who only exist in the fog-soaked brains of petit-bourgeois rationalizers of capitalism" (7).

In the same month in which he wrote this review, Rahv published a long article in the *New Masses,* called "The Literary Class War." Proceeding from the assumption that bourgeois literature was in a state of decay, he again criticizes contemporary middle-class writers. He asserts, for instance, that "the novels of a writer like William Faulkner leave the reader with nothing" (7). In Joyce's *Ulysses* he finds "a certain magnitude, but only in a negative sense." "It is the magnitude of death, not of life," he explains (8).

Considering the possibility of recruiting "fellow travellers" into the movement, he is pessimistic. "It is quite certain," he predicts, "that following the economic interests of their class, most bourgeois writers will swing toward fascism . . . " (10). He therefore advises caution in dealing with them, and warns: "Only their ability and willingness to master Marxian theory will insure their loyalty. . . . [O]nce it becomes clear that his bourgeois class roots are too strong, he should be neatly and rapidly dispatched on the road back" (10).

While Michael Gold's occasional Proletcult excess in 1930 is commonly seen as typical of his approach to literature, the views Rahv expresses here, two years later, are either overlooked or downplayed. James Gilbert refers to the "over-enthusiastic generalities" of Rahv's early essays (114), while Terry Cooney suggests that they were the product of youthful impetuosity, the "hyperbolic rhetoric . . . that one might expect from a 'super-revolutionary' young radical" (41). Discussing Rahv's essay in the *New Masses,* Cooney does not mention his remarks on Faulkner and Joyce, nor his position on "fellow travellers." William Barrett, a member of the *Partisan Review* in the forties, contends that Rahv was simply adhering to the line of the movement's leadership during this period. A "straightforward party-line scribe," Rahv "simply put on a uniform" when he wrote his 1932 *New Masses* article (42). One exception here is Eric Homberger, who recognizes that "Philip Rahv, at the age of 24, was the voice of leftism . . . " (136). He contrasts Rahv's rigid separation of everything bourgeois and proletarian with the statement Serafina Gopner made at the Charkov Conference in the name of the Comintern: "The organization of revolutionary writers must not erect a superfluous barrier between itself and those whose revolutionary instinct is greatly developed, but who have not succeeded as yet to come to any definite standpoint, who have not yet acquired firm Marxist views" (qtd. in Homberger 136). The publication of a long article criticizing Rahv a few months later in the *New Masses* revealed the increasing focus on leftism by the leadership of the proletarian-literature movement at this time. The author of the article was A. B. Magil, who was a member of the IURW's executive council.

In criticizing Rahv's remarks on modern bourgeois literature Magil cites both Lunacharsky's article "Marxism and Art"—which had appeared in the *New Masses* a month before—as well as the Charkov Conference.

Lunacharsky, he states, "has pointed out that even in the period of its decline the art of a dying class is still capable of making significant contributions in the field of form," and that "the innovations of individual bourgeois writers . . . can . . . serve to enrich the arsenal of proletarian art and make possible a fuller and truer picture of objective reality" ("Pity and Terror" 18). Magil indicates that the Charkov Conference "recognized the positive value of some of the experimental movements . . . " ("Pity and Terror" 18), and insists that "one cannot simply sweep away all these new experimental forms as so much chaff" ("Pity and Terror" 18). He finds that Rahv has overlooked the element of protest against the existing order in some of the "florid outbursts" of modernist writers ("Pity and Terror" 18). He mentions Mayakovsky and Johannes Becher as proof that "individual writers and even entire groups may under certain conditions be won over to the side of the revolutionary proletariat" ("Pity and Terror" 18).

Magil describes Rahv's attitude as "fatalistic" and "capitulatory," a mixture of "didactic condescension" and "suspicion and distrust" ("Pity and Terror" 18). The categorical assertion that they must become Marxists if they are not to " 'desert and re-join the bourgeoisie,' " Magil writes, will "probably be shattering news to Theodore Dreiser and Romain Rolland who are not at all likely to 'make the Marxian world-view their own' and who are now faced with the certainty of sliding back into the bourgeois mire" ("Pity and Terror" 18). He again cites the Charkov Conference, where it was stated that the movement of fellow travellers toward Communism was a "most complicated and responsible task. . . . a problem of guidance, not of command" (qtd. in "Pity and Terror" 18). Finally, the term which Freeman had employed against Communists who disparaged literature in the twenties, and which the IURW leadership had applied in criticizing American delegates at Charkov, appears once again as Magil characterizes Rahv's attitudes as leftist ("Pity and Terror" 18).

Thus, though commonly characterized as a forerunner in the criticism of leftism in the American proletarian-literature movement, Rahv in fact found himself on the opposite side in the first major confrontation over the heritage, modernism, and relations with sympathetic, non-Communist writers.

Notes

1. Information on German-American socialist literature and theater can be found in Poore, chapter 4.

2. Alan Calmer deals with this tradition in his article "Early American Labor and Literature."

3. Information on Reed and the pageant are in Aaron 17–18, 37–41.

4. Daniel Aaron provides an extensive account of the early history of the *New Masses* and the John Reed Clubs in his book *Writers on the Left.*

5. *Daily Worker* 23 Nov. 1933: 5.

6. Ibid. A number of Soviet works were serialized in English translation in the *Daily Worker* in the mid-twenties. Among these were Yuri Libedinsky's "A Week," Boris Pilnyak's *At the Doors,* and stories by Vsevolod Ivanov and Ivan Kasatkin.

7. *Daily Worker* 23 Nov. 1933: 5.

8. Details on this are given in Aaron 135.

9. Among the writers who attribute various of these positions to Gold are Pells, Rideout, and Gilbert.

10. The article, "Towards Proletarian Art," appeared in the *Liberator* in February 1921 under Gold's real name, Irwin Granich. Rpt. in Folsom 62–70.

11. "Notes of the Month," *New Masses* Sept. 1930: 5.

12. Ibid.

13. Ibid.

14. *New Masses* Apr. 1930: 4.

15. "Notes of the Month," *New Masses* Sept. 1930: 5.

16. *New Masses* Dec. 1929: 7.

17. "Notes of the Month," *New Masses* Sept. 1930: 5.

18. *New Masses* Dec. 1929: 16.

19. The original Russian title of the article and its date of publication are not given in the *New Masses.*

Part Two | The Discussion in the Mid-Thirties

4

Aesthetic Theory in
International Literature

The First Five-Year Plan and the Restructuring
of Writers' Groups in the Soviet Union

ON APRIL 23, 1932 the Central Committee of the Communist party issued a short statement in *Pravda* announcing the disbanding of the RAPP as well as all other proletarian cultural organizations in the Soviet Union. In explaining this move it pointed to changes in the area of culture and in Soviet society in general. "Significant success in the building of socialism," it explained, had been accompanied by the emergence of new writers and artists from the "mills, factories and collective farms," so that it was no longer necessary to help proletarian writers consolidate their position. The proletarian literary-artistic organizations now appeared too narrow, and threatened to become exclusive circles, "divorced from contemporary political problems and from a significant group of the writers and artists who sympathize with the building of socialism." In their place a single union of Soviet writers was to be established, uniting "all writers supporting the platform of Soviet power and aspiring to participate in the building of socialism" ("On the Reformation" 120). Not mentioned, of course, was the fact that a single organization would also provide the government with an effective instrument of control. In August a fifty-member organizing committee (Orgcommittee) with Maxim Gorky as president began laying the groundwork for the new writers' union (James 83), which was finally established at the First Congress of Soviet Writers in the summer of 1934 (Lomidse and Timofjew 162).

The successes referred to in the Central Committee's statement involved the completion of the First Five-Year Plan in three years, during which time agriculture was forcibly collectivized—at an enormous cost in human lives—and the basis laid for heavy industry. These developments, following the defeat of the groups around Trotsky and Zinoviev, and later Bukharin, made the government appear stronger than ever. Writers who throughout the twenties had been counting on its gradual collapse now saw their hopes disappointed, while others seemed genuinely enthusiastic about the phenomenal growth of industry and the economy.

Anxious to accommodate the growing numbers of non-Communist writers who now, whether out of conviction or resignation, supported the government, the Central Committee concluded that the RAPP was not suited to this task, since it had made too many enemies in the course of its numerous disputes. Criticism of the RAPP's sectarianism did not, however, emerge suddenly in 1932 as has sometimes been claimed. While David Pike maintains that "Party spokesmen never reproached RAPP prior to 1932 for its treatment of the fellow travellers . . . " (*Lukacs and Brecht* 27), in fact as early as October 1929 a long article appeared in *Pravda* relating the complaints of non-Communist writers that the RAPP was not fulfilling the Central Committee's 1925 resolution concerning cooperation between fellow travelers and the "cultural forces of Communism" (Ol'chovyj 390). The RAPP was reminded that the Party did not grant any literary organization a monopoly position in representing its opinion on literary matters (Ol'chovyj 389). The author further suggested that the RAPP was using the Federation of Organizations of Soviet Writers (FOSP)—the organization formed in 1927 uniting Communist and non-Communist writers' associations—to promote its own interests, and advised it instead to work to make the FOSP an organization that would "help in the transformation of the fellow travellers to the ideological position of Communism" (Ol'chovyj 391). In the same month, Lunacharsky reminded the RAPP and the other proletarian-writers' organizations that none of them were in a position to declare that "the Central Committee and the whole Party are on our side" ("Unsere Aufgaben" 392).

Conflict with the Central Committee had also developed over the RAPP's criticism of Gorky after his return to the Soviet Union in 1928. In *Na literaturnom Postu* he was characterized as unreliable and was attacked for his defense in *Pravda* of a minor poet called Molchanov, who had been satirized by Mayakovsky in "Kop—the Bedbug." The issue involved was the approach to be taken toward unpolished, nonprofessional proletarian writers. While the RAPP was critical of Molchanov, Gorky felt that such writers should be "valued and taught, not yelled and barked at" (qtd. in James 73). In return, Auerbach accused Gorky of conceit and condescension and questioned his loyalty to the proletariat, while *Pravda* took Gorky's part. When a Siberian writers organization took up the attack, calling him a "crafty, disguised class enemy" (qtd. in James 74), the Central Committee stepped in on July 25, 1929 with a resolution that characterized the accusations as "grossly mistaken and bordering on hooliganism" (qtd. in

James 74). The Siberian Party Committee was instructed to fight left-wing deviations in the literary organizations (James 74).[1]

While some of the writers attacked by the RAPP were also criticized in *Pravda,* the Party felt that the RAPP occasionally went too far and engendered unnecessary conflict. Boris Pilnyak was a case in point. In 1929 Pilnyak published a novel outside the Soviet Union, entitled *Mahagoni,* which painted a bleak picture of Soviet reality and presented a sympathetic portrayal of a Trotsky supporter (Lefevre 43). Starting in August of the same year, he was attacked by RAPP members and others in various publications. On September 18 an article in *Pravda* mentioned him as an example of the type of "fellow traveller" who rejected the revolution when it proceeded to the task of socialist construction. What was meant here was the First Five-Year Plan.[2] On the other hand, Joseph Freeman related that Pilnyak, in the course of a five-month stay at Freeman's house in 1931, showed him documents "in which the Party reversed various of RAPP's actions against him."[3] Answering Max Eastman's claim that the RAPP enjoyed unlimited power among writers, Freeman pointed out:

> ... in 1930 ... Boris Pilnyak earned more money than any single individual in the Soviet Union, regardless of position or profession. ... For although RAPP opposed him and attacked him, the State Publishing House issued his books and thousands of Soviet citizens bought them.
>
> Similarly Afinogenov, whose plays aroused RAPP's ire, was able to produce those plays and to EARN huge sums of money.

The same was true of the Moscow Art Theater, which Freeman describes as "another of RAPP's betes noires."[4]

After the demise of the RAPP the conciliatory approach toward non-Communist writers was also reflected in criticism of the RAPP's use of the term *dialectical materialism* as a slogan. At the first plenary session of the Orgcommittee of the Soviet Writers' Union In October 1932, the Secretary, Valeri Kirpotin, explained that the slogan often led to an oversimplified view of the connection between ideology and artistic creation. The fact was overlooked that "the artist sometimes arrives at true and instructive conclusions in art, despite his world outlook. ... " The approach to such writers was to be one of "ideological guidance" rather than "administrative 'compulsion' " (Kirpotin 143). At the second plenary session three months later Lunacharsky took up the same point again, arguing that the artist "presenting the socialist revolution in the practice of which he is immersed" can "instinctively uncover many most important traits" of Soviet reality.

He explained: "What is important is, that you have revolutionary feeling, that you understand the basic problems of the revolution in the given stage, that you are artistically sensitive and that you possess a style that stirs the reader and successfully conveys your thoughts and feelings" ("Problems" 92).

While Max Eastman, Malcolm Cowley, and Lawrence Schwartz describe theoretical developments in the Soviet Union after 1932 as a complete break with the RAPP's ideas, criticism of the RAPP was, in fact, mixed with recognition of the group's achievements. In his speech Kirpotin pointed out: "The growth of proletarian literature, the growth of its influence, its ideologically leading role in Soviet literature as a whole, achieved with the help of the party and through the RAPP are the best justification of the support at one time afforded by the party to the RAPP. And this increase could never have been brought about but for the struggle waged under the leadership of the party and the RAPP against the various hostile anti-Marxian, anti-Leninist tendencies in the sphere of literature" (Kirpotin 142).

Accordingly, many of the RAPP's leaders, including Auerbach, were taken onto the Orgcommittee of the Soviet Writers' Union (Ermolaev 133). Fadeyev played an important role in the discussion over socialist realism,[5] and Dinamov, who had been editor of *Na literaturnom Postu,* became editor-in-chief of *International Literature.*[6] Finally, criticism of the misuse of the slogan of dialectical materialism did not mean a rejection of the aesthetic theory behind it. As Kirpotin stated: " . . . only that criticism which is guided by the method of dialectical-materialism . . . can be fruitful. . . . We are in favor of dialectical materialism in art . . . " (Kirpotin 143). In fact, the aesthetic concepts that had evolved within the proletarian-literature movement were largely incorporated into the theory of socialist realism.

The Propaganda Question

The reorganization of writers' groups in the Soviet Union marked the beginning of a broad discussion on aesthetics, in which various writings of Marx, Engels,s and Lenin on art and literature provided the basis. Starting in 1933 this material was published in *International Literature* and played a crucial part in the American discussion over leftism. The influence of Marx's and Engels's analysis of Balzac was obvious in Granville Hicks' approach to non-Communist writers such as Marcel Proust and

Andre Malraux, while a key article in the *Partisan Review* on leftism quoted Engels's letter to Margaret Harkness. In *New Theatre,* remarks of Marx and Engels were cited in criticism of tendentiousness. In his book *Left-Wing Dramatic Theory in the American Theatre* Ira Levine mistakenly suggests that the relevant writings of Marx and Engels only appeared in the late thirties. "Most of their opinions," he writes, "were unavailable to the American radical community during the years with which this study is concerned" (xiii). He mentions only the volume *Marx and Engels on Literature,* which was compiled by Franc Schiller and Mikhail Lifschitz and appeared in English translation in 1937, and ignores the publication of Marx's and Engels's writings in *International Literature.*

Of particular importance was a series of recently discovered letters dealing with the relation between literature and propaganda. The clarification of Marx's and Engels's views on this question confirmed the direction within the proletarian literature movement, which had begun with Plekhanov and Mehring and had culminated in the distinction between tendentiousness and partisanship. Underlying Marx's and Engels's approach to the propaganda question, was, again, the distinction between the methods or art and science: while science presented the laws of social and natural development abstractly, art and literature combined essence and appearance, the general and particular in concrete images. In elucidating the laws of social development the writer was to portray characters and situations that were historically and socially typical, avoiding excessive abstractness, on the one hand, and the photographic reflection of the inessential, on the other.

Marx and Engels criticized the first tendency in letters addressed in 1859 to Ferdinand LaSalle, who had recently completed a historical drama called *Franz von Sickingen.* Both consider lack of concreteness the play's main weakness, manifested in the characters' tendency to become, in Marx's words, "mere mouthpieces of the spirit of the time," engaging in long argumentative discussions with each other (Marx to LaSalle 118). Behind this approach to character they see the influence of the German romantic poet and dramatist Friedrich Schiller. Engels writes: " . . . the principal characters in fact represent definite classes and tendencies and hence definite ideas of their time and the motives of their actions are to be found not in trivial individual desires but in the historical stream upon which they are being carried. However, the next step forward should be in making these motives more lively, active, so to say, spontaneously occupying the foreground by the course of the action . . . "(Engels to

LaSalle 120). The goal should be that "the argumentative speeches become unnecessary" (Engels to LaSalle 120). Engels continues: "According to my views on the drama, the realistic should not be overlooked because of the intellectual elements . . . " (Engels to LaSalle 121). Like Marx, he suggests to LaSalle that he take Shakespeare as a model rather than Schiller.

In a letter addressed to an English writer, Margaret Harkness, in 1888, Engels criticizes the opposite tendency: concentrating on realistic detail, Harkness overlooks the essential motive forces of development and change. Anticipating the distinction between tendentiousness and partisanship, he goes on from here to suggest a form of realism in which socialist bias is not expressed in rhetorical pathos or idealized characters, but rather in the undistorted reflection of the actual trends of social and historical development. Engels's letter was accompanied in *International Literature* by a long commentary by Franc Schiller. As Hans Günther points out in his book *Die Verstaatlichung der Literatur,* Schiller, Mikhail Lifschitz and Georg Lukacs were all members of a group centered around the magazine *Literaturnyj Kritik,* which took on the task of publishing and interpreting Marx's and Engels' writings on art and literature (9). The Russian edition of Schiller's and Lifschitz's anthology of these writings appeared in 1933, with a preface by Lukacs (Günther 9).

In his analysis of Engels's letter to Harkness, Schiller asserted that it bore out "the correctness of a number of artistic slogans put forward by the RAPP" ("Marx and Engels on Balzac" 124). The English writer had recently completed a novel in which she described the destitution of working girls. In his remarks on the novel Engels, like Plekhanov and Mehring, called for the portrayal of the proletariat as revolutionary subject, so that the writer's bias became the bias of reality itself. While praising the "realistic truth" of the novel, he finds: " . . . it is not quite realistic enough. Realism, to my mind, implies, besides truth of detail, the truthful reproduction of the principle that the emancipation of the working class ought to be the cause of the working class itself. The revolutionary reaction of the working class against the oppression that surrounds them, their convulsive attempts—half conscious or conscious—to attain their rights as human beings, belongs to history and may therefore lay claim to a place in the domain of realism" (Engels to Harkness 113). Engels insists that he does not, however, mean a tendentious novel, glorifying "the social and political views of the author," but instead a work that expresses the actual developmental forces of society (Engels to Harkness 114). He holds up

Balzac as an example of an author who, in spite of his aristocratic sympathies, recognized the historical necessity of the nobility's downfall and accurately portrayed the rise of the bourgeoisie, presenting thereby "a complete history of French society" (Engels to Harkness 114).

Engels had more to say on the question of bias in another letter that was described in *International Literature* as a "document of enormous significance for the solution of the question of Marxist-Leninist art criticism" (F. Schiller, "Friedrich Engels" 122). He was writing this time to Minna Kautsky, a popular writer and journalist among social-democrats in pre–World War I Austria and Germany. In 1885 he received her recently completed novel, *The Old and the New*, which centered around the lives of salt miners in a village in Austria and the struggle between religious fatalism and gloom, on the one side, and humanism and faith in science, on the other (F. Schiller, "Friedrich Engels" 123).

Engels's criticism of the novel focuses on the way in which the author expresses her social convictions. While she succeeds in creating a number of typical characters—each one "type, but at the same time a completely defined personality"—her hero is abstract and idealized. Arnold, he points out, is "too good for this world"; in him "personality is entirely dissolved in principle." Another figure, Elsa, "is also somewhat idealized." Engels sees this as symptomatic of a general weakness in the novel, the author's need to publicly declare her convictions, "bearing witness to them before the whole world" (Engels to Minna Kautsky 122).

What Engels questions is not the aesthetic validity of bias as such. The works of Aeschylus, Aristophanes, Dante, and Cervantes, as well as the best contemporary Russian and Norwegian writers, he maintains, all contained bias. Nevertheless, he explains:

> ...the bias should flow by itself from the situation and action, without particular indications, and...the writer is not obliged to obtrude on the reader the future historical solution of the social conflicts pictured. And especially in our conditions the novel appeals mostly to readers of bourgeois circles, that is, not directly related to us, and therefore a socialist biased novel fully achieves its purpose, in my view, if by conscientiously describing the real mutual relations, breaking down conventional illusions about them, it shatters the optimism of the bourgeois world, instills doubt as to the eternal domination of the existing order, although the author does not offer

any definite solution or does not even line up openly on any particular side. (Engels to Minna Kautsky 122–23)

In a long commentary which accompanied Engels's letter in *International Literature,* Franc Schiller defines bias as class outlook, and asserts: "All the greatest creations of world literature are completely permeated with the outlook of various social classes" ("Friedrich Engels" 125). Paraphrasing Engels, he states: " ... the thought which the writer wishes to express should not have the character of subjective preaching to the reader of a line not arising out of the action itself" ("Friedrich Engels" 126). He traces Kautsky's weakness to what Lukacs called the undialectical conception of the subjective factor: representing social demands as proceeding from an extra-social moral ideal instead of arising through historical necessity, out of the objective conditions of class struggle. Failing to comprehend the "external circumstances" and "class grounds" for the development of the new, she creates heroes that are " 'incarnations of a principle' ... prepared models of ideal new people, standing outside society" ("Friedrich Engels 124). "Not analyzing the real live forces of social development Kautsky ardently strives for the 'new' principles by means of declarations, standardized propaganda ... " ("Friedrich Engels" 125).

The Bourgeois Literary Heritage

As in the case of the propaganda question, the clarification of Marx's and Engels's views on the bourgeois heritage conformed with the RAPP's insistence that proletarian writers learn from their bourgeois predecessors, particularly nineteenth-century realists. By the early thirties the extreme Proletcult view that there was nothing to be learned from the literature of the past had long been rejected by the leadership of the proletarian literature movement. After the Proletcult controversy in the Soviet Union in 1920, the need to build upon the bourgeois heritage had become axiomatic to the Soviet party's position on culture. The October Group had insisted on it in its dispute with the Kúznitsa, and later on it had been a main point of disagreement between the RAPP and the LEF. Information on the Soviet discussion had provided moral support to writers such as Joseph Freeman and Moissaye Olgin in their confrontation with extreme Proletcult views in the American party in the mid- and late twenties, and in Germany the leadership of the BPRS had received the backing of the IURW in their struggle against the same views.

The articles in *International Literature* on Marx's and Engels's writings on aesthetics indicated, once again, that both were deeply interested in literature. Among Marx's unfulfilled projects was a work on aesthetics and a book on Balzac. The authors he preferred included Aeschylus—whose works he read in the original every year—Homer, Dante, Cervantes, Diderot, Fielding, and Goethe. He was a particular admirer of Shakespeare, whom he frequently quotes in *Das Kapital*. Engels shared his enthusiasm for Balzac and Shakespeare, and in general preferred the same writers (Troschenko 138–40; F. Schiller, "Marx and Engels" 120).

It was pointed out that Marx was interested in literature of a "rich socio-historical content and intellectual content," regarding it as an invaluable source of information in studying the history of society (Troschenko 139). Referring to the English novelists Thackeray, Dickens and Charlotte Brontë, he wrote in the *New York Tribune* in 1854: "The brilliant modern school of English novelists have uncovered more political and social truths with their graphic and eloquent portrayals than all the politicians, publicists and moralists taken together" (qtd. in Troschenko 139). Similarly, Engels related that he had learned more about French society from Balzac than from "all the professional historians, economists and statisticians of the period together" (qtd. in F. Schiller, "Marx and Engels" 114).

As one commentator pointed out, Marx's and Engels's esteem for these authors reflected a preference for realism over romanticism. This in turn was traced to the principle that when an author took social reality as his starting point, he was sometimes able to grasp the motive forces of development even if he was reactionary in his sympathies. This contradiction was not possible in subjective idealist writers such as Schiller, who reduced characters and plot to vehicles of abstract ideas (Troschenko 142, 144).

Engels pointed to the possibility of this contradiction in his letter to Margaret Harkness. He calls it "one of the greatest triumphs of realism" that Balzac, in spite of his sympathy for the nobility was "compelled to go against his own class sympathies and political prejudices," that he "saw the necessity of the downfall of his favorite nobles and described them as people deserving no better fate, that he saw the real men of the future . . . " (qtd. in F. Schiller, "Marx and Engels" 114). Lenin perceived the same kind of contradiction in Tolstoy, whose point of view was that of the "patriarchal, naive peasant" (qtd. in "Lenin on Tolstoy" 92), but who nevertheless created "incomparable pictures of Russian life" and reflected "some of the more essential phases of the revolution" (qtd. in "Lenin on Tolstoy" 85).

For Marxist literary critics, Marx's, Engels's, and Lenin's remarks on nineteenth-century realists were a warning against hasty generalizations about bourgeois authors, tracing all features of their writing to their class origin. In his last letter dealing with literature, which was written in 1890, Engels was explicit on this point. It was addressed to a young writer and critic, Paul Ernst, who, Franc Schiller explained, "traced literature directly to economics," denying the possibility of a bourgeois writer's "going beyond the limits of his class ideology" ("Engels Against" 83–84). Proceeding from an idea of philistinism derived from German conditions, Ernst applied the term in criticizing non-German writers, ignoring the specific differences in their respective countries. Discussing Ibsen, he saw Norwegian society permeated with philistinism and dismissed his dramas as a reflection of this condition. Commenting on this situation, Engels warns him that "the materialist method is turned into its opposite when used . . . as a ready templet to which historical facts are stretched and recut" (Engels to Paul Ernst 81). Engels devotes most of his letter toward explaining the differences between the historical development and social conditions in Germany and Norway. "I consider it essential," he insists, "for one to make a study of all this before venturing an opinion" (Engels to Paul Ernst 82).

Modernism

One question that was vehemently discussed but remained unresolved in *International Literature* in 1934 and 1935 was whether the bourgeois heritage would include contemporaries who deviated from the conventions of nineteenth-century realism. While Malcolm Cowley and Alan Wald have maintained that modernism was the main issue dividing the *Partisan Review* editors from their orthodox opponents in the *New Masses,* in fact there was no orthodox position at this time. Both in *International Literature* as well as in the *New Masses* and *Daily Worker,* a wide spectrum of opinion appeared on this question.

Setting the stage for the discussion was the concept of decadence as it had developed from Plekhanov to Lukacs. When a class was no longer the motor of social progress, the argument went, its ideologues lost the ability to see society as a developing, organic whole, shaped by human action. The consequence was a split between the subjective and objective, with certain writers striving for a kind of photographic objectivity while others concentrated on the individual psyche, isolated from its social surroundings.

In order to compensate for the general loss of content from which their work suffered, writers from declining classes tended toward formal experimentation and art for art's sake.

Also conditioning the debate in the thirties was the discussion over formalism, which had taken place in the Soviet Union in the preceding decade. The formalist movement emerged about 1915 as an attempt to define the study of literature as a discipline. Common to all the theoreticians of the school—including Boris Eichenbaum, Victor Sklovsky and Yuri Tinyanov—was their focus on the evolution of literary forms, examined in isolation from the social and historical context. Among those who participated in the attack on formalism in the twenties was Trotsky, Bukharin, and Lunacharsky, all of whom pointed to its basis in idealism and insisted on viewing literature in relation to social development.[7] By 1930 the term *formalist* had become an epithet against both the theoreticians of the school as well as writers who engaged in formal experimentation.

On the other hand, it was argued that a changing society constantly provided new content. Since form and content were inseparable, it was equally formalist to canonize nineteenth-century norms of realism. Accordingly, proletarian writers were urged to assimilate the heritage "critically," that is, while learning from their bourgeois predecessors, they were not to imitate them. Militating against a general dismissal of the formal innovations of contemporary bourgeois writers was Engels's idea that the new and developing could also be reflected, albeit imperfectly, by writers whose ideology was hostile to working-class interests. Similarly Plekhanov, Mehring, Lunacharsky, and others had pointed out that decadence was a general process, and did not imply that individual bourgeois writers could not still create outstanding works. Even in the most negative work of art, Lunacharsky argued, it was possible to find "something which is very useful from the technical point of view" ("Marxism and Art" 14).

Since the writings of Marx and Engels predated the rise of what came to be known as "modernism," they did not specifically address the question as to how genuine innovation was to be distinguished from formal experiment for its own sake. Nevertheless their warnings against mechanically applying the base-superstructure idea provided a broad guideline in the approach to the question. In analyzing any manifestation in the superstructure, Engels pointed out, it was necessary to consider not only the economic base, but also the interaction of various elements within the superstructure itself: "Political, legal, philosophical, religious literary, artistic, etc. development is based on economic development. But they also all react upon each other and upon the economic base. The economic situation is not alone active, as cause, and everything else mere passive effect. Rather there is interaction, resting on the foundation of an economic necessity that *ultimately* always asserts itself." ("Engels to W. Borgius" 32).

Another guideline was provided by Lenin's idea that art should be accessible to the masses. In 1920 in conversation with Clara Zetkin, one of the founders of the KPD, he stated: "Art belongs to the people. It must be rooted in the broad working masses. It must be understood and cherished by them" (qtd. in Zetkin, "Erinnerungen" 75). Furthermore he made no secret of his aversion to modern art: "Why idolize the new like a god that must be obeyed just because it's 'new'. . . . I can't extol the works of expressionism, futurism, cubism and the other 'isms' as the highest manifestation of artistic genius. I don't understand them. I get no pleasure out of them" (Zetkin, "Erinnerungen" 74–75). Lenin did not, however, generalize his distaste into a stricture for artists and writers, but instead suggested that he might simply be behind the times in this area (Zetkin, "Erinnerungen" 75).

Despite Marx's and Engels's warnings about mechanical materialism, one tendency that recurred in discussions over modernism was to simplify the relationship between base and superstructure, and to consider departures from nineteenth-century realistic norms only in terms of the subjective-objective dichotomy. Ignoring such an obvious factor as the development of the camera, Lunacharsky wrote an article in 1913 in which he dismissed all modern schools of French painting, equating their departure from photograph-like resemblance with a retreat into subjectivism.[8] The RAPP's criticism of the LEF as well as Lukacs's categorical rejection of all attempts to combine literature and journalism were also marked by the tendency to ignore all factors except ideology, and to reduce such attempts to the disintegration of consciousness of a declining class.

This tendency emerged again in *International Literature* in an article by one of the major participants in the discussion over modernism, Dmitri Mirsky. Mirsky was a member of the prerevolutionary aristocracy who had recently returned from exile in England where he had become acquainted with James Joyce's writing (Schmitt and Schramm 205). In considering Joyce's technical innovations, he reduces everything to ideology and the subjective-objective dichotomy. He sees both extremes in the inner monologue, which he describes as naturalistic, stenographic reporting, on the one hand, and a manifestation of ultrapsychologism, the product of idleness and finesse, on the other. He rejects the possibility of its being used by Soviet writers on the grounds that it is "too intimately tied up with the ultra-subjectivism of the coupon cutting bourgeoisie and totally inapplicable to the art of socialism under construction" ("James Joyce" 102). Similarly, Joyce's word creation is characterized as "cubistic voluntarism," the "style of a falling bourgeoisie that wants to encompass reality in forms of its own choosing . . . " ("James Joyce" 99). Mirsky categorizes *Ulysses* as a whole as "esthetic, formalistic naturalism" ("James Joyce" 100), and describes Joyce as the epitome of the pure artist.

The other articles in *International Literature* dealing with modernism did not center around Joyce, about whom most Soviet writers probably had little or no direct knowledge, but rather John Dos Passos. There was a great deal of interest in Dos Passos among young writers in the Soviet Union at this time. One reason was that, next to Theodore Dreiser and Sherwood Anderson, he was the most prominent of the American leftist-liberal writers who had moved toward the Communist party in the late twenties and early thirties. The other reason involved his use of modernist technique in socially critical novels. In his trilogy, *U.S.A.*, stream-of-consciousness appeared in the "camera eye" sections, and the barrier between fiction and journalism was loosened through the incorporation of news flashes and short biographical sketches of historical figures into the narrative.

In March 1933 the Orgcommittee of the Soviet Writers' Union co-sponsored a discussion on Dos Passos that lasted three evenings. As reported in *International Literature:* "A substantial paper by A. Leites, (Soviet literary critic) entitled 'Dos Passos' Course' and an additional paper by the well known Soviet dramatist V. Vishnevsky, were read, after which there was a lively discussion by a number of Soviet writers and critics. The discussion raised a tremendous amount of interest among Soviet writers generally" ("Soviet Literature and Dos Passos" 103).

If Mirsky's article on Joyce represented one extreme in the discussion over modernism, the paper read by Vishnevsky, who had initiated the discussion, was at the other. Although his position was a minority one (Günther 68), he was given almost twice as much space in *International Literature* as Leites. He begins by repeating the necessity of developing new forms to express the new content provided by Soviet society. Describing what he sees as the weaknesses of Soviet literary criticism, he states:

The analyses of art, analyses of artistic works today leave us very much dissatisfied. Language, color, image, composition, manner, style—all this is left out of consideration and comprehension. Much is made of formalism: "Beware of it!" There isn't a gathering lately at which the evils of formalism are not mentioned. I would advise however a little thought on the matter. Do not forget that we are also talking about the form we are beginning to master. . . . We shouldn't just spit at form. There is no art without form. (Vishnevsky 106)

Turning to the discussion on Dos Passos, he warns: "We cannot deduce style, genre, fluctuations, trends from a purely economic basis" (Vishnevsky 106). Lamenting the "schoolmaster's tone" (106) that he detects at the conference, he states: "Dos Passos gives one a feeling of the tremendously many phases of life, and you simply come to him and say: naughty—naughty! you are a mechanist! why have you got the "camera eye"? and so on" (Vishnevsky 108). Echoing Engels's advice to Paul Ernst he asks: "Don't you think Dos Passos will continue to be formed under the influence of events in the U.S.A. and not those demands you address to him from here? Where is the consideration of the specifically American and Dos Passos' place in American literature, his influence upon it, etc.?" (Vishnevsky 106).

Addressing the question of Western literature in general, he reminds the audience that bourgeois writers are also capable of reflecting important aspects of contemporary society:

In the West there is a crisis, decay, the signs of disintegration, etc. I want to ask our critics: you, dialecticians, do you really fail to understand that in the regularity of the disintegration, the decay, the perishing of a descending class, something tremendously new is regularly rising? And when we look at Grosz, look at Proust, look at Picasso who got to things entirely dead—we should be able to see that behind them, beside them, a tremendously new seed is already sprouting. One must understand where it is and grasp it, taking culture as a whole under investigation "even" the enemy, "even" bourgeois culture. (Vishnevsky 107)

In regard to Joyce, he argues like Joseph Freeman in 1926 that "*Ulysses* exposes modern conditions of existence in the West" and is " 'an indict-ment of Europe' " (Vishnevsky 110). In addition Joyce "compels the search for deeper form" (Vishnevsky 110). He concludes that, while imitation should be avoided, the methods of Joyce and Dos Passos "must be utilized" (Vishnevsky 110): "There is no phenomena in the realm of art or culture which should be tabu to the Soviet artist.... Only people incapable of living a full life try to dictate to those that can, a sort of 'rules' for writers. A totally fruitless work. It will leave no trace in the history of our literature and culture except some articles in *Pravda* correcting our critics" (Vishnevsky 107).

In the final article on Dos Passos in 1934, the Soviet literary critic M. Bleiman once again attacks the simpleminded approach to Western literature that attributes all formal innovation to decadence. Like Vishnevsky he traces this to ignorance of the specific context from which individual works emerge. Failure to see the evolution of the writer in the light of "the general movement of literature," to analyze "phenomena in motion," leads critics to classify works according to "external features" and "to consider every attempt to break away from the form of the novel traditional to the nineteenth century as due to the same cause," namely "disintegration of consciousness." Thus novels are classified, not according to intellectual content, but along formal lines, so that "Revolutionary literature is put on the same shelf as reactionary literature" (Bleiman 98).

While he grants that the decline of realism is a hallmark of a declining class, he argues that one must distinguish between writers whose formal experimentation derives from lack of content and those whose innovations are an attempt to approach reality. He places Dos Passos in the latter category, seeing "genuine innovation" in "his ability, by means of the introduction of elements of actual reality into the woof of the tale, to define the development of the characters in his books, to establish, perhaps imperfectly, the social characteristics of phenomena and the connection between social existence and individual consciousness" (Bleiman 106).

He repeats the argument that the development of society and of consciousness demands new forms: "The classical form of the bourgeois novel can therefore not be taken as a criterion, a canon, any deviation from which is incontravertible evidence of incurable disease" (Bleiman 99). Formalism, he reiterates, includes the freezing of form, "not taking into account the fact that the movement of social consciousness predicates literary form as one of the means of expressing this consciousness" (Bleiman 99).

Proletarian Literature and Socialist Realism

Writers such as Max Eastman, Malcolm Cowley, and Lawrence Schwartz, who see in the propagation of socialist realism a purely administrative measure and an abandonment of the RAPP's concept of proletarian literature overlook the continuity and liveliness of the discussion that actually took place.[9] This continuity is best demonstrated in the concept of the typical, which was derived from Marx's and Engels's commentaries, and at the same time summarized the whole analysis of the subjective and objective, the abstract and concrete, from Plekhanov's and Mehring's early adaptations of Hegel's aesthetics to Lukacs's essays in the *Linkskurve*. In *International Literature* Kirpotin thus defines socialist realism as a reflection of society in its revolutionary movement and development, and contrasts it with subjective idealism, on the one hand, and the reproduction of inessential details, on the other:

> By socialist realism we mean the reflection in art of the external world ... in all its essential circumstances and with the aid of essential and typical characterisation. We mean the faithful description of life in all its aspects, with the victorious principle of the forces of the socialist revolution.... We set socialist realism against idealism, subjectivism, the literature of illusion in any form whatsoever, as an untrue and distorted reflection of reality. (Kirpotin 145).

He adds that the "insistence upon unessential details ... and sketchiness prevent completeness of social realism" (Kirpotin 145). In calling for the union of the abstract and concrete in the typical he paraphrases Engels: "Only along the path of socialist realism shall we achieve the ideal of art described by Engels: the combination of historical consciousness with the liveliness and power of characterization of a Shakespeare" (Kirpotin 145).

Another component of the theory of socialist realism that incorporated positions put forth by RAPP was the concept of partisanship. From its beginnings in the early twenties the October Group had differentiated itself from the Proletcult by its recognition of the leading role of the Party. In his 1928 speech Fadayev had stated: "The artist of the proletariat is no 'loner' ... but rather a proletarian revolutionary, who works with his class and party, employing the methods of art in recognizing and transforming the world" ("Der Hauptweg" 30).

Commonly cited in connection with the concept of partisanship was an article of Lenin's called "Party Organization and Party Literature." Writing after the relaxation of the censorship in the wake of the 1905 revolution, he developed guidelines for future Party work in the publishing field. Rejecting the notion that writing was a private, individual matter, he asserted: "Literature must become a component of organized, planned and integrated Social-Democratic Party work" (104). At the same time he insisted that writers must be granted wide latitude for "personal initiative, individual inclination, thought and fantasy, form and content" (104). Literature, he stated, "is least of all subject to mechanical adjustment or levelling to the rule of the majority over the minority" (104).

The question of whether Lenin was referring here only to writing that appeared in the Party press, or to literature in general has been a matter of dispute. The wording of the article does not allow for a definitive answer. In any case it was interpreted in the Statutes of the Soviet Writers' Union to mean that in postrevolutionary society the writer joined in "active work of socialist construction" (166), a task commonly expressed in the description of the writer as "engineer of the human soul." While this expression has usually been attributed to Stalin, the idea behind it had been propagated by the RAPP in its dispute with the LEF in the late twenties and was argued by critics of utilitarianism in the American movement in the mid-thirties. In opposing the separation of reflection and praxis and the LEF's idea of the writer as craftsman carrying out assignments and creating products of immediate social and political utility, Fadeyev had argued in 1928: " . . . the art of the proletariat, permeated with Marxism . . . acts upon the whole psyche of the human being, transforming it in the direction of socialism ("Der Hauptweg" 29). In describing the role of the writer in Soviet society, the Statutes of the Writers' Union likewise insisted on the unity of reflection and praxis: the "veracity and historical concreteness of artistic portrayals" was to be "combined with the tasks of the ideological remoulding and education of toiling people in the spirit of Socialism" (166).

One element of socialist realism that had not been explicitly formulated in the RAPP's concept of proletarian literature was "revolutionary romanticism."[10] The main source of this concept were statements of Lenin in "What to Do?" He, in turn, had been influenced by the ideas of the Russian revolutionary democrats of the mid-nineteenth century on the educational function of art. One of them, Dmitri Pisarev, had differentiated between escapist dreams, which pointed away from reality, lulling people into inaction, and those which had the effect of a vision, supporting and strengthening morale. The latter were compared to the imagined picture of a finished building when it was still in the beginning stages. Commenting on the distinction made by Pisarev, Lenin wrote: "Unfortunately we have too little of such dreaming in our movement" (qtd. in James 25).

Another source was Maxim Gorky. Expanding on the idea that proletarian literature was to grasp the trends of development, and portray the positive hero working for the socialist transformation of society, he had defended the writer's freedom to exaggerate those features of reality that pointed to the future (*Zur Theorie* 114). The influence of both Gorky and Lenin is evident in Kirpotin's description of revolutionary romanticism. Employing the image of the incompleted building, he states:

> This future is actually among us, it stands amid its scaffolding. . . . The heroism, the exploits, the selfless devotion to the revolution, the fulfillment of our realistic dream, all these are characteristic and essential features of our age, of our days. The artist is performing a useful, a necessary task, in magnifying these features, even when, leaving out insignificant aspects, every day life, unimportant details he idealises them, so long as he shows the integrity of life, its huge scope, towards which the whole of our construction is leading. (145)

Its validity depended on whether it expressed the real forces of development: "Red revolutionary romanticism is a legitimate and valuable principle . . . so long as it fulfills the demand for the faithful description of life, of socialist realism" (145).

The careful wording that was often used in connection with this concept suggests awareness of the danger of its being used to justify the kind of distortion of character and coloring of reality that writers were asked to avoid. It was usually stated that romanticism, thus defined, was an acceptable, though not necessary, element of socialist realism. Kirpotin, for example, states: "When we speak of socialist realism we do not mean to imply that revolutionary romanticism is in any way at loggerheads with it" (145).

In early formulations of socialist realism the freedom of the writer in regard to form, style and genre was repeatedly stressed. In the case of revolutionary romanticism the door was to be left open to a whole school of literature which the RAPP had disparaged. Thus Lunacharsky stated: "There is no need for shutting out a means of artistic prognosis. . . . Socialist realism is a broad program which includes many different methods."

("Problems" 90–91). He anticipates it being employed, not in the theater or novel, but in other literary and artistic forms:

> Why then can our art have no grand synthetic images—if not in the novel or the drama, at least in the opera or in collossal pageants where tens of thousands of people are gathered? Because it is not realistic? True—there are traces of romanticism in this as the combined elements have not the likeness of truth. But they truthfully represent this truth. It uncovers the inner features of development, becomes its pennant and there is no reason for us to deny the need for us of such an art. . . .
>
> And so we see that together with the tremendous problem of socialist realism to give a picture full of truth, based on a close description of an object of reality, giving it so, however, that development, motion, struggle are evident, together with this form it is really possible to have a Socialist romanticism. . . . " ("Problems" 90–91)

What remained unclarified in the discussion over socialist realism was the status of proletarian literature within the newly formulated theory. With Marx's and Engels's observations on Balzac as a probable model, Kirpotin and Lunacharsky defined the socialist realist writer in broad terms to include non-Communist authors who were favorable to socialism and succeeded in conveying basic trends of development in Soviet society. Within this group proletarian Communist writers were to have the "ideologically leading role" (Kirpotkin 144). Lunacharsky stated: "The proletarian realist examining reality realizes that the fundamental, moving historical force in the past, at present, and in the nearest future is the class struggle. One can of course imagine a Socialist realist to whom this is not yet clear . . . " ("Problems" 89).

The logical corollary to the distinction between these two kinds of writers would have been to define proletarian literature as a subcategory of socialist realism. Preventing this was the overlapping of the two theories. While a writer who grasped important aspects of Soviet reality might be classified as a socialist realist, socialist realism itself, like proletarian literature, was defined according to ideology. At the Soviet Writers Congress in 1934 Bukharin explained: "The philosophical prerequisite of socialist realism is *dialectical materialism.* . . . [Socialist realism] corresponds with dialectical materialism, it is the transference of the latter to the realm of art" ("Referat" 339).

As Hans Günther points out in his book, *Die Verstaatlichung der*

Literatur, what was involved in the usage of these terms in the Soviet Union in the mid-thirties was a general shift in emphasis from "proletarian" to "socialist." At the Seventeenth Party Congress of the CPUSSR in early 1932, the First Five-Year Plan was seen as having laid the groundwork for a classless, socialist society. With the adoption of the new Soviet constitution in 1936, Stalin declared that Soviet workers could no longer be called proletarian since they were not exploited by capitalists (Günther 12).

While the precise relation between proletarian literature and socialist realism remained undefined in *International Literature* in the mid-thirties, in practice the latter term was mainly confined to Soviet literature, while socialist-oriented works by writers in capitalist countries continued to be referred to as "proletarian."

Notes

1. Gorky also intervened on behalf of other writers, including Pilnyak and Zamyatin. See Eimermacher 56–57.

2. This article can be found in a German translation in Eimermacher 387–88.

3. *Daily Worker* 24 Nov. 1933: 5.

4. Ibid. 27 Nov. 1933: 5.

5. Fadeyev authored one of the first essays on socialist realism to appear in the Soviet Union. It was published in two parts in the magazine *Literaturnaya Gazeta* on 29 Oct. and 11 Nov. 1932. It has been reprinted in German under the title "Über sozialistischen Realismus" (see bibliography).

6. See Freeman, "Letters from Sergei Dinamov" 92.

7. Trotsky criticized formalism in his book *Literature and Revolution;* in a speech delivered on 13 Mar. 1925 Bukharin took a position similar to Trotsky's; Lunacharsky criticized formalism in a 1924 essay. The position of all three are discussed in Günther and Heilscher.

8. This article appears in a German translation under the title "Pariser Briefe" in the collection of Lunacharsky's essays and articles, *Die Revolution und die Kunst* (see bibliography).

9. For another view on this, stressing the continuity between the RAPP's concept of proletarian literature and the theory of socialist realism see Ermolaev 204 and Günther 13.

10. It is commonly claimed that the RAPP rejected romanticism as incompatible with realism. See, for example, Brown, *Russian Literature* 173; James 72; Lomidse and Timofejew 155–58. Hans Günther, however, sees the essence of the idea of revolutionary romanticism in a speech which Fadeyev delivered on 22 Sept. 1929, although Fadeyev avoided the term *romanticism.* See Günther 36.

5

Criticism of Leftism
in the United States

Historical and Political Background

THE DISCUSSION over aesthetics after 1933 in the United States took place in the context of a cultural movement that had expanded considerably since the late twenties. An important factor in this development was a general increase in the Communist party's influence, which was manifested in the mass activity it helped organize in the wake of the economic collapse. A high point in this activity was reached in March 1930 when Communists organized unemployment demonstrations throughout the country in what one historian has described as "the first concerted, large-scale protest in this country against the downward economic trend" (Leab 308). While Party efforts to establish labor unions independent of the AFL in the late twenties and early thirties met with only limited success, Communist-led unions did manage to organize some of the most militant strikes of the period, including the one in the coal industry in Harlan County, Kentucky in 1931.[1]

The growing prestige of the Communist party was also manifested in the large numbers of writers and other intellectuals who endorsed its policies, a development begun before the stock market crash. Seriously disillusioned about the nature of the American judicial system after the execution of Sacco and Vanzetti in 1927, John Dos Passos, Sherwood Anderson, and others worked with Communists toward the end of the twenties in defending prisoners who had been arrested in connection with labor-union activity.[2] In 1931 the National Committee for the Defense of Political Prisoners was formed on the initiative of Theodore Dreiser in order to assist International Labor Defense—the American affiliate of International Red Aid—in drawing public attention to individual cases. Among the Committee's members were, again, Dos Passos and Anderson, as well as Lincoln Steffens and novelist Waldo Frank. In the following year, with the economy approaching a standstill and millions out of work throughout the country, the above writers were joined by a long list of other professionals—including Edmund

Wilson, Langston Hughes, and Malcolm Cowley—who signed a public statement announcing their support for the Communist party candidates for president and vice-president, William Z. Foster and James Ford.[3]

Depression conditions and the growing prestige of the Party provided fertile ground for the cultural movement that had been spawned in the late twenties. By 1934 the John Reed Clubs could boast of thirty branches across the country, with a total membership of 1200, and a series of magazines featuring the reportage, poetry, and short fiction of club members. The most prominent of these publications was the *Partisan Review,* the organ of the New York John Reed Club. Others were *Leftward* (Boston), the *Partisan* (Hollywood), the *Cauldron* (Grand Rapids), *Left Review* (Philadelphia), *New Force* (Detroit), the *Hammer* (Hartford, Connecticut) and *Left Front* (Chicago) (Aaron 431).

In addition to these, a number of magazines published proletarian literature without being affiliated with a John Reed Club. The best known was the *Anvil,* which specialized in short fiction and was edited by Jack Conroy, the author of the novel, *The Disinherited. Blast,* a New York magazine, likewise published short fiction, as did *Scope. Dynamo* concentrated on the poetry of writers active in the movement, such as Michael Gold, Joseph Freeman, and Horace Gregory. The *New Masses,* while not officially connected with any of the clubs, continued publishing the work of individual members as well as articles by well-known professional writers who remained outside the clubs.

The proletarian literature of the thirties was not limited to the short forms that appeared in these magazines, but included the novel as well. Walter Rideout, in his book *The Radical Novel in the United States,* lists fifty between 1930 and 1936. Two of the more widely read were *The Disinherited* and Gold's *Jews Without Money.* Like Conroy and Gold, most of the authors were well known in the movement, and many had published their first literary efforts in its magazines.

Finally, there were the workers' theaters, of which about two hundred existed by 1932 (Cosgrave 207). Most of them were connected with cultural organizations of ethnic minorities and performed agitprop sketches in workers halls, before picket lines and in front of factory gates. The best known of these were located in New York: *The Arbeter Theater Ferband* (ARTEF), a Jewish group; the German-language *Proletbühne;* and the Workers Lab. In 1932 about one hundred groups joined the League of Workers' Theatres—later renamed the New Theatre League—and became affiliated with the Soviet-based International Workers' Dramatic Union. In addition to the workers amateur theaters, a professional group, the

Theatre Union, was formed toward the end of 1933 (Brüning 22–26, 30–35).

The growth of the movement was qualitative as well as quantitative. By 1933 a number of novels of undeniable literary merit had appeared, and favorable reviews became common in such publications as the *Saturday Review of Literature* and the *New York Times Book Review*. The workers' theaters attracted national attention with the production of a series of one-act plays including Clifford Odets's *Waiting for Lefty,* Albert Maltz's *Private Hicks* and Irwin Shaw's *Bury the Dead*. The influence of the movement was also reflected in the radically expanded readership of the *New Masses* after it became a weekly in 1934,[4] and in the large number of well-known writers who contributed to it, such as William Saroyan, Erskine Caldwell and Theodore Dreiser.

The consolidation of the early thirties and the increased participation of professional writers supplied the precondition for the fulfillment of a long-range goal, which had initially been set for Soviet proletarian literature, but which had seemed too ambitious to participants in the movement in other countries. In its 1925 statement the Central Committee had called on Soviet writers to go beyond agitprop and workers correspondence and to draw upon the literary heritage in creating a literature as varied in theme and form as its bourgeois predecessor. It was in the pursuance of this goal that the RAPP had formulated its theory of dialectical materialism and the living person, insisting on the importance of the bourgeois literary heritage, while attacking tendentiousness and the LEF's strictly utilitarian approach to literature.

Outside the Soviet Union, where proletarian-revolutionary writers did not have the resources of the government at their disposal, the call for this kind of expansion seemed unrealistic to many, particularly in the early stages of the movement. In the German BPRS there were members such as Maxim Vallentin and Erich Steffen, who felt that proletarian writers should concentrate on agitprop and worker correspondence, and that political effectiveness should be the sole criterion in judging individual works. On the other side were the *Linkskurve* editors, who launched an all-out attack on proletcult attitudes, tendentiousness and utilitarianism, and called for the great proletarian epic, combining reflection and praxis.

Despite IURW criticism, there had been no equivalent development in the *New Masses* for almost two years after the Charkov Conference. Aside from the ambiguity in *Literature of the World Revolution* in regard to literary criticism and theory, one possible explanation for the lag in the United States was unfamiliarity with the aesthetic concepts that had been formulated within the RAPP and the BPRS. While individual articles by

Gold, Freeman, and Olgin had anticipated various aspects of the theory of the living person and dialectical materialism in the years before the conference, there had been no discussion in the *New Masses* over aesthetics, such as had taken place in the BPRS in 1930. In their critical analysis of Mehring's writings, the editors of the *Linkskurve* had come much closer to the RAPP's theory than their *New Masses* counterparts. Thus Auerbach's Charkov speech on creative method contained little that was new to them except for some terminology that was adopted in the *Linkskurve* shortly thereafter. In the *New Masses* there was no commentary on Auerbach's speech, nor did this terminology start to appear until early 1933.

Another possible explanation for the delay in the United States is that in Germany, where the KPD was already a mass party in the twenties, the leaders of the cultural movement felt that it was sufficiently consolidated by 1930 to allow for increased emphasis on quality and large forms. The kind of criticism Lukacs directed at Willi Bredel would have been of doubtful usefulness in the United States at that time, with young John Reed Club members making their first halting efforts at writing, and many professional writers only starting to show interest in the movement.

Nevertheless, by the end of 1932 major confrontations over various aspects of leftism had taken place in the John Reed Clubs, the *New Masses,* and in the theater movement. The role that Lukacs and the other *Linkskurve* editors had played in the BPRS was assumed in the United States by various literary critics and leaders of the movement, such as Nathaniel Buchwald for the theater, Granville Hicks and other *New Masses'* editors, and members of the *Partisan Review* staff. As had been the case in Germany, discussion focused initially on the theater. The reason for this was obvious. The workers' theater movement had consisted almost exclusively of amateur, agitprop groups, so that critics, in calling for thematic and formal diversification, found it necessary to point up the difference between the purposes and methods of the short political sketch and the full-length drama. The situation in the novel was somewhat different. The vast majority of American proletarian novelists were professionals. Only a handful had gone the way of Willi Bredel from worker correspondent to fiction writer. Furthermore, the length of time usually involved in writing a novel meant that the form itself was ill suited to agitprop addressing events of the moment. It was probably for these reasons that tendentiousness was less an issue here. As the *Partisan Review* editors pointed out in 1934, the novel was the form that was most free of leftism.[5]

Nevertheless novelists, too, were urged to expand beyond the theme of direct class confrontation, and to learn from bourgeois literature in moving toward the great proletarian epic. As in the Soviet Union and Germany, the approach to the heritage was strongly influenced by Marx's and Engels's views on Balzac, and on Lenin's remarks on Tolstoy. Likewise, the distinction between partisanship and tendentiousness, as defined in Lukacs's 1932 article, became a guiding principle in criticism of proletarian literature and drama.

The demand for a high-quality proletarian literature, which was to be broad in theme and form, and therefore suited to addressing not only Party members and supporters but a wide spectrum of the population, was reinforced by political developments. After the division of the working class in Germany cleared the way for the Nazi takeover, the rejection of tendentiousness, utilitarianism and proletcult attitudes in the international proletarian literature movement became incorporated into a general campaign against leftism and sectarianism.

According to Gilbert, Rideout, and others, this campaign was directed against views that were dominant within the movement and were only abandoned in connection with the Popular Front. In reality the attack on leftism was largely based on views that had a long history within the movement and were propagated in its central organ, *International Literature*. Numerous writers and critics testified to the influence and importance of this magazine. The June 1934 issue contained the following quote from Philip Rahv: "*International Literature* is rapidly acquiring in this country the esteem and popularity which is its due as the central organ of revolutionary literature. Time and again the writer has observed workers discussing the contents of this magazine. He has seen them coming into bookshops inquiring whether a new number of the magazine had arrived. The magazine is also read by writers and artists in search of theoretical guidance" (151). In the same issue, Herman Spector, one of the editors of *Dynamo*, described *International Literature* as "the most stimulating and advanced magazine that we see in America" (151). John Dos Passos wrote in the first issue for 1935: "I've been greatly enjoying the copies of *International Literature* I've been getting. I think you are publishing a very good magazine" (111). Similar comments by Dreiser, Langston Hughes, Waldo Frank, and others could also be cited.

Of particular importance to the American discussion were letters of Marx and Engels on literature, which appeared in *International Literature* in early 1933, for the first time in English, and were accompanied by commentaries by Franc Schiller. Three of the main participants in the debate over leftism placed special value on this material. Granville Hicks wrote: "Perhaps the most interesting and valuable critical material . . . may be found in the various letters on literary questions by Marx and Engels with comments by F. Schiller" ("Of the World Revolution" 26). In the July 1934 issue of *International Literature* future *Partisan Review* editor Alan Calmer stated: "As to *International Literature,* what we need here is more basic essays on the problems of Marxism, art and literature like those in the past year by F. Schiller." (159) Finally, Philip Rahv pointed out in the *Daily Worker* in early 1934: "In literary criticism . . . the issue [no. 4 (1934) of *International Literature*] presents the long-awaited Marx and Engels correspondence with La Salle, dealing with his dramatic tragedy, *Franz von Sickingen.* The concrete and profound insights of Marx and Engels into the problems of tragedy and the revolutionary viewpoint in literature will undoubtedly illuminate many dark corners in our young proletarian criticism . . . " (" 'International Literature' Grows" 5).

The Discussion in the Workers' Theater Movement

In his 1985 book, *Left-Wing Dramatic Theory in the American Theatre,* Ira A. Levine divides the development of the theater movement in the first half of the thirties into two phases. In the first years of the decade the emphasis was on the mobile theater and the short agitprop sketch, while in 1934 and 1935 the stationary theater and "revolutionary realism" prevailed. He sees Soviet and German influence behind the first, and identifies it with the "dogged proletarianism of American Communist critics," including Gold and Freeman, who insisted on "a clear-cut demarcation between heroic workers and villainous or decadent capitalists" (87–88). The expansion toward realistic, evening-filling drama, on the other hand, is described as "primarily an indigenous American development . . . " (108), in which fellow travelers played an important role. Unlike Communist critics, he writes, " . . . noncommunist Marxists . . . were prepared to study the expertise of the commercial theatre and, later in the decade, to learn especially from the techniques of bourgeois realism" (84). Following the pattern established in the literature on leftism, he portrays the expansion toward stationary theaters and realism as a reflection of politics, namely the transition from the "Third Period" to the Popular Front (102–3).

Contrary to Levine's interpretation, the call for stationary theaters and evening-filling drama was expressed some months after the founding of an international organization of workers theaters in 1929, in keeping with the long-range goal of a broad proletarian culture, encompassing large forms. At the very beginning of the American workers-theater movement, in 1927, it was a Communist, Moissaye Olgin, who rejected the abstractness of agitprop and insisted on living characters ("For a Workers' Theatre" 2:4). In the early thirties another Communist party member, Nathaniel Buchwald, was among the first to endorse and propagate the establishment of stationary theaters performing full-length dramas, and to attack what he called " 'leftist' vulgarization" ("The First International" 140).

In December 1929 the International Workers' Dramatic Union (IWDU) was founded in Moscow on the initiative of the German *Arbeiter-Theater-Bund*. At the first conference of the IWDU, which was held the following June, disagreement arose over the concept of proletarian culture—encompassing large literary and theatrical forms—that had developed in the Soviet Union after the Proletcult controversy of the early twenties. On the one side were a number of Soviet delegates who called on workers' theaters in other countries to expand beyond small mobile groups performing short agitprop pieces. On the other side were German and other foreign representatives. A report on the conference in the German magazine *Arbeiterbühne und Film* related: "Some Russian comrades, although in favor of the activity of the workers' theaters in the capitalist countries, with the agit-prop troupes, spoke against the neglect of the large, evening-filling drama. The foreign representatives, however, unanimously stressed the great importance of the agit-prop troupes and at the same time described the difficulties that accompanied the performance of large pieces" ("Der erste Kongress" 15).

Like Maxim Vallentin in the *Linkskurve,* the editors of *Arbeiterbühne und Film* argue for a "utilitarian" theater, addressing events of the moment: "The workers' theater in the capitalist countries must be a theater of struggle, it must take a clear position in the daily struggles of the proletariat, it is the battle drum of the revolution. For technical and financial reasons the large-scale drama can hardly at all, or only seldom, fulfill these tasks" ("Der erste Kongress" 15–16). Nevertheless in the resolution that was adopted at the conference the door was left open to the kind of expansion the Soviet delegates had called for. The IWDU, it stated, "is not only to concern itself with the workers amateur theaters but must also where possible extend its influence over the revolutionary leftist theater and its personnel and draw them into its work" ("Wege und Formen" 10). The American workers' theaters had not yet formed a central organization in 1929, which perhaps explains why no delegates were sent to the IWDU conference. However, here, too, a conflict arose, which was similar to that which had occurred at the conference and had sprung up between Vallentin and the *Linkskurve* editors in Germany. On the one side was John Bonn, the director of the Proletbühne, while Nathaniel Buchwald, one of the founders of the ARTEF, was on the other.

Before immigrating to the United States in 1928, Bonn, whose original name was Hans Bohn, had worked in the State Theater in Berlin and had produced a political revue in Leipzig entitled "Was Uns Fehlt." Having spent a lot of time in Berlin in the twenties, Bonn was no doubt familiar with the productions of Erwin Piscator and had witnessed the growth of the local agitprop workers' theaters (Cosgrave 202).

When Bonn became head in 1928, the Proletbühne had been in existence for two years as the dramatic section of a workers' club in the Yorkville section of Manhattan. Under his direction the group developed into what one writer has called "the vanguard of American revolutionary theatre" (Cosgrave 201). Like its counterparts in the old country and in the earlier German-American workers' theaters, the productions of the Proletbühne consisted of short, militant pieces presented at political meetings, before picket lines, and at the waterfront, with a minimum of props. The speech was abstract, the mass chant being a frequently employed device, and the characters were generally stereotypes of capitalists, policemen, politicians, and workers.

Like agitprop groups elsewhere, such as Maxim Vallentin's Das rote Sprachrohr, the Proletbühne saw its productions as the antithesis of the bourgeois theater, and propagated a purely utilitarian approach. That is, its emphasis was on political events of the moment, and the goal was the mobilization of the audience.

The conflict that arose in early 1932 involved the undifferentiated condemnation of the bourgeois theater. In the beginning of the year, the League of American Workers' Theatres had been set up on the initiative of the Proletbühne and the Workers' Lab, both of which had been publishing the magazine *Workers Theatre* since April 1931.[6] In preparation for a "National Spartakiade of Workers' Theatres" to be held in April 1932, the March issue of *Workers Theatre* described the upcoming event as "a mobilization of all workers against the bourgeois theater for the workers theatre" (qtd. in McNamara and Schuman 99). In an essay on the history of the Proletbühne, Stuart Cosgrave indicates that the Spartakiade "was severly criticized by the Marxist press" (209). In this connection he cites a review in *Workers Theatre* by Communist party member Nathaniel Buchwald[7] of Bonn's "Red Revue," which had won first prize.

While Ira Levine mentions Buchwald, in passing, as "ARTEF's leading theoretician" (67), he fails to analyze the role he played in the discussion in the workers' theater movement. Already in his remarks on "Red Revue," Buchwald presaged the direction the discussion would take in the workers' theater movement over the next few years. Thus he criticized what he regarded as excessive sloganizing, and expressed doubt about the effectiveness of the Proletbühne's kind of agitprop for non-Communist audiences:

> . . . it is questionable whether the 15-minute *Red Revue* would impress a neutral or an unfriendly proletarian audience. . . .
>
> In general, the work of the Prolet-buehne, though outstanding in the field of agit-prop theatre, leans too heavily on direction and delivery of lines and too little on the literary and dramaturgical shaping of its plays. . . . [T]he plays themselves are frequently devoid of effective theatrical form and the vocabulary leans to the conventional propagandistic jargon. . . .
>
> The virtue of simplicity of direction is developed by the Prolet-Buehne director to a fault. While the use of placards is quite effective it tends to grow dull with repetition. . . . Its [the revue's] lines ring with the overtones of sectarian phraseology and formulation. ("The Prize-Winners" 110)

Buchwald's criticism mirrored developments in his own group, the ARTEF, which by this time had already established a stationary theater and was performing full-length plays in addition to the short agitprop pieces which its mobile groups continued to perform.

Writing some months after Buchwald's article, Bonn demonstrated a conciliatory attitude on the issue of stationary workers' theaters, and mentioned Piscator's theater and the ARTEF as models. At the same time he emphasized a point that would be repeated by others over the following years, namely that expansion did not mean the replacement of one form of theater for another: " . . . the other form of theatre, the stationary theatre, should not be neglected or condemned. . . . There exists a demand for the stationary workers theatre with its more elaborate technical means, with its more emotional approach toward the audience. . . . The question is not: Agitprop theatre or stationary theatre. Our task is to develope both types" ("Situation and Tasks" 8).

The "Constitution of the League of Workers Theatres in the U.S.A.," which was drawn up in 1932, pointed in the same direction as the "Draft Manifesto of the John Reed Clubs," which was issued in the same year. That is, cooperation with professional, sympathetic, non-Communist writers was sought, in keeping with the demand for expansion of the movement. Thus the League declared its intention to "establish contacts with all sympathetic elements in the bourgeois theater and to make it possible for them to participate in the workers theatre movement" (14).

The question of the nature and goals of the proletarian-revolutionary theater was taken up again in 1933 at the First International Olympiad of Revolutionary Theatres, which was organized by the IWDU and was described in *International Literature* as "mainly a critical review of the content and forms of the revolutionary theatre" (Buchwald, "The First International" 139). Between May 25 and 31, agitprop groups from the USSR and sixteen other countries performed in Moscow. By this time, the movement of intellectuals toward the Communist party presented new possibilities for expanding in the proposed direction, while the new political situation made such an expansion seem all the more imperative.

In a report on the Olympiad in *International Literature* Nathaniel Buchwald developed his earlier line of criticism, attacking the same tendency as the *Linkskurve* editors in 1930, namely "raising the technical limitations of the agitprop theater, imposed by the circumstances, to the level and dignity of a principle" ("The First International" 140). As a result, he explained, "every technical means, such as scenery, costume, make-up, etc. was rejected and decried as bourgeois and every attempt at systematic training was ridiculed as bourgeois intellectualism. . . . " The "agit-prop style . . . degenerated into a cliché, into a rigid form which stifled the spirit of the script and which grew duller and duller with repetition" ("The First International" 140).

The term he applies to these attitudes is " 'leftist' vulgarization," which, he indicates, the IWDU "waged a consistent struggle against" ("The First International" 140). He traces the new "emphasis of *quality,*" the campaign against "sketchiness and superficiality," to the second plenum of the IWDU, which had been held in November 1932 ("The First International" 142). "In the light of these theses," he writes, "the agit-prop theater abroad began reorganizing its work" ("The First International" 142). Like

Bonn, he indicates that reorganization does not mean the replacement of the short agitprop piece by the full-length drama: "It cannot be expected of the agit-prop groups abroad to discard entirely the sketchy symbols of the characters in agit-prop plays and to go in for profound, searching character portrayal" ("The First International" 142). Rather, they were to strive for "better literary and dramatical quality of the scripts and greater technical and scenic inventiveness . . . new forms of revolutionary theatre, with a minimum of expenditure of time, money and materials" ("The First International" 142). Meanwhile no opportunity was to be lost "to establish stationary revolutionary theatres utilizing the services of the art intelligentsia . . . " ("The First International" 142). In keeping with the desire to accomodate professionals from all classes, the name of the central organization was changed from the IWDU to the "International Union of Revolutionary Theatres" at this time ("The First International" 137).

A few months later Buchwald pointed to the Workers' Lab as an example of a group moving in the right direction. He praised them for abandoning "the slogan-ridden script, in favor of swift and racy colloquialisms," and the "barren 'agitprop' clichés" for "native theatrical idiom" ("Workers' Theatre Movement" 5). He explained: "The tendency away from the sloganized agitprop stencils and in the direction of live, truly popular and truly entertaining revolutionary theatre is characteristic of the whole workers' theatre movement in the present phase" ("Workers' Theatre Movement" 5).

The need for the proletarian theater to achieve the variety of form and theme of the bourgeois theater was expressed once again in the first issue of *New Theatre*, the successor of *Workers Theatre*. A new stage in relations between the German and American movements was reached as the two dramatists in exile, Erwin Piscator and Friedrich Wolf, joined Michael Gold, Joseph Freeman, and others as contributing editors. John Bonn was retained as associate editor. In regard to the change in the magazine's name, it was explained that, while both magazines endorsed a theater "whose viewpoint . . . is that of the revolutionary working class," the new title signified "a broader conception of the revolutionary workers theatre as the historical successor of the bourgeois theatre." The editors noted: "The workers theatre now understands that it must study the technique of the theatre of the past, adapting the best of the old to the service of the masses. . . . The workers theatre now understands that these professional theatre workers and artists who are being expelled by the thousands from the bourgeois theatre must be attracted to the revolutionary theatre. . . . *New Theatre* will welcome every sincerely progressive trend in the American theatre."[8]

Coming toward the end of 1933 this declaration can easily be interpreted as a mere reaction to the changed political situation, as a harbinger of the Popular Front. In contrast to statements in the early *Workers Theatre,* this was after all an unequivocal repudiation of the all-or-nothing approach to culture that rigidly separated everything proletarian and bourgeois, and summarily rejected contemporary non-Communist theater. Also, as the change in the magazine's title indicated, there was a de-emphasis on the class origin of the participants and a move toward professionalism. On the other hand, the definition of proletarian culture according to ideological viewpoint, and the insistence on the importance of the heritage were positions that had been formulated in the early Proletcult debates in the Soviet Union. The demand to enlist sympathetic non-Communist writers into the movement had been issued as soon as the IURW and the IUDW had been set up, and had already been written into the Constitution of the League of Workers Theatres and the Draft Manifesto of the John Reed Clubs in 1932.

The criteria that were applied over the next few years in guiding the movement toward large forms also had a long history by this time. They were based on the distinction between the methods of art and science, which had been a basic element of Mehring's and Plekhanov's aesthetic theory and had been formulated in the correspondence of Marx and Engels. In the United States it had been propagated in the late twenties, at the very beginning of the theater movement, by Moissaye Olgin.

Harold Edgar, who had a regular column on the theater in the *Daily Worker* in 1933, insisted on the following need for living characters: "To be exciting and convincing in the theater, the audience must feel that the workers represented are not ideological abstractions, but men and women whom they know well."[9] Reviewing a short play in his column on November 10, he differentiated between the methods of agitprop and drama: "In a short vaudeville skit or a mass recitation the simplest slogan eloquently or colorfully stated carries weight, but in a play with a more involved story and a background that needs explanation, the mind begins to question the authenticity of the incident unless every character is properly motivated, every turn of the plot is realistically justified. If the play fails in this, its propaganda value is undermined" (5).

In evaluating *Stevedore,* a full-length play produced by the Theatre

Union, Michael Gold applied the same criteria. Of probable influence on Gold's analysis was Engels's criticism of "argumentative speeches" (Engels to LaSalle 120), and his insistence that the "bias should flow by itself from the situation and action . . . " (Engels to Minna Kautsky 122). Describing *Stevedore* as "the most successful attempt at a proletarian drama we have yet had in America," he points out:

> Yet this is only a beginning. The rough plastering still shows of the new house. Stevedore is crowded with those set "propaganda" speeches that are really a technical blunder, in any playwright's play. It is not the content of these speeches that one objects to, but the fact that they are not worked into the action skillfully enough. We are just beginning to learn things in America, and one of the things a crystallizing Marxist criticism of literature is teaching us is that the dialectics of action and imagery are the tools of literature, and not the "idealistic" speeches that are superimposed like decorations; in other words, the structure must be functional, it must teach its own moral. When it fails, all the added words and speeches in the world will only further bungle the matter.
>
> Stevedore has this structure, but did not seem to trust in itself or the intelligence of its audience sufficiently, at various points.
>
> It has another fault, that of its lapses into photographic realism in dialogue. . . . The proletarian drama is epic, heroic, satirical, poetic, in its aims and content; it must of necessity find a different speech than the drab prosy naturalism of the Broadway merchants. ("Stevedore" 29)

While the distinction between the methods of art and science was commonly employed in criticism of the full-length drama, opinions differed on whether the same criteria should be applied to the short, agitprop piece. What was indirectly involved here was the question of whether the one form should supplement the other or replace it. Like Edgar and Buchwald, Gold felt that both should be promoted and that separate criteria should be applied to each. Thus, although he evaluated *Stevedore* according to criteria formulated by Engels in his remarks on LaSalle's full-length drama and Minna Kautsky's novel, he had allowed for abstraction and caricature a month before in a review of the production of two amateur, agitprop groups. While praising *New Theatre* for the "intense self-criticism by which it [the theater movement] grows," he asserts: "What was clear in the performances of both groups was that subtle realism and psychology have little place in the workers' theatre." Noting the "broad poster style" used in portraying the exploitation of Ukrainian-American workers, he states: "This theme is crude propaganda, I can hear Mr. Krutch . . . declare." Noting that audiences nevertheless liked it and responded to it, Gold concluded: "For the time being let this fact be enough" ("The Stage" 29).

Other critics at this time made no distinction between the professional and amateur branches of the theater movement and applied the same criteria to both. In the *New Masses* Ben Blake wrote: "Most of the younger worker-writers in the workers' theatre, and even most of the professional playwrights who come over to the revolutionary viewpoint, understand too mechanically the thesis that all art is propaganda. They write plays whose 'propaganda' consists all too little of realistic action by well-developed characters and all too much of political talk by unconvincing abstractions of capitalists, sheriffs, and revolutionary workers. Referring to the author of *They Shall Not Die,* a dramatization of the Scottsboro case, he writes: "But John Wexley has not fallen into this. He has created real human beings, whose speech and action grow naturally out of their character and social background. His play thus offers a lesson to revolutionary dramatists: careful characterization and motivation are artistically and ideologically far more convincing than 'type' abstractions and politically correct but mechanically motivated action" (26).

In an article in *New Theatre* toward the end of 1934 Herbert Kline, the editor of the magazine, takes the same position as Blake in criticizing the scripts of the League of Workers' Theatres. He lists as the most glaring faults: "Stiff, over-written dialogue, carry-all plots, poor timing, failure to even try for characterization and the tendency to substitute long expository or argumentative conversation for dramatic images and action . . . " ("Writing" 22). The result, he explains, is "schematic plays . . . that only scratch the surface of the complex and intense life they seek to portray" ("Writing" 22).

Kline's article is particularly significant in that it clearly demonstrates that the criticism of these characteristics—all of which were eventually defined as leftist by the *Partisan Review's* editors—were not based on allegedly dissident views proceeding from that magazine, but rather on the writings of Marx and Engels in regard to the novel and the full-length play. Behind all of the qualities he criticizes, Kline sees "a fundamental lack of understanding of the approach of the class-conscious playwright to his material" (22). He goes on to quote long passages from Marx's and

Engels's letters and observes: "When they called for rich characterization, colorful representation of peasant life, the juxtaposition of individualized characters and the blending of intellectual depth with the social content in quick and vivacious dialogue they struck at the heart of the workers repertoire problem today" (23). On the basis of the letters quoted, he asserts that the workers do not want "long, dull speeches and fight talks," but rather "plays with real people in them" (23). He attacks in particular the sudden conversion and the caricature: "They [the worker audience] cannot be convinced by a fake character who opens a scene as a duped and discouraged dolt and becomes ten minutes later a revolutionary leader. ... And would it be 'counterrevolutionary' to picture in our workers stage a different kind of capitalist than the usual Morgan caricature. Is a 'scab' always the slinky rat or is he sometimes a self-concerned worker who is driven by the need of his family to steal his class brother's job?" (23).

Kline sees one possibility for expanding the repertoire in choosing scenes from plays by Moliere, Gogol, or Gorky. In this connection he writes: "The workers theater, and the playwrights especially, must fight against disdainful disregard of the old cultural inheritance, and toward the masters of theatre art. There is much to be learned from plays that are sometimes referred to disparagingly as 'bourgeois.' " (23)

In regard to the reception of individual, full-length plays, there was a major controversy over Albert Maltz's *Black Pit*, which was presented by the Theatre Union in 1935. Again discussion centered around the need for a broad proletarian theater, covering a wide spectrum of themes. In this case a threat to expansion was perceived in the demand for positive heroes and upbeat, militant endings. Ira Levine maintains that, in the *Daily Worker* and the *New Masses,* Communist critics, as a group, called for "heroic workers" and insisted that plays "should conclude on a positive note ... " (88). This is not borne out in the discussion over Maltz's play. The controversy started in the *New Masses* with a review by one of the editors, Joseph North, which was generally favorable, but objected to the choice of a miner who turns stool-pigeon as the main character.[10] In the *Daily Worker* most of the commentators, including Michael Gold and Communist party union leader Jack Stachel, disagreed with North. Gold stated: "Joseph North, of the New Masses, thinks the play a mistake, because it emphasizes the problem of stool-pigeoning, instead of presenting a positive type of militant leader. Jack Stachel ... believes that the play is important and useful.... " Siding with Stachel, he writes that while the union leader "sees proletarian literature as a great, broad current that should reflect all of the working class world," North "wants to keep it as narrow as it was years ago; he wants to impose a formula on it, a formula that be it good or bad, is sure to strangle all future growth."[11]

Probably the closest to what may be considered an official summary of the results of the discussion in the theater movement was presented at the American Writers Congress by Nathaniel Buchwald and Michael Blankfort, a member of the Theatre Union. Their speech on the theater was included in the collection issued by the Communist party publishing house, International Publishers, in 1935 under the title *American Writers Congress.* As in Buchwald's 1933 article in *International Literature,* the two writers distinguish between the methods of agitprop and the professional theater, while attacking the tendency to make virtue of necessity. The agitprop theater, they write, "made a virtue of its crudity and started off on the wrong foot by proclaiming its independence not only from the content of the bourgeois theater but also from its forms and techniques. They went so far as to officially condemn orthodox theatrical forms as little short of counter-revolutionary" ("Social Trends" 131–32).

Unlike Blake and Kline, Buchwald and Blankfurt make it clear that improved quality and assimilation of the heritage do not necessarily mean imitation of the bourgeois realistic theater. Instead they point to the possibilities of the popular stage: "Gradually the agitprop theater grew out of its infancy and began to show a decent respect for competent acting, staging, writing, etc. . . . It rediscovered and adapted the native American forms of entertainment, such as vaudeville, the minstrel show with its interlocutor and end-men, the 'harmony gang,' slapstick and burlesque low comedy" (132). The agitprop theater, they indicate, has borrowed from the popular stage to create its own forms, namely "the mobile theater with its short-skits . . . which can be produced quickly, and everywhere, without the use of stage trappings," and "the mass pageant with its effective use of groups, commentators and dancers, and revelatory playlets within the pageant . . . " (132).

They describe the development of forms from the popular stage as one direction within the agitprop theater. The other is toward the longer play which leaves behind it "the staccato thrusts of caricature and treats its subject matter realistically" (132). They mention Clifford Odets's *Waiting for Lefty* as an example. "Both these approaches," they insist, "are praiseworthy," and they warn playwrights that to "relegate the mobile theater to a minor place is to dull one of the sharpest edges of the theater weapon" (132).

Turning to the professional revolutionary theater, they apply the same criteria as Gold, Edgar, and Kline:

> In many of the plays . . . social and political revelations seemed stuck in or tacked on. Dealing in most cases with a worker or intellectual swinging leftward, these plays, "pendulum plays," were hampered by too great a schematicism. Essentially plays of plot and action rather than of character, they based themselves on an ideological design and tried to fit in scenes and characters with which to illustrate it. It appeared as though the revolutionary theater, although advanced in content, had to fall back, in its treatment, to a sort of morality level. (133)

They go on to praise *Black Pit* as a step in the right direction. "This play is important," they assert, "because it indicates a different type of selection of material and a different treatment." While other plays, such as *Stevedore*, "portray man resisting the onslaughts of capitalism, fighting it head on, and conquering it, at least temporarily, then *Black Pit* deals with man crushed." "Both types of plays reveal the forces of oppression," they explain, and both are "equally effective propaganda." They see the future of the revolutionary drama in the combination of a play "which strikes an effective balance between inner conflict and outer events, between the drama of the individual and the drama of his class" (134).

As in the theater movement, the goal of a broad proletarian culture, as varied in form and content as its bourgeois predecessor, was to determine the course of the discussion over proletarian literature in the mid thirties.

The Application of the IURW's Aesthetic Theory in the *Daily Worker* and the *New Masses*

In describing the dispute between the original *Partisan Review* and the *New Masses,* Phillips, Rahv, and Alan Calmer claimed that critics in the latter magazine took a utilitarian approach to proletarian literature: they insisted on militant themes of immediate political import, encouraged abstractness and tendentiousness, and ignored questions of form and technique. Among the historians who give a similar description of *New Masses* criticism are James Gilbert and Walter Rideout. In his book, *The Radical Novel in the United States,* Rideout states: " . . . the pressure of two leading shapers of *New Masses* literary policy [Hicks and Gold] was generally toward persuading the proletarian novelists . . . that they should deal with the more obvious aspects of the class struggle, melodramatize their characters into good workers versus evil *bourgeoisie,* and end on a carefully affirmative note whether the internal logic of the novel demanded such a conclusion or its opposite . . . " (228).

In reality, the approach to proletarian literature in the *New Masses* and *Daily Worker* closely paralleled that which was taken toward the full-length drama in the theater movement. As in the *Linkskurve,* insistence on artistic quality was coupled with the demand for thematic diversification. Thus, writers were called upon to proceed beyond factory themes and the portrayal of immediate class confrontation toward a literature that would reflect all of social reality from a Marxist viewpoint, while avoiding the tendentiousness and abstractness of agitprop.

While the statements that Michael Gold made in 1930 during the Wilder dispute are cited by Malcolm Cowley and others as characteristic of Communist critics' disregard for form and technique, the need for proletarian writers to achieve mastery in this area was repeatedly stressed by Gold in his *Daily Worker* column in 1933 and 1934. On September 30, 1933, he pointed to the lack of qualified Marxist criticism in the United States and admitted his own limitations in this area:

> I haven't the critical temperament, and don't ever expect to be a really good Marxian critic of literature. But it sometimes grieves me to see how our critics lag behind the actual movements in the literary field. . . .
>
> No proletarian critic that I know has paid much attention to the difficult problem of style, of creative writing. They are historians and polemicists, a vital and necessary job at present. The young proletarian writer has little creative guidance. (7)

A week later he held up the German proletarian writer Hans Marchwitza as an example to Americans. Referring to a recently completed novel of his, he stated: "He wrote and rewrote the book at least thirty times. He had to learn his technique step by painful step."[12] Reporting on a conference of the Soviet Orgcommittee, Gold takes up the theme again, quoting the writer Vsevolod Ivanov on the importance of form. "I should like to have our new organization of writers," Ivanov had stated, "direct its attention also to questions of FORM. It is extremely important to strive after form."[13]

At the end of 1933 Gold devoted a whole column to the proletarian writer's need to master technique: " . . . out of the hundreds who strive to learn the technique of writing, I have found that there are never more than a handful who try to grapple with the problem in any systematic way." In contrast to his 1930 position that the proletarian writer would learn to express himself if he wrote long enough,[14] he now asserts that the young worker unwilling to go through a long apprenticeship in technique "will never be much of a writer." Gold concludes: "He may learn, if he persists long enough, to write cheap detective and cowboy stories for the pulp magazines, but he will never become the real thing."[15]

Filling in for Gold in the *Daily Worker* in November 1933, Joseph Freeman again emphasized the importance of technique, and called for living, believable characters in proletarian literature. Freeman's remarks were in answer to a letter he had received a year before from Sherwood Anderson, who had apparently wanted to review a proletarian novel for the *New Masses*, but felt that criticism of its shortcomings would not be acceptable. To this Freeman quotes the reply he sent to Anderson in November 1932: "We, by no means, want to praise books whose intention may be good, but whose execution is poor. . . . [I]n regard to the general question of 'representing people as they are,' I agree with you. I would add that a book is not only bad art, but bad propaganda when it fails to represent people as they are." In this connection he emphasizes: "THE REVOLUTIONARY WRITER NOT ONLY CAN AFFORD TO TELL THE TRUTH BUT MUST TELL THE TRUTH. THE TRUTH IS ON HIS SIDE."[16]

Another writer, filling in for Gold at around the same time, addressed the problem of abstractness in poetry. Edwin Rolfe, a member of the Young Communist League and a poet himself, insisted on the need to fuse feeling and idea, the abstract and concrete, and attacked lifeless, sloganized verse. "The poetry of the revolutionary movement in the United States is still in its adolescence," he indicated, in that many poets were maintaining "a rigid isolation of themselves as human beings from their writings." He went on to explain: "One cannot sit down and say 'I am going to write a revolutionary poem.' This is an artificial approach, and it will be apparent in the finished poem, which may contain all the correct slogans, all the perfectly phrased correct ideas on the subject, and yet remain lifeless, stilted, false." Rolfe concludes: "Revolutionary poetry of a high order" can only be created when the writer's experience and world-view are "perfectly blended."[17]

A month later in Gold's column Joseph Freeman supported Rolfe on this point: "It is only too common to find people who are Communists in thought and action and bourgeois in their feelings. Our emotions develop more slowly and painfully than our ideas. Some of us attempt to conceal or overcome this disparity by writing verse that represents only their ideas. In most cases the result is flat, stale and unprofitable.[18]

In one of his first articles in the *New Masses,* in early 1933, Granville Hicks concurs with Gold on the need for qualified Marxist literary criticism. In keeping with the general trend away from the forms and methods of agitprop he criticizes simplifiers who judge literature on its ability to directly induce workers to do some specific thing. One weakness of this approach, he explains, is that it provides no means of evaluating most of the literature of the past and present, which possesses little or no agitational value. Second, it implies a constant shift in literary standards. In rejecting agitational value as the sole criterion of literary criticism, Hicks argues along the same lines as the RAPP in its dispute with the LEF, and the *Linkskurve* editors in their remarks on Vallentin and Steffen. Thus he assumes the unity of reflection and praxis, and describes the political effect of literature as an indirect one, forming the psyche of the reader. He asserts that "that class is most likely to approximate objective truth which has most to gain by such an approximation and least to gain by distortion" ("The Crisis" 5). The effect of an accurate reflection of reality is not usually, however, to directly stimulate action of some kind. Marxist critics are, therefore, not to approach literature with this demand, but instead to ask if the work in question creates "an attitude capable of extension and of adaptation to any situation," and impresses on the reader "the complete unworthiness of the existing system and the hope and power of the working class" ("The Crisis" 5). Such an effect can be achieved, he adds, not only by revolutionary writers, but by bourgeois authors as well, insofar as they accurately reflect social reality. As an example Hicks cites Proust, whose *Remembrance of Things Past,* in his view, "gives a finer, clearer, more convincing picture of the decay of bourgeois civilization" than any novel he has found "written from the revolutionary point of view" ("The Crisis" 5).

Having attacked critics who attempted to reduce proletarian literature to agitprop, Hicks turned his attention to proletarian writers, urging them on to thematic and formal diversification. Finding "a striking lack of variety" ("The Past" 29) in proletarian fiction, he wrote a seven-part series in the *New Masses* in 1934, entitled "Revolution and the Novel." While elaborating on various possibilities that he felt writers might explore, he formulated aesthetic principles for the movement. Again the overriding one was the need to combine the abstract and concrete in living, typical characters and plausible situations.

Discussing what he calls the "dramatic novel," he writes: "The situation . . . must be representative; the characters must be recognizable men and women and not mere puppets; and the order of events must correspond to a credible conception of cause and effect" ("Drama and Biography" 35). In regard to plausibility of character development he criticizes, in another article in the series, the sudden conversion of the hero in *The Disinherited* and *Jews Without Money*. In reference to an article by Dos Passos in which he had stressed the importance of living, rounded characters in fiction,[19] Hicks wrote: " . . . [Gold and Conroy] should have remembered what Dos Passos calls the business of the novelist. . . . Each book ends with the awakening of the central character to class-consciousness. But in both books this awakening comes as a surprise. Something is missing, for otherwise the reader would feel that the climax of the book followed inevitably from everything that had gone before" ("The Problem" 55).

Elsewhere in the series he turn to the portrayal of capitalists, and explains:

> Proletarian novelists . . . are not likely to fall into the liberal fallacy of attributing to personal wickedness the evils of a system. . . . He might or might not illustrate the ways in which the millionaire falls below his professed moral standards, but he would not in any case assume that such delinquencies were the key to the man's character and career. . . . Without attempting to make him a monster, he would show clearly and concretely the process of exploitation. . . . It is fatal to the substance and reality of a book to reduce the central character to his economic function; the millionaire in fiction must be as many-sided as the millionaire in life. ("Characters and Classes" 41)

Rejecting abstract moralizing and distortion, Hicks declares that the revolutionary writer "knows that slogans and sermons will not serve his purpose, and he will not resort to falsification" ("Characters and Classes" 43).

Another form of abstractness that Hicks urges proletarian writers to avoid is editorializing. Here his critical observations on Upton Sinclair recall Lukacs's analysis of the journalistic novel. In *The Jungle*, he states, Sinclair "sees . . . both the conditions and the response to the conditions as part of a larger whole. . . . But there are also long passages of straight exposition, in which we are conscious of the author as observer and muckraker. . . . Direct observation is suddenly substituted for imaginative recreation . . . " Hicks insists that "every such interruption is destructive" ("The Problem" 57).

Like Lukacs, Hicks combines his criticism of abstractness and tendentiousness with the call for a great proletarian novel. Generalizing about the quality of proletarian novels up to then, he finds that "the whole is usually more successful than the parts" ("The Future" 63), and anticipates a future "proletarian masterpiece," which would "do justice to all the many-sided richness of its characters, exploring with Proustian persistance the deepest recesses of individuality and at the same time exhibiting that individuality as essentially a social phenomenon" ("The Future" 65).

Not surprisingly, the first book review in the *New Masses* that showed the unmistakable influence of the IURW was written by A. B. Magil, a member of the executive council of the central organization. In February 1933 he analyzed Grace Lumpkin's novel *To Make My Bread,* which was based on the Communist-led strike in the textile industry in Gastonia, North Carolina, in 1929. The author was a professional journalist and writer, whose work had been appearing in the *New Masses* since the twenties. Magil directs most of his criticism against the twin poles of naturalism and abstractness, tracing both tendencies to the author's failure to correctly relate subjectivity and objectivity, and to grasp society as a developing whole, shaped by human action. He states: "Instead of drama, we have an accumulation of accurate detail, a monotone of cautious, even-paced narrative. . . . a flatland of people and events, seen through an elegiac mist" ("To Make" 19). He contrasts this kind of static objectivity—which "at best . . . can produce only penetrating 'slices of life' "—with one that perceives the "objective world as an evolving process, changing through the clash of contradictory elements, moving in a certain direction . . . " ("To Make" 19). The precondition for comprehending the dynamics of social change in this manner, he asserts, is the viewpoint of "that class which is destined to do away with all classes" ("To Make" 19). Only from "the mountain-top of dialectical materialism," he states, is "a truer and deeper picture of the objective world" possible ("To Make" 19–20).

In Magil's review, for the first time in the *New Masses,* dialectical materialism is related to the creation of living characters and the avoidance of abstractness. In the "most revolutionary section" of the novel he finds the author's greatest artistic failure: "Her characters lose all individuality, the organizer from the North, Tom Moore, is a complete blur, and the entire section fails to flow organically out of the body of the book. Instead of a creative condensation of her material, we have a slurring over and a failure to motivate action properly" ("To Make" 20). The portrayal of the conflict between labor and capital, the "unity of Negro and white workers" and the "power of the working class to create its own leadership" and "win its freedom" must be accomplished, Magil insists, "not in formal declarations, but as part of the creative process, in the warp and woof of a story. . . . " Postulating the unity of reflection and praxis, he states that the kind of realism he is describing is both a "critique of the existing order," as well as "an instrument of its transformation a challenge and a prophecy" ("To Make" 20).

Reviewing Jack Conroy's novel *The Disinherited* in the *Daily Worker*, Michael Gold likewise pointed to the need to combine subjectivity and objectivity, essence and appearance, in living characters, and criticized the book's sketchiness:

> Your novel shows the internal stress of the man under fire or the young proletarian writer writing a first report of a strange life. There are too many unprecedented facts, and he is so involved in each one, that sometimes he cannot piece them together in any satisfactory pattern. Hence, the sketch-form which predominates in your book, and which is a dominant proletarian form today.
>
> For it is noteworthy that your novel has many of the same faults and virtues as other first novels by proletarians. It is semi-autobiographic, which is a virtue. However, in avoiding the sickly introspection of the bourgeois autobiographers of youth, the psychological reality often escapes our young authors. They neglect the major problem of all fiction, which the creation of full-blooded character. Your characters aren't complete. . . . Facts are not enough. There must be a living human man portrayed through whose mind all this is reflected. . . .
>
> In your novel too many of the characters are social reports and eccentrics. They are not typical enough. It isn't easy to fuse the typical and the individual in one true and breathing portrait, and yet that is our chief fictional problem. ("A Letter to" 215–16, 219)

In early 1935 Granville Hicks once again complained of the failure of proletarian novelists to successfully combine the individual and the general in the depiction of capitalists. "The portrayal of a member of the ruling class in such a way as both to make him a human being and to show his social role," he indicated, "is a problem still to be solved" ("The Novel and the Middle Class" 278). He finds an exception in Josephine Herbst's novel, *The Executioner Awaits:*

> The people in *The Executioner Awaits* are representative of millions of Americans, and yet they are sharply and unmistakeably individuals. They are living human beings, eagerly pursuing their own ends, and yet they are the instruments of great impersonal forces. The reader never thinks of Miss Herbst as imposing Marxist conceptions on the material of the novel; these conceptions inevitably emerge from the substance of the story ("The Novel and the Middle Class" 279).

He criticizes two other, more militant novels for not achieving this. He finds Arnold B. Armstrong's *Parched Earth* to be at times "schematic," and attributes this to "a certain disparity between Armstrong's knowledge of social tendencies and his understanding of human beings . . . " ("The Novel and the Middle Class" 279). Maxwell Bodenheim's *Slow Vision,* he states, "is weakened . . . by a great deal of direct exposition" ("The Novel and the Middle Class" 280).

In one book review in the *Daily Worker* in 1935 the connection was made between the theory of socialist realism and the campaign against abstractness and tendentiousness in proletarian literature. Commenting on the anthology *Proletarian Literature in the United States,* Moissaye Olgin wrote:

> . . . the literary production here collected succeeds in being class literature without appearing to be "propaganda." Hardly any critic with a sense of literary values will be able to say that the facts as here recorded by the writers have been so marshalled as to prove a thesis. The editors were particularly careful to avoid the pitfall of cajoling reality to conform to theory. They rightly assumed that the life of the proletariat as it is contains enough revolutionary implications. There is a happy avoidance of sermonizing in the volume, and wherever there appears revolutionary action, it seems to grow out of the very soil of the workers' lives.

> If socialist realism consists in truthfully depicting reality by showing the essential, not some accidental or illusory, traits of reality, by revealing the historical tendencies inherent in that reality and by making clear the inevitability of the victory of the new over the old

social forces, then the bulk of this volume is socialist realism. ("First Choice" 5)

As in the case of the play *Black Pit,* a number of reviews of proletarian novels in the mid-thirties reflected the need for thematic diversification and attacked various kinds of restrictive demands. While Ira Levine includes Michael Gold and Joseph Freeman among the "Party's literati," who "stipulated that all revolutionary art must serve a propagandistic function, that it must focus on proletarian subject matter, and treat the class struggle" (87), in fact Gold and Freeman defended the author's right to depart from the theme of direct class confrontation. The issue arose in connection with Edward Newhouse's novel *You Can't Sleep Here,* a rather light-hearted, largely autobiographical account of a newspaperman's experiences after he loses his job. Alluding to Gold's *Jews Without Money,* Freeman recalled: "In 1930, when a revolutionary writer published a moving novel of his youth on the East Side, our sectarians attacked him not for what he wrote, but for what he omitted . . . " ("You Can Fight Here" 25). The fact is that Gold's novel had received a rather negative review in his own magazine. Among other things, he was taken to task for not writing about the struggles of the garment workers on the East Side. Replying to his critics at that time, Gold had taken the same position as Freeman now in his defense of Newhouse: "Comrade Levy . . . is disappointed because I . . . did not include the Triangle and the great garment strikes. Yet I could do nothing else honestly and emotionally at the time. I could only describe what I had seen with my own eyes. I did not want to falsify the emotional values and bring in material that I did not feel. I do not believe any good writing can come out of this mechanical application of proletarian literature" (qtd. in Wilson 537–38). In Gold's column in the *Daily Worker* in November 1933, Freeman had likewise insisted that poets should proceed from what they knew and felt, rather than impose undigested Marxist ideas on their work. In regard to the novelist on the Left, he now observed:

> . . . [he] can confine himself to a section of America and describe it with the skill of an artist presenting life, rather than the insistence of the agitator driving home a point. If he is a good artist as well as a revolutionist he makes the point anyway; in the long run, his art is stirring propaganda. . . .
>
> By the time the hero participates in an unemployed [sic] demonstration, gets beaten up and lands in the hospital, his drift toward the

revolutionary movement has the inevitability of personal character.
The idea is never imposed from above.... ("You Can Fight Here"
25–26)

Michael Gold's position on *Black Pit* was paralleled by his defense of
Fielding Burke's *Call Home the Heart,* another novel based on the Gastonia
strike. A *Daily Worker* reader, Jeanette Pearl, had attacked the book for its
downbeat ending, in which the heroine retires to her mountain home after
the defeat of the strike. Remarking on the demand for militant, upbeat
conclusions, Gold wrote:

> Anybody can write the first two acts of a revolutionary play. It is the
> last act, the act that resolves the conflicts, that has baffled almost
> every revolutionary playwright and novelist in this country.
>   For you can't truthfully say in your last act or last chapter, that
> there has been a victorious Communist revolution in this country. It
> would be a lie if you did, yet many of our comrades like Jeanette Pearl
> almost demand that an author falsify in this manner.[20]

Burke's novel, he argues, has "revolutionary import," even if the author is
lacking in the "historic Marxian outlook" that would enable her to
convey "a historic picture that includes the past and future." Criticism of
revolutionary literature, Gold concludes, must not be conducted with a
"meat-axe," but should rather be constructive.[21]
    Reviewing Erskine Caldwell's short story "Kneel to the Rising Sun" a
year and a half later in the *Daily Worker,* Philip Rahv takes the same
position as Gold on this question: "Inevitably, sectarian critics will be
found who will read a defeatist political line into the working out of the
story's plot.... No method in criticism is as false as the judgement of a
work of art by the formal denouement of the action; repeated examples in
proletarian literature have proven that a so-called 'defeatist' ending does
not necessarily imply a defeatist line. 'Black Pit' is a case in point. A work
must be judged by the aggregate of its components" ("New Standards" 5).
    Writing at the end of 1935, Gold sees the lack of thematic diversifica-
tion as a continuing problem. Reviewing the anthology *Proletarian Literature in the United States,* he comments on the limited range of subjects.
Again the goal is a proletarian literature as broad in theme as its bourgeois
predecessor. "Capitalist art," he writes, "is still ahead of our proletarian
art because it presents a better-rounded picture of all the variegated, rich
nature of humanity." While he sees in the anthology "the best demonstra-

tion of the maturity of the literary movement," he laments its "narrowness of range": "Strikes and industrial accidents are the main concern of our authors—the worker as soldier, the worker as victim. . . . " As in his 1928 criticism of Upton Sinclair, in which he expressed his preference for "the variety of life to abstraction" ("In Foggy California" 169), he notes the failure of writers in the anthology to present "the worker as creator, as lover, as sensuous, free healthy animal."[22]

Parallel to the controversy in the theater over *Black Pit,* there was a dispute in 1935 over a novel. The *New Masses* had the practice of accepting book reviews from numerous unknown contributors. On February 12, an unsigned commentary on Henry Roth's novel, *Call it Sleep,* appeared among a number of short reviews. Roth had employed symbolism and stream-of-consciousness in describing the psychological development of a young immigrant boy growing up in Brooklyn and the Lower East Side of New York. The initial review gave no indication of the novel's high literary quality and was almost entirely negative. It ended with the remark: "It is a pity that so many young writers drawn from the proletariat can make no better use of their working class experience than as material for introspective and febrile novels" (27). Several readers protested and the editors announced a further critical discussion of Roth's novel.

The result was a long essay entitled "Caesar or Nothing," which appeared in the following month. The author, Edwin Seaver, was a long-time member of the *New Masses* as well as editor of the magazine *Soviet Russia Today.* In spite of Seaver's position within the movement, Walter Rideout includes him among the "Centrists" around the *Partisan Review,* and describes his article as an intrusion of views that were dissident and alien to the *New Masses* and were now only tolerated in anticipation of the Popular Front: "During the early months of 1935 . . . the 'Centrists' carried the fight into the strongest enemy position when a whole series of protests against 'Leftism' began appearing in *The New Masses* itself. One of the first was Edwin Seaver's 'Caesar or Nothing' . . . " (231). Actually there was nothing in the article that was not in keeping with the main direction of the American movement over the previous two years.

Like others in the *New Masses* and *Daily Worker,* Seaver attacked tendentiousness and abstractness in proletarian literature, and insisted on the need for writers to proceed from their own experience and depart from the theme of direct class confrontation. Behind the review of *Call It Sleep* he sees an attitude that he describes as "schematicism." Among writers, he explains, it takes the form of "offering ideas or slogans without benefit of the creative act; without, that is, clothing such ideas and slogans in flesh and blood. . . . " In criticism it manifests itself in the tendency "to kill a book because it does not bring out certain desired 'truths' which fall outside the scope of the particular work." Here Seaver repeats points that Freeman had made two months earlier in defending *Jews Without Money* and *You Can't Sleep Here,* and which Gold had touched on in his review of Burke's *Call Home the Heart.* Seaver asks: "What better use could Roth have made of his working-class experience as a child than to have shown honestly and greatly exactly what that experience consisted of? Should little David Shearl have joined the Young Pioneers, a non-existent organisation? Should David's working-class father have been a socialist when he wasn't? Should the author himself have turned Jehovah and moved history forward to satisfy his critics?"

Seaver extends to literary critics the advice that the Soviet playwright Vishnevsky had given to critics in his country. Seaver explains: "As with the creative writer, the proletarian ideology must become flesh and blood of the critic if he is to function in his ripest capacity. He will not then see the political, aesthetic and other aspects of a novel as separate entities, but as an amalgam, with each aspect modified and conditioned by the others." Like Gold in his review of *Call Home the Heart,* he concludes, "What is wanted are not killers, but leaders" ("Caesar or Nothing" 21).

One possible reason why Seaver's article has been interpreted as an attack on *New Masses* criticism is that, at one point, he directs his remarks at Granville Hicks, citing as an example of "wish-fulfillment" his reading of revolutionary symbolism into the novel *Parched Earth.* Actually, there was nothing unusual in one *New Masses* editor criticizing another, as was demonstrated by Gold's disagreement with Joseph North over similar issues, which arose a few months later in connection with *Black Pit.* Furthermore, this was not the first time that criticism was directed against Hicks from within the movement, as will be shown.

Completely overlooked by Rideout is the rave review of *Call It Sleep* which appeared in the *Daily Worker.* Here Alfred Hayes asserted: "There has appeared in America no novel to rival the veracity of this childhood. It is as honest as Dreiser's 'Dawn,' but far more sensitive and ably written. It is as brilliant as Joyce's 'Portrait of the Artist,' but with a wider scope, a richer emotion, a deeper realism" ("Fine Recreation" 5). Hayes goes on to praise Roth's "virtuoso use of language," his conveying of "a new barbarous English, studded with Yiddish idioms, twisted out of shape into a dialect as local and picturesque in its way as Kentucky backwoodsman's speech, or Synge's Aran islanders" ("Fine Recreation" 5). The only thing that Hayes criticizes is that the novel is overladen with symbolism, forcing the reader to "fish around and guess for 'ultimate' meanings.'" He concludes: "... the significance of *Call It Sleep* resides securely not in any mystical universal 'symbols,' but in the extraordinary social reality of the picture, the honesty of its documentation, the artistic integrity and courage of the author, the sheer writing ability, and the warm clear regard for the people who live and labor in the tenements in Brownsville and on Ave D." ("Fine Recreation" 5).

The Approach to Nonproletarian Literature:
The Question of the Heritage and Modernism

The contention of James Gilbert, Jack Salzman, and Alvin Starr that *New Masses* literary critics rejected the bourgeois heritage has no basis in fact. Among the critics in that magazine and in the *Daily Worker* in the mid-thirties, the position that proletarian writers had nothing to learn from bourgeois literature had no adherents. For those who were new to the movement and had not followed the discussion in the twenties, the publication of Marx's and Engels's letters had settled this issue, although certain questions remained unanswered and disagreement continued over specific writers.

At the same time as he was emphasizing to proletarian writers the importance of form and technique, Michael Gold returned to the question of the heritage in his *Daily Worker* column. In earlier articles in the *New Masses* he had held up nineteenth-century writers such as Thoreau, Emerson, Whitman, and Twain as standards by which he measured the literature of the present.[23] In regard to contemporary writers he had distinguished between "escapists," such as Thornton Wilder, and the "pioneers of a new realism," among whom he included Dreiser, Anderson, Sinclair Lewis, and Carl Sandburg.[24] The latter group he recommended as models for proletarian writers.

While Alan Calmer, writing in 1937, suggested that Gold, Hicks, and other *New Masses* critics had opposed the efforts of young proletarian writers to "assert and deepen the native quality of modern American writing" ("Portrait" 14), Gold had repeated this very demand throughout the twenties and thirties. On September 30, 1933, he added Ring Lardner, William Carlos Williams and, Edgar Lee Masters to the lists of "discoverers of the real America" and once again rejected gentility and derivativeness:

It has always been there, this submerged American continent, but it was less known to literature than the life of the Eskimo. Mark Twain and Walt Whitman had described it in their day, but gentility had set in, and the continent sank beneath waves of plush and prissiness.

The discoverers of the real America did a great job. What they lacked, of course, was a way out of all the meanness, tragedy, stupidity and real horror they described.

He concludes that proletarian writers have more to learn from writers like Lardner than from "the Thornton Wilders, Cabells, O'Neills and other stuffed shirt escapists" (7).

On October 12, 1933, he took up the question once again in an article in the *Daily Worker* on William Carlos Williams: "When somebody writes the future history of the pioneer beginnings of proletarian literature in America, I am sure W. C. Williams will be somewhere large in the table of contents. . . . Williams has never written about a strike or a labor union. What he has done, however, is to reflect as in a faithful mirror the raw powerful force of the unorganized American worker, and the horrors of the slum life he leads" (5).

When Gold returned to the subject of the heritage in the *Daily Worker*, October 17, 1935, after the introduction of the Popular Front, the only noticeable difference was that he placed the demand for nativism in the context of the struggle against fascism. "The chief battleground in the defense of culture against fascist barbarism," he wrote, "is in this question of the national tradition." He again mentions Whitman, Thoreau, Twain, and Emerson, describing them as "the spiritual forefathers of the proletarian writers of America, and the champions of the American people" (5).

The other writer most closely associated with *New Masses* criticism, Granville Hicks, explained his approach to nonproletarian literature in two essays in 1932 and 1933. Taking up the point Freeman had made in the late twenties, he criticized V. F. Calverton's sociological method and rejected "oversimplification" in classifying books and authors. "Obviously," he insisted, "it does not help us much to know that James, Howells and Mark Twain were all members of the bourgeoisie . . . " ("The Crisis" 7). Sociological classification, he argues, is only the beginning of the critic's task. This did not mean, however, that he was to proceed to an evaluation of craftsmanship, isolated from content, as Calverton sometimes suggested. Like Plekhanov, Hicks considered the degree to which the writer comprehended the dynamics of social development as an important criterion of criticism, and pointed out that, although the "proletarian point of view" was a prerequisite for an "accurate and clarifying" interpretation of contemporary society, it was not uncommon to find upper-class writers who were capable of reproducing life with "considerable, though fragmentary, insight" ("Literary Criticism" 47).

In the *New Masses* toward the end of 1934 he cites Proust as an example of such a writer. The influence of Marx's and Engels's observations on Balzac are evident in Hicks's remarks on the contradiction between Proust's class sympathies and his realism. He notes: "There is a great deal of evidence to show that Proust was a snob, that he placed an almost ludicrously high value on his association with the aristocracy. But, as not infrequently happens, the writer was better than the man. He was sometimes deceived by the false standard of the class with which he tried to identify himself, but by and large he saw through its pretenses. . . . The characters who come from 'the people', though in no sense class-conscious, are all stronger and finer than the Guermantes and their kind" ("Proust" 208). While pointing out Proust's limitations, he described certain features of his writing that were of value to revolutionary writers, in particular his ability to create living, rounded characters and to show the connection between the individual and the social: "Proust has found a way of showing us his characters from many points of view instead of only one. . . . We know more about his people than we know about people in most novels. He probes deeply, and he looks at them from all sides. But what we are chiefly aware of is that, taken together, all these varied revelations of a great variety of persons form a picture, an extraordinarily full and detailed picture, of a certain society" ("Proust" 207–8).

In André Malraux, Hicks saw another example of a nonrevolutionary writer who succeeded in this. In the late summer of 1934 there was a controversy in the *New Masses* over the French writer's novel *Man's Fate,* which deals with revolutionaries in China. The initial review, by Alfred Hirsch, dismissed the novel as nonrevolutionary, while another reader declared it to be one of the best revolutionary novels to appear up to then. Commenting on the dispute, Hicks wrote in the September 4 issue of THE *New Masses:* "I have read *Man's Fate* since the review of it appeared in the NEW MASSES. . . . To me the reading of the novel, especially after Alfred Hirsch's review, was a startling experience. Hirsch had not given me the slightest inkling of the book's extraordinary intensity" (28). While he agreed that the novel was not revolutionary, Hicks attacked what Seaver would characterize some months later as a "Caesar or Nothing" attitude toward literature:

> Hirsch's mistakes are . . . mistakes of omission, but they are important mistakes, and they invalidate his estimate of the book. . . . Though a great deal of the revolution escapes Malraux, a great deal is in his book, and there are moments when he transcends his limitations and gives the reader a real sense of the power and greatness of the revolutionary movement. . . . The review of his book in THE NEW MASSES should, I believe, have dealt as generously with what he succeeded in doing as it did cogently with what he failed to do. (29–30)

Hicks addressed the question of the specifically American heritage of proletarian writers in his book *The Great Tradition,* a review of fiction and poetry from the Civil War to the thirties, which he wrote before becoming literary editor of the *New Masses.* The line of tradition he establishes extends, like Gold's, from Emerson, Thoreau, Whitman, and Twain to the realists of the twenties. The book was an ambitious undertaking, and provided ample material for critics, both inside and outside of the movement. Aware of this, Hicks predicted in the second issue of *International Literature* in 1933, before his book appeared: "Of course sound Marxists will find all sorts of flaws in it, but the truth is that Marxist criticism is still in its infancy in America, and I have had to go my own blundering way" (129).

In the following year criticism was, in fact, directed at the book in *International Literature* by John Strachey, the English correspondent to the *New Masses.* His remarks were made in a long article called "Fascism and Culture," which was the extended version of a lecture he had delivered in New York as part of a fund-raising campaign to launch the New York John Reed Club's projected magazine, *Partisan Review.* Discussing the need to defend culture against the fascist onslaught, Strachey starts by acknowledging Hicks's achievement in *The Great Tradition:*

> Let me say at once that the American revolutionary movement should be immensely proud of the fact that at this early stage in its history it has been able to produce a work of such scope and maturity. . . .
>
> The supreme merit of Granville Hicks' book is his irrefutable demonstration that American revolutionary writers are the heirs to the essential tradition of American literature: that they are, to put it

paradoxically, political revolutionaries just because they are cultural conservatives. (108)

Having said this, he goes on to observe that Hicks's analyses of some of the "young bourgeois writers of the present day" are "less satisfactory" (109). As an example he mentions his discussion of Hemingway.

Hicks's evaluation of this writer differed in one important respect from that of Gold and Freeman. Although Gold counted Hemingway among the "escapists," he nevertheless held him up to proletarian writers as a model of style and technique. Similarly, Freeman had brought him to the attention of Soviet writers and had been responsible for the first translation of his writing into Russian. In addition there had been Dos Passos's adulatory review of *Farewell to Arms* in the *New Masses* in 1929.

In his four page analysis of Hemingway, Hicks, in contrast, says hardly a word about his accomplishments as a writer. In a strongly moralizing tone he limits himself to demonstrating that Hemingway is an escapist, describing his concern with physical activity as "an evasion of responsibility." He ends with the prognosis: "It seems unlikely that he will ever transcend his limitations" (275–76). A section on William Faulkner was similar in approach.

Commenting on his evaluation of these two writers, Strachey sees Hicks falling into "an error which . . . is a tempting one for Marxist critics," and observes: "He hardly seems to pay enough attention to the merits of writers as writers. . . . And yet, as Hicks shows in a dozen places in his book, he has a most sensitive and genuine appreciation of literature. It would be a thousand pities if his strong sense of his responsibility, as the foremost Marxist literary critic of America, which he certainly is, should force him to stifle his aesthetic sensibility" (110).

The tendency that Strachey criticized was also evident in an article Hicks had written for *International Literature* some months before the publication of his book. Here he was discussing the movement of middle-class writers toward the Communist party and the literary traditions they might draw upon in their writing. Comparing the situation in fiction and in poetry, he wrote: "Whereas the revolutionary novelist may, at least to a certain point, learn from the more critical of his bourgeois predecessors, the revolutionary poet has no earlier stage of revolt to which he can look for guidance" ("Problems of" 109). He criticizes young poets such as Horace Gregory for attempting "to adopt to their purpose the forms and idioms of the experimental reactionary poets," among whom he includes

Eliot. In contrast to A. B. Magil, who had maintained in the *New Masses* that something could be learned from even the most politically conservative writers ("Pity and Terror" 18), Hicks states: "Eliot and kindred reactionaries have evolved forms that express their own restlessness and futility. The attempt to use their technical devices for the expression of the revolutionary spirit inevitably involves a fundamental contradiction and the resulting poems are confused and ineffective" ("Problems of" 109).

On the basis of these remarks one might expect Hicks to have taken a position on modernism close to that of Mirsky in the Soviet Union. In his book *The Revolutionary Imagination* Alan Wald mentions Dos Passos's trilogy, *U.S.A.,* as evidence of the "pervasive impact of modernism on political writers" of the thirties (14) and attributes an antimodernist position to the "leading Party critics" (13). In fact, Hicks's analysis of Dos Passos in *The Great Tradition* suggests a favorable attitude toward his use of stream-of-consciousness and montage. Referring to *The Forty-second Parallel* and *1919* he writes:

> ... to give us the fullest possible sense of the mass emotions and actions that lie behind the comparatively few lives he has singled out to describe, he employs three devices: in the "Newsreels" we find the raw material of history, the actual and undigested stuff of experience, out of which the narrative sections have been fashioned; "the Camera's Eye" [*sic*], with its impressionistic bits of autobiography, strengthens the effect of reality by suggesting that the author, too, has been part of what he describes; the portraits, records of human heroism, meanness, bewilderment, victory, defeat, set before us the gods, demigods, and devils of our time, and give the novels an epic scope. (289–90)

Like Gold in 1929, he praises Dos Passos for "creating new forms for the just representation of both the forces of life and the forces of death in our war-torn society." The term he uses to define the form of *The Forty-second Parallel* and *1919* is "the complex novel," which deals with a series of individuals "whose stories are only loosely or not at all related." He describes it as a "natural expression of the sense of absence of unity that Henry Adams regarded as characteristic of the modern era," and recommends it to proletarian novelists. "Unity of plot," he explains, "is discarded at the outset; unity of time and place is not necessary; unity of mood may or may not be desirable. What is essential is the unity that comes from an understanding of the actual connections of apparently unrelated events" (316). Dos Passos, he maintains, succeeds in doing this. The characters in *1919* and *Forty-second Parallel,* he states, "belong together because they are being swept along by the same forces, a fact that Dos Passos indicates by interrupting the story of one to tell the story of another, and emphasizes by making his reader aware of broad social movements in the background" (289).

In *The Great Tradition* Hicks summed up his position on formal innovation thus: "The revolutionary novelist will say what he has to say as fully as possible, and there can be no excuse for slovenly adopting other writers' patterns or filching their devices. But he will not be concerned with novelty of form as an end in itself. If his vision demands something that is manifestly new, he will create it, but if the novelty is subtler, he will be just as well pleased" (318).

While Alan Wald claims that antimodernism was "official Communist dogma" at this time (*The Revolutionary* 3), in fact the *Daily Worker* and *New Masses* published varying positions on this issue, as was the case in *International Literature.* Although proletarian writers were occasionally advised against imitating Joyce, Eliot, and others, reviews of individual novels and plays revealed a generally favorable attitude toward experiment, as long as the final product was intelligible to the average reader. At no time in the thirties was there a campaign against "decadence" or "formalism" in the American movement, and some of the most highly praised proletar ian novels employed modernist technique.

The first long article in the *New Masses* on Joyce appeared in February 1934. The author was "Wallace Phelps," who was soon to become coeditor of the *Partisan Review* under his real name, William Phillips. While acknowledging the psychological depth of Joyce's characters, and his ability to portray " 'nuances of mood, the emotional responses which are scarcely reflected in speech or gestures or facial expression,' " Phillips notes that "these merits have been achieved at the expense of immediate intelligibility to a reader with an average background of experience" ("The Methods" 26). While *Ulysses* represents "the fullest possible exploitation of language for the purposes Joyce has evidently set himself," Phillips argues that "there is a limit to the load which language can bear and still remain a medium of communication; and there is a limit to the use to which any literary method can be put if it is not to become sheer method" ("The Methods" 26).

Like Mirsky, Phillips relates Joyce's failure to adequately reflect the "Irish revolutionary movement" to his method, which he finds unsuited "to present social conflict or human conflict against a background of class struggle." Having stated these reservations, he declares:

> ... the sensibility of Joyce is an important reaction to the contemporary world, and the technical devices in *Ulysses* are effective for exploring parts of that world. *Ulysses* is now part of our literary heritage. And it is likely that proletarian writers will use variants of the Joycean method in some portions of their novels for presenting, for example, a flow of memories, a merging of thought with conversation and action, a sense of multiple meaning in a scene, or, as Dos Passos has done, for relating the lives of diverse characters to a social situation. ("The Methods" 26)

In the *Daily Worker,* Gold likewise insisted that proletarian literature must remain accessible to the masses while writers searched for new forms:

> I think a new content often demands a new form, but when the new form gets so far ahead of all of us that we can't understand its content, it is time to write letters to the press. . . .
> If the truth were told, I have gotten to the point where I believe Communist art now needs a Tolstoy more than it does a James Joyce.
> That is, if it can't have both.[25]

A few days later he advised proletarian poets against imitating T. S. Eliot.[26]

What was possibly the most explicitly antimodernist article in the *Daily Worker* in the mid-thirties appeared in July 1934. The author, Maxwell Bodenheim, was the prototype of the middle-class writer who, in renouncing his class origins, wound up at the extreme left wing of the movement. Discussing the heritage of proletarian writers, he excludes not only Joyce, but two writers whom Gold and Hicks had recommended. "It is impossible," he argues, "to divide the style from the motivated flesh-and-blood of E. Hemingway, Marcel Proust, and James Joyce. . . . " Calling for simplicity and directness, he asserts: "The revolutionary writer . . . should regard these united styles and contents as nothing more than real, or imaginary, immersions in the bacteria of pretense, escape, futility and decay!"[27]

Information on the Soviet discussion on modernism was also supplied in 1934 and 1935. In April 1934 Mirsky's article on Joyce appeared in the *New Masses,* and in the *Daily Worker* a report on the Soviet Writers'

Congress touched on the issue. The author of the report, Vern Smith, emphasized the wide spectrum of opinion on "purely stylistic matters." He quoted as an example Leonid Leonov and Isaac Babel, both of whom had been asked by the American delegate, Ben Fields, what they thought of American writers:

> Both Babel and Leonov fixed at once on Dos Passos, probably, Babel said, "because he is beautifully translated."
>
> "I like Dos Passos," said Babel, "and his influence is growing."
>
> "I don't like Dos Passos," said Leonov. "I don't like literary tricks. And when a writer comes out in public, I think he should have his clothes buttoned up; he should have thought out his ideas." ("Soviet Authors" 5)

Three days later the *Daily Worker* published excerpts of a speech by Ilya Ehrenbourg, in which he warned against imitating nineteenth-century literature, and called for new forms ("To Depict" 5).

A year later Edwin Seaver reviewed a book containing various speeches from the Congress, and quoted Radek's observations on Joyce and Dos Passos. At the Congress Radek had agreed with the principle that, in matters of form, Soviet writers were to learn not only "from the classics of the old literature but also from the literature of dying capitalism" ("Radek" 203). Though he recognized Joyce as a writer of genius, he nevertheless discouraged Soviet writers from adopting his techniques. Like Mirsky, he described his method as photographic and microscopic, incapable of portraying social movement and development, and therefore at odds with the principles of socialist realism. In regard to Dos Passos, Radek connected his method to the lack of an "integral view of life" (qtd. in Seaver, "Socialist Realism" 24). Commenting on Radek's views on Joyce, Edwin Seaver finds "a cogency of argument that is pretty hard to refute" ("Socialist Realism" 23). As for Dos Passos, Seaver describes Radek's criticism as "succinct" ("Socialist Realism" 24).

While statements such as this suggested an antimodernist attitude, in actual practice, writers in the *Daily Worker* and *New Masses* were generally undogmatic on this issue. Seaver's own praise for Henry Roth's novel, *Call It Sleep,* in his article "Caesar or Nothing" serves as an example. A further example was the reception afforded William Rollins, Jr.'s strike novel, *The Shadow Before,* which Walter Rideout calls "the classic example of proletarian experimentalism" (209). Phillips's predictions of how proletarian writers would adapt Joyce's innovations adequately describe

Rollins's method. In his portrayal of the Gastonia textile strike in 1929, he makes liberal use of stream-of-consciousness, merging "thought with conversation and action" to convey "a sense of multiple meaning in a scene" (Phelps, "The Methods" 26).

Like Dos Passos, Rollins makes use of newspaper headlines and stanzas of songs, although he does not separate these off into "newsreel" sections, but rather integrates them into the narrative. The reaction within the movement was overwhelmingly favorable, and nowhere was the author rebuked for employing these devices. On the contrary, his book was held up as an example of the successful use to which the techniques of Joyce and Dos Passos could be put. The review in the *Daily Worker* pointed out:

> Rollins has drawn upon the works of Dos Passos and Joyce for his form. In doing so, I believe he has answered for all revolutionary writers the problem that has concerned them so, what can we take and what must we leave untouched in decadent literature. . . . From Joyce he has taken the tools that permit him to reveal the psychological flux and fusion within his characters, that make him succeed in creating the most subtle relationships and atmospheres. He has taken those positive elements from decadence that allow him to disclose the tensions, complexities, rhythms and neuroses of modern life. (Adler 7)

In the theater movement the issue of modernism arose in connection with two plays presented in 1935 and early 1936. One was an adaptation by Erwin Piscator of Theodore Dreiser's novel *An American Tragedy,* the other was Brecht's *The Mother.* Emerging from the Dada school after World War I, Piscator had developed a concept of "proletarian" or "political" theater, in which he proposed to avoid naturalism, at the one extreme, and psychologism at the other. As in the RAPP's approach to the novel, the defining element was in the elucidation of the connection between personal, individual conflict, and class struggle. His method of conveying this connection differed, however, from that propagated by the RAPP, and later Lukacs. Arguing that the drama did not present the same possibilities as the novel for depicting the historical, social background of personal conflict, he attempted to compensate for this through the use of film clips and slides, which he interjected between scenes, as a kind of commentary on the action. The analogy to Dos Passos's use of montage in his trilogy was obvious. The literary critic in the KPD's news-

paper, Die Rote Fahne, initially rejected his experiments as an attempt to reduce art to propaganda, but in the mid-twenties he presented two political revues in cooperation with the Party. In the early thirties he was named head of the IURT.[28]

Shortly after Dreiser's novel appeared in translation in Germany, Piscator got the idea of adapting it for the stage. He collaborated on this with Lena Goldschmidt, and they were preparing to produce it when the Nazis came to power. Once in the United States he resumed the project, and *The Case of Clyde Griffiths* opened at the Ethel Barrymore Theater in New York on March 11, 1936, with Lee Strasberg as director ("The Case" 7).

The play consists of various episodes from the novel, which are supplemented by cinematic flashes. A speaker, who stands outside the action and addresses both the characters and the audience, is intended to proved cohesion. Describing his method in the *Daily Worker,* Piscator acknowledged his debt to modern writers and pointed to technological developments as a factor influencing changes in form:

> In combining theatrical and cinema technique in "Case of Clyde Griffiths," I have been aided by the new ideas which have been introduced not only into theatre literature, but in the novel as well. Through the works of Joyce, Dos Passos, Döblin and others, a new method in fiction has been developed—a workmanlike realistic analysis of mankind. The boundary line between all the major arts of today—the cinema, the theatre and the novel—have been to a large extent effaced. . . . The cinema is not the theatre; neither is the novel. But both, in their modern forms, are children of new scientific techniques. Technical invention gives to both forms, and to the play devised from their essential elements, a new technical and thus a new artistic form. (qtd. in "Piscator Describes" 6)

Brecht's approach to the theater was similar in several respects to Piscator's, and in fact the two had worked together for a while. In 1928 Brecht adapted Jaroslav Haseks book, *Schweik,* for Piscator's theater (Mittenzwei, *Brechts Verhältnis"* 140–41). Both dramatists stressed the didactic function of the theater and incorporated elements of the agitprop stage into some of their plays. In *The Mother,* for example, which was presented by the Theatre Union in 1935, songs provide commentary on the action, and the mass chant is employed by a chorus that represents the Party and addresses characters and audience. Like other plays of Brecht's and Piscator's, it was "open," in the sense that the "fourth wall" was abolished and the action was suspended and commented upon. Like Piscator Brecht felt that the revolutionary writer could learn technique from modernists like Joyce, Proust and Kafka.[29]

The issue raised by the innovations of Piscator, Brecht and Dos Passos involved the distinction between science and literature which had formed the basis of Hegel's aesthetics, and had been a fundamental element of Marxist literary theory since Plekhanov and Mehring. Within the proletarian literature movement in the USSR, Germany, and the United States, this distinction had been used primarily in attacking abstractness in the form of stereotyped, lifeless characters, sloganized out-of-character speeches, and the manipulation of character and plot to introduce documentary material. The question now was, what about writers who avoided all this, but broke with the conventions of nineteenth-century realistic literature and drama in suspending action to introduce commentary and documentary material. Lukacs, at one extreme, extended his criticism of Sinclair's and Ottwalt's journalistic novels to an a priori rejection of all attempts to combine journalism and literature in open forms. Others were less rigid on this question. One proposal for reconciling the demand for living persons and dialectical materialism with the open form was made by Andor Gabor, a BPRS member. "Quotations and reportage," he wrote in the *Linkskurve* in 1932, "can be essential elements, but only after reality has been grasped and represented in artistically-formed figures" (Zwei Bühnenereignisse" 30). In an article which appeared in the RAPP's organ, *Na literaturnom Postu,* in 1928, Lunacharsky quoted Plekhanov in stating that literature operated with images, so that "every intrusion of pure thought, pure propaganda is always a move in the wrong direction in a work" (Lunacharsky, "Thesen über" 172). However, he goes on to qualify this statement: "Of course this criterion of Plekhanov's is not absolute. There are outstanding works . . . that noticeably offend against this criterion, but that only proves that hybrid literary phenomena of a belletristic-journalistic nature are possible" ("Thesen über" 172).

In his book *The Revolutionary Imagination,* Alan Wald suggests that in "Communist publications the leading Party critics" supported Lukacs on this issue (14–15). The reaction in the *Daily Worker* and *New Masses* to Brecht's and Piscator's plays indicate, however, that both publications tended more toward Gabor and Lunacharsky. Commenting on *The Mother,* Moissaye Olgin, like Gabor, conceives of a montage-like combination of living characters and journalistic commentary. Describing an imaginary dramatization of Marx's *Das Kapital* employing methods such as those of Piscator, he writes:

> The spectacle would have to consist of many episodes, selected scenes. The connection between the scenes would have to be "told" from the stage or from back stage by declamation or reading or some other method. Perhaps the screen would have to be resorted to, to supplement the things that happen on the stage. . . . A cinema screen is spread over the stage. On the screen are thrown supplementary scenes which cannot be enacted on the stage because they would require either too much time or too many people. Beside the stage proper is placed the chorus which declaims or sings in accompaniment of the stage action. . . . The workers, capitalists and state officials who appear in such a play can be living human beings, men and women of flesh and blood. In other words, they can be real. It is true, however, that this would be realism of a special kind. (" 'Mother' " 5)

In fact the Theatre Union had misinterpreted Brecht's intentions and had tried to remain within the normal conventions of the realistic theater in presenting *The Mother*. Olgin noted: "The realism of the Theatre Union often violated the special realism required by Brecht's conception and this jeopardized artistic unity." Recognizing the significance of the issues raised by Brecht's concepts, he concludes: "The spectacle has already become a subject of controversy and this in itself shows that we are dealing here with a phenomenon of prime importance in the development of our proletarian theater" (" 'Mother' " 5).

Like Olgin, Michael Gold considered *The Mother* "a fine play," but criticized the Theater Union's interpretation. While expressing his approval of experiment in the theater, he argued that the Theatre Union should stick to more conventional productions and native themes:

> *Mother* . . . is well worth seeing as an example of a stylistic experiment of Germany's most illustrious revolutionary playwright, Bert Brecht.
>
> In the American direction, however, some of the starkness of the original idea is lost. It is, also, an agit-prop play, with a strongly German flavor, and as such I don't see how the Theatre Union directors misjudged their typical audience by presenting it. Once having accepted it, however, they should have allowed Bert Brecht

and Hanns Eisler to produce it, since these men are great artists and surely know what they wanted to do.[30]

The following day in the *Daily Worker* he added:

> *Mother* is a fine play, well worth producing and seeing. But does it belong in a pioneer theatre that presumably set out to explore the virgin continent of proletarian American life?
>
> Nobody expects the Theatre Union to dabble in expressionism, futurism, constructivism, or any other interesting style of stage experiment. If such experiment is needed, and it certainly is, let it be done in some small studio theatre, newly established for the purpose.[31]

In the *New Masses* two articles appeared on Brecht in December 1935. One consisted of a long explanation of his theory by Eva Goldbeck. While Ira Levine claims that at this time "American exposure to Brecht's theory was almost nil" (146), Lee Baxandall describes Goldbeck's article as the "best exposition of Brecht's principles to appear in English in the '30s" (*Marxism and Aesthetics* 48). The other article was a defense of Brecht's concept of the epic theater by Stanley Burnshaw:

> There is the question of "didactic" drama, which has long been a bogey of criticism. Brecht is not afraid of forthright didacticism because didactic art when suffused with revolutionary meaning is simply political art; and as such it touches the very root of Marxian purpose. If Mother, like many well-intentioned products, were didactic in an inorganic sense, it could be dismissed as a failure. But Brecht has fused the form and the content of his play in such a way that its didacticism is part of the very texture. ("The Theatre Union" 28)

In keeping with the position taken at the American Writers Congress, Burnshaw concludes: "The realistic play can be powerful revolutionary drama, the agit-prop play (*Waiting for Lefty, Mother*) can be powerful revolutionary drama. One form does not exclude the other, and there is no question of 'choice.' Our theater needs both kinds of plays and will need a great many new kinds as yet uncreated" ("The Theatre Union" 28).

In regard to Piscator's play, which closed after only a few weeks, more reservations were expressed. In *New Theatre,* John Gassner weighed the pros and cons of his method, without drawing any firm conclusions. He argues: Its novelty and crass directness can provide a tonic to jaded theatre-going nerves, and any procedure which will shake the average spectator's complacency deserves a blue ribbon" ("Drama" 9). Furthermore he sees the techniques employed by Piscator as a means of "condensing the vast bulk of Dreiser's novel, of achieving condensation without emasculation." "It is not easy," he recognizes, "to compress a social system into the so-called 'well-made play.' " Nevertheless, he finds that the "Speaker's interruptions of the flow of the drama are sometimes disconcerting, and his explanations occasionally superfluous and bald. . . . " The "harangues and explication basic in the style" are problematic, in Gassner's view, since "the pre-convinced part of the audience finds much repetition in them, while the stiff-necked tribe of unbelievers is not apt to humble itself in dust and ashes before a direct assault" ("Drama" 9).

In the second half of the thirties the case against modernism hardened in the Soviet Union. On January 28, 1936, Shostakovich's twelve-tone opera, *Lady Macbeth of Msensk,* came under heavy fire in *Pravda,* and a few years later Meyerhold's experimental theater in Moscow was closed. In 1938 Lukacs declared emphatically in *International Literature* that the "super-modern developments in the field of the arts" were "characteristic of the imperialist era," and he advised Soviet writers and painters to reject "the artistic tendencies of the immediate present" ("On Socialist Realism" 88, 90). Among German writers in exile a heated discussion over expressionism—later known as the Brecht-Lukacs debate, although Brecht did not directly participate in it—sprang up in the Soviet-based magazine *Das Wort.* In the United States, in contrast, there was neither a campaign against formalism at this time, nor was there any equivalent of the Brecht-Lukacs debate. One probable reason was that among the major critics of the Communist party press and the *New Masses* there was no one who was as consistent as Lukacs in identifying formal experiment with decadence. In the *Daily Worker* and *New Masses* a favorable attitude toward modernism persisted to the end of the decade.[32]

Notes

1. This strike is discussed in Bernstein 358–91.

2. For information on the Sacco-Vanzetti case and its after-effects on writers see Aaron 169–73.

3. Accounts of the left-wing political activities of writers in the early thirties can be found in Aaron, Rideout, Carter, Schevill, Elias, Landsberg, Swanberg, and Klehr.

4. The circulation of the *New Masses* increased from 4,000 in September 1933 to 25,000 by early 1935. See Rideout 150.

5. In their June 1934 article, "Problems and Perspectives," Phillips and Rahv concluded their remarks on leftism with the observation: " ... only in the novel, the most successful genre of our literature, have any far-reaching attempts been made toward the solution of these problems" (18).

6. Editorial, *New Theatre* Sept.–Oct. 1933: 3.

7. Buchwald's Communist party membership is mentioned in Taylor 140.

8. Editorial, *New Theatre* Sept.–Oct. 1933: 3.

9. *Daily Worker* 25 Oct. 1933: 5.

10. "Theatre Union's 'Black Pit,' " *New Masses* 2 Apr. 1935: 42–43.

11. *Daily Worker* 6 May 1935: 5.

12. Ibid. 5 Oct. 1933: 5.

13. Ibid. 30 Oct. 1933: 5.

14. *New Masses* June 1930: 22.

15. *Daily Worker* 29 Dec. 1933: 5.

16. Ibid. 20 Nov. 1933: 5.

17. Ibid. 13 Oct. 1933: 5.

18. Ibid. 17 Nov. 1933: 5.

19. "The Business of a Novelist," *New Republic* 4 Apr. 1934: 220.

20. *Daily Worker* 9 Feb. 1934: 5.

21. Ibid.

22. Ibid. 7 Oct. 1935: 5.

23. See "O Californians ... " 124–25; "Wilder: Prophet ... " 201.

24. See *New Masses* Apr. 1930: 3–4.

25. *Daily Worker* 11 June 1934: 5.

26. Ibid. 14 June 1934: 5.

27. Ibid. 3 July 1934: 5.

28. Piscator's concept of the theater is described in Gallas 23, 90–91; the KPD's initial opposition is discussed in Fähnders and Rector 1: 115 and in Schrader 138–46; the two revues which Piscator presented in cooperation with the KPD were "Roter Rummel" and "Trotz Alledem" (see Simons, "Der Bund" 130); Piscator's connection with Dada is mentioned in Schrader 95–96.

29. Brecht's position on these writers is discussed in Mittenzwei, *Brechts Verhältnis ...* 137–38. Piscator's and Brecht's concepts of the theater are explained in Kändler.

30. *Daily Worker* 5 Dec. 1935: 7.

31. Ibid. 6 Dec. 1935: 9.

32. See Erskine Caldwell's remarks on Edwin Seaver's use of montage, *New Masses* 16 Mar. 1937: 20; Seaver, "Realism and Abstraction in Contemporary Art," *Daily Worker* 15 July 1937: 7; Rhodes's remarks on Picasso in "Modern Goya," *Daily Worker* 22 Aug. 1937: 10; Seaver on Kafka, *Daily Worker* 25 Oct. 1937: 7; Sebastian, "Charles Ives at Last," *New Masses* 7 Feb. 1939: 30–31; Burgum, "Faulkner's New Novel," *New Masses* 7 Feb. 1939: 23; Michael Gold on modern art, *Daily Worker* 10 Aug. 1937: 9.

6

The Position of the Original
Partisan Review

Criticism of Leftism in Proletarian Literature

JAMES GILBERT contends that the "first shots" in the controversy over leftism in the United States were fired in the *Partisan Review* in 1934 (122). In actuality, rejection of the tendencies in proletarian literature and criticism that Phillips, Rahv, Calmer and Farrell defined as leftist between 1934 and 1936 was well underway by this time. All that was new in their analysis of shortcomings in proletarian literature was their extension of the definition of leftism to include tendentiousness and utilitarianism, both of which had been criticized for years—particularly in the theater movement—in keeping with the goal of a broad proletarian culture encompassing large forms. Far from being dissident, their rejection of leftism in proletarian literature closely paralleled the views of Georg Lukacs, presented at the beginning of the thirties in the *Linkskurve*.

In February 1934 the first issue of the *Partisan Review*, the organ of the New York John Reed Club, appeared. Initially the editorial board included members of the *New Masses* staff, such as Joseph Freeman, Joshua Kunitz, and Edwin Seaver. However, as Phillips explained in his autobiography, it was "understood from the beginning" that he and Rahv "were the main force behind the magazine and its chief editors" (*A Partisan View* 37). In the middle of 1935 Alan Calmer, the National Head of the John Reed Clubs, joined the staff. After the magazine merged with *The Anvil* in 1936, Jack Conroy was taken on as editor, and James T. Farrell contributed a regular column on the theater. The last issue of the original *Partisan Review*, which appeared in October 1936, listed only Phillips, Rahv, and Calmer as editors.

By the time the first issue of the magazine went on the stands, criticism of tendentiousness, utilitarianism, and proletcult attitudes toward the heritage was already assuming the proportions of a campaign. However, although Granville Hicks had dealt with aesthetics in a number of articles, there still had been no equivalent in the American movement of the kind of long theoretical essay that had appeared in the *Linkskurve* between 1930 and 1932. This was therefore to be one of the tasks the new magazine assumed. While there was nothing new in the views the editors presented in their articles on leftism, they succeeded in summarizing the results of the discussion over aesthetics in the proletarian literature movement in a way that the *New Masses* had not. Furthermore, their insistence that critics devote more attention to specifically literary matters in reviewing books helped correct the tendency that John Strachey had criticized in his article in *International Literature*. While these contributions were recognized within the movement, the manner in which the *Partisan Review* editors occasionally presented their analyses of shortcomings in proletarian literature and in American Marxist literary criticism engendered irritation and personal conflict.

Like James Gilbert, Jack Salzman places the *Partisan Review* in the vanguard of the proletarian literature movement in its insistence that "the Left could learn from bourgeois writers" (41). However, an article by Rahv in *International Literature* in June 1934 reveals no difference between his general approach to the heritage and that which prevailed in the movement as a whole. In regard to modern writers, his remarks retain the negative tone of his 1932 *New Masses* article which A. B. Magil had criticized as leftist (Magil, "Pity and Terror" 18). He begins by defending Marxist criticism against former *Nation* editor Henry Hazlitt, who had defined Marxism as "economic determinism," and maintained that Marxists dismissed "practically all existing culture by the mere process of labelling it bourgeois" (qtd. in Rahv, "Marxist Criticism" 113). Countering these allegations Rahv observes that Hazlitt "is totally innocent of any knowledge of Marxism" and has "completely falsified Marxian criticism" ("Marxist Criticism" 113).

In explaining the actual position of Marxists on the heritage, Rahv elaborates on the distinction between the historical phases of classes: "During the period of social ascent a class is able to produce powerful works of art that are mainly materialist in conception; during its decline its spiritual production likewise deteriorates, and is transformed into the most rabid forms of idealism" ("Marxist Criticism" 115). He includes in the "proletarian heritage" that literature which "to a large measure identified itself with the elements of social growth and combatted the reaction of its period" (Marxist Criticism" 114). Idealists, on the other hand, "who chose the road of reaction, who withheld themselves from history" are

included in the heritage "as historical material, but not as living things . . . "
("Marxist Criticism" 114). From the "symbolists and the romantics," he
declares, "the proletarian writers can learn little . . . " ("Marxist Criticism"
114). At the same time Rahv warns against a hasty, over-simplified political classification of writers. Citing Lenin's approach to Tolstoy, he insists:
"One cannot, at all times, draw a hard and fast line separating progress
from reaction. Frequently the positive and negative exist side by side in
the same work" ("Marxist Criticism" 114).

In regard to modernism Rahv argues that in the declining phase of a
class, its writers resort to formal experiment in order to compensate for
loss of content: "The bulk of contemporary bourgeois literature, by
reason of the degeneration of its social basis and the duty of defending its
class through the varnishing and suppression of reality, is no longer
capable of assimilating significant content" ("Marxist Criticism" 115). The
"sophisticated bourgeois writers" whom Hazlitt had defended in the
Nation, Rahv claims, "attempt to escape extinction by wrenching form
out of its dialectic relation to content and elevating it to a unique position
in the creative process" ("Marxist Criticism" 115). Whereas Magil had seen
an element of protest in the formal innovations of modern writers, Rahv
sees in modernism "Endless, ideologically barren experimentation and
superficial cleverness; esthetic and intellectual dandyism without a breath
of life . . . " ("Marxist Criticism" 115). He adds that this does not mean
that "formal effectiveness" is not still possible in the declining phase
of a class, but that Marxist criticism must constantly expose "the preda-
tory class visage behind the esthetic veil" ("Marxist Criticism" 115).

The tone that had brought upon Rahv the charge of leftism in 1932
reemerged in the first long editorial in *Partisan Review,* which appeared in
the same month as Rahv's article in *International Literature.* Taking the
approach that Hicks was to criticize in his remarks on Malraux and that
Seaver later attacked in his "Caesar or Nothing" article, Phillips and Rahv
assail the "right-wing writer" within the movement, whose "acceptance
of the revolutionary philosophy is half-hearted, though he makes sporadic
use of it." At the root of this attitude the editors see "political fence-
straddling, disinterest in Marxism, and lack of faith in the proletariat."
Dos Passos's novels are cited as "a prototype of this viewpoint." Like
Hicks, they name Horace Gregory as one of several young poets in the
movement who "have adopted the obscurantism of the verse in the
bourgeois-esthetic little magazines." His criticism and poetry are seen as
exemplifying the "semi-revolutionary approach, which really amounts

to little more than liberalism" ("Problems and Perspectives" 6). In this connection they accuse other unnamed Marxist critics of political opportunism, in going too easy on such writers: "No doubt many fellow-travelers resent criticism, especially Marxian criticism, and some of our revolutionary editors and critics, unfortunately, in their endeavor to strike the proper note in their relations with fellow travelers, frequently seem unable to distinguish between diplomacy and analysis..." ("Problems and Perspectives" 6–7).

One can only speculate as to who was meant, but it is not unlikely that these remarks were a delayed response to Magil's 1932 article, "Pity and Terror," in which he had accused Rahv of sectarianism in his approach to bourgeois writers. Other possible addressees were Edwin Rolfe and Joseph Freeman, both of whom had dealt with the question of the sympathetic, middle-class writer a few months before in Gold's *Daily Worker* column. Rolfe had mentioned Horace Gregory in illustrating that it was better for fellow travelers to write honestly about their own feelings and experiences than to impose undigested Marxist ideas onto their poetry. Freeman had supported him on this. Another critic whom Phillips and Rahv might have had in mind was Hicks, whose analysis of Dos Passos in *The Great Tradition* had been laudatory.

In the same editorial in which they attacked "right-wing writers" and opportunism among Marxist critics, Phillips and Rahv criticized leftism in proletarian literature:

> The most striking tendency, and the most natural one in a young revolutionary literature, is what is commonly called "leftism." ... Its zeal to steep literature overnight in the political program of Communism results in the attempt to force the reader's responses through a barrage of sloganized and inorganic writing. "Leftism," by tacking on political perspectives to awkward literary forms, drains literature of its more specific qualities. ... [It] distorts and vulgarizes the complexity of human nature, the motives of action and their expression in thought and feeling. ("Problems and Perspectives" 5)

The only thing new in these remarks on leftism is the extension of the term's definition. While it had hitherto been employed in attacking sectarianism in relations with non-Communist writers and extreme Proletcult attitudes toward the bourgeois literary heritage, they now use it in reference to tendentiousness and abstractness—qualities that had long been criticized within the movement.

In the preceding issue of the *Partisan Review* Lukacs's 1932 *Linkskurve* article "Tendenz oder Parteilichkeit" had appeared in translation. James Gilbert denies that this article played any role in the formulation of the *Partisan Review*'s position on leftism and the propaganda question. Referring to Lukacs analysis, he writes: "This sophisticated justification for proletarian art was really a dismissal of the problem of art versus propaganda as the magazine [*Partisan Review*] saw it rather than a successful answer. Four months later in the *Little Magazine* Rahv dismissed Lukacs's proposals. The critic's use of the word 'propaganda' to denote recreation of objective reality was irrelevant to Americans, Rahv argued, because writers here did not understand the term in this way" (126).

Far from dismissing Lukacs's distinction between partisanship and tendentiousness, Rahv enthusiastically endorsed it in the *Little Magazine*. Only at the end of his article did he express reservations about the definition of propaganda. The problem here was one of faulty translation. In the English version the word *propaganda* was used for the German term *Tendenz*, thereby distorting Lukacs's analysis. Rahv stated:

> George Lukacs, a foremost European Marxist, brings to bear the full equipment of materialist dialectics to the solution of the [propaganda] problem. Lukacs defines propaganda in literature as "subjective wish on the author's part," as the recreating of reality in "a subjective, moralizing and preaching manner," and as a "demand, a summons, an ideal, which the writer contrasts with reality." There are two kinds of propaganda writers: those who seemingly repudiate propaganda (the esthetes, the formalists, the neutrals) and those proletarian writers who accept it in order to contrast it with art, thus laboring under the delusion that Marxism recognizes such a duality. The result of Lukacs' critical operations is a blow both to "pure" art and to the "leftists" in the proletarian camp. Proletarian art, says Lukacs, is that art which portrays reality objectively—"its actual motive forces and its actual trends of development"—and such an objective portrayal cannot be given except by those who are partisans on the side of the working class, for Marxism alone makes possible a dialectical, objective view of the entire process of our time. Paradoxically enough, Lukacs has here turned the tables on the esthetes. If propaganda is the portrayal of an ideal, subjective reality, then surely estheticism is out and out propaganda. ("Valedictory" 2)

Rahv concludes: "To my mind, Lukacs is perfectly correct if we accept his definition of the term. But this we cannot do, inasmuch as people do not always *mean his meaning* when they use the word" ("Valedictory" 2).

In an article entitled "The Novelist as Partisan," which appeared in the same issue of the *Partisan Review* as Lukacs's essay, Rahv applied the Hungarian writer's concepts in remarks on two proletarian novels, Arnold B. Armstrong's *Parched Earth* and William Rollins, Jr.'s *The Shadow Before*. In regard to the latter he stresses the author's success in combining the general and the particular, the subjective and objective: "Rollins employs the psychological method in revealing the working out of these [class] interests in the detailed action, and he does this successfully because each of his psychological perceptions is a projection of social character, and as such is rooted in class reality" (51). Rahv finds that both novelists reveal contradiction and suggest solutions without resorting to abstract polemics:

> The primary merit of *Parched Earth* and *The Shadow Before* lies in the fact that their authors are acutely conscious of the *material* reality of act and character. And it is precisely this consciousness of the economic factor as the leading factor in the determinism of life under capitalism that makes it possible for them not merely to state the mounting contradiction between the classes but also to resolve it. In both novels the solution is definitely established: not externally, through the well-known device of preaching and finger-pointing, but internally, through the inevitable logic of social necessity materializing in highly articulate images of existing life. ("The Novelist" 50)

The articles by a *Partisan Review* editor that most closely paralleled Lukacs's appeared in the *New Masses* in 1935. The author of both was Alan Calmer. The source of the critical concepts he applies was not necessarily Lukacs himself, but might just as well have been Franc Schiller, whose commentaries on Marx's and Engels's letters in *International Literature* were praised by Calmer. In the first article he insists, like Hicks in the *New Masses* and Herbert Kline in the *New Theatre,* on plausibility of character development and criticizes the conversion ending. The authors of proletarian short stories, he notes, frequently have their characters "act exactly as they *wish* all people would act." He continues: "This method of forcing the desires of the writer down the throat of his characters (or, to express the same thing in esthetic terminology, this *subjective tendentiousness*) proves to be a boomerang. It produces idealized black-and-white abstractions, bearing little relation to the flesh and blood of life and realistic literature" ("The Proletarian Short Story" 17).

Two months later he reported the results of a contest, sponsored by the John Day publishing company, for the best proletarian novel written by a nonprofessional. The only thing that distinguishes Calmer's article from numerous others in the *Daily Worker, New Theatre,* and *New Masses* criticizing tendentiousness is the harsh, supercilious tone he employs in discussing the deficiencies of what was, after all, the work of amateur writers. He begins by criticizing the tendency that Gold had noted in Conroy's *The Disinherited:* "Many of them were packed with actual happenings which were not *re-created* as fiction, but were simply recorded as fact. . . . Their authors seemed unable to do more than report facts badly. These writers lacked the artistic sensibility which would enable them to churn a mass of experience into literary form" ("Reader's Report" 23).

Like Gold in the *Daily Worker,* he insists on the need for proletarian writers to master form and technique and to learn from bourgeois literature: "Since there is still so much disdain for literary tradition in the American labor movement, it is worth repeating here that no worker (or anybody else for that matter) is likely to be a skilled writer if he does not serve his literary apprenticeship under the best and most advanced masters of his craft" ("Reader's Report" 23).

The most frequent deficiency that Calmer notes is abstractness. Here both the content of his remarks as well as the tone recall Lukacs's analysis of the worker-writer Willi Bredel. He describes "the worst scourge of proletarian literature" thus:

> . . . the tendency of writers to sloganize, to preach the principles of the class struggles directly to the reader, to impose "propaganda" *upon* the story instead of making it arise out of the story itself. Like most deliberately "tendentious" novels (proletarian or otherwise), such books are full of sermons which violate the integrity of the original situations upon which they are based. . . .
>
> As a rule, this editorializing is put into the form of didactic conversations and interminable speeches. . . . A certain amount of literary ingenuity is needed in order to mold such substance into literary form. It is distressing to find most of these writers completely unconcerned with such matters. ("Reader's Report" 23)

"Sermonizing and sloganizing" along with the " 'conversion ending' " Calmer finds symptomatic of "the vulgar 'leftist' approach to literature"

("Reader's Report" 23). Only on the issue of modernism does he differ with Lukacs. Noting a tendency toward derivativeness and nineteenth-century Victorian gentility in some of the writers in the contest, he asserts: "All of them could stand a stiff dose of modern fiction—Hemingway and Faulkner, Joyce and Proust, as well as proletarian novelists" ("Reader's Report" 23)

In at least two book reviews in the *Partisan Review* the concepts applied in literary criticism by Calmer and Rahv were indirectly associated with socialist realism. Commenting on the Soviet author Mikhail Sholokhov's novel *Seeds of Tomorrow*, Jack Conroy points up the writer's success in connecting the subjective and objective, the individual and the whole in living characters, and praises his ability to portray the new and developing in Soviet society:

> For the first time in my experience the collectivization campaign of the Soviet government has been interpreted in terms of flesh and blood. *Seeds of Tomorrow* . . . is a living record of these crucial days. The book translates the effects of a political decree into the actions and thoughts of breathing human beings, and at the same time manages to remain an exciting and swiftly moving tale of adventure, love, humor, intrigue and murder. . . . The phenomena of nature are here as fully and vividly delineated as in lesser novels by those who timorously dodge the social overtones dominating *Seeds of Tomorrow*. The new life whose birthpangs are attended by sweat, pain and blood; the agony of tearing asunder the umbilical cord fastened to the past. Each character, though endowed with motivations and attributes distinct from the others, fits inevitably into the major theme, enriching it and fulfilling it. . . . The seeds of tomorrow are sprouting on the steppes, in the factories, in a new literature of which Sholokhov's book is a distinguished harbinger. ("A World Won" 30–31)

Reviewing *And Quiet Flows the Don* by the same author, William Rollins, Jr. applies the distinction made in the *Partisan Review* between partisanship and propaganda. He observes that, while Sholokhov is partisan, his portrayal of characters and events is free of distortion and tendentiousness:

> I can imagine some people's reading the book through without knowing the writer's stand. For his bias appears subtly (though not

intentionally so); it is there only because the life of his cause—*and the fact that his cause is a living thing—is there.* There are no heroes or villains in the book (except that all his chief characters are at times heroic and at times ferociously villainous, which seems characteristic of all figures in Russian fiction). . . .

There is no propaganda, as I say; there is only the *life* of the thing of which Sholokov writes, and in which he obviously believes so fully and simply that it does not seem necessary to him . . . to distort the picture in the slightest, to gloss over any of the meanness and ferocity that marked on both sides the bloody civil war in the Don country with which he ends his story. ("The Collective Novel" 60–61)

The campaign against leftism in the *Partisan Review* has been described as a general assault on the proletarian literature movement. James Gilbert maintains that the character of the magazine reflected Phillips and Rahv's "criticisms of the existing Communist movement" (110). Terry Cooncy characterizes the criticism of leftism as a "recognition of what proletarian literature had thus far been," as opposed to the *Partisan Review*'s "vision of what it might be . . . " (78). It is therefore important to establish which works the attack on leftism was directed against. In his article in the *New Masses* on the proletarian short story, Calmer found tendentiousness to be prevalent in this form but reserved favorable comment for Albert Maltz's stories "Man on a Road" and "The Scab," Joseph Kalar's "Collar," and James T. Farrell's "The Buddies" ("The Proletarian Short Story" 17–18). In regard to the novel, his remarks were directed not against published works, but rather material that had been submitted by amateurs. In the July 1935 issue of *International Literature* he noted the "steady appearance of outstanding working-class novels in every season's publishing lists" and pointed out that proletarian literature had "reached heights which have won the acclaim of the most reactionary critics" ("A New Period" 74). In the first editorial in the *Partisan Review* criticizing leftism Phillips and Rahv cited as examples the poetry of Maxwell Bodenheim and H. H. Lewis, a novel called *The Road* by George Marlen, the short stories of Joseph Vogel, and the "majority of the manuscripts" submitted to the *Partisan Review,* most of which were presumably written by amateur writers in the New York John Reed Club ("Problems and Perspectives" 5, 9). On the other hand Phillips and Rahv, like Calmer, described the novel as "the most successful genre of our literature." Here, they indicated, "far-reaching attempts" had been made toward the solution of the problems they discussed ("Problems and Perspectives" 8).

Reviewing Robert Cantwell's novel *Land of Plenty* some months before, Rahv again had pointed to the high quality of recent proletarian novels:

> The publication of *The Land of Plenty* makes it plain that in the realm of the novel revolutionary literature in America is fast outstripping anything that the bourgeoisie can still lay claim to as its own. . . . What with Jack Conroy's *The Disinherited,* William Rollins' *The Shadow Before* and now *The Land of Plenty,* revolutionary literature in America has reached a higher stage of development this year, setting new standards for the army of proletarian art. (" 'Land of Plenty' " 5)

In regard to poetry, Phillips praised the high selective level of the magazine *Dynamo* ("Phelps," "Poetry Journal" 5) in May 1935, and a year later he and Rahv stated that most revolutionary poetry was free of leftism: "The fact is that revolutionary poetry teems with personal tonalities, and is composed of many strains and tendencies. It is true, of course, that the work of a small scattered group of 'leftists,' poaching on the fringes of revolutionary poetry, does illustrate in several ways the charges of impersonality and barren publicism" ("Private Experience" 100).

In February 1936 the anthology *Proletarian Literature in the United States* was reviewed in the *Partisan Review* by Newton Arvin. Again criticism was mixed with praise, and the general tone was favorable. In fact Alan Calmer was among those who had compiled the anthology. Arwin begins his critical remarks by observing: "There can't be any doubt that this book announces unmistakably a new and, now, a healthy chapter in American literature at the same time that it shows how an old promise, an old potentiality present in our culture from the beginning, is going to be fulfilled and made a reality" (12). Comparing the various sections of the book, he finds the drama and fiction to be among the most successful. In regard to the first, he praises Clifford Odets's "prodigal endowment for the writing of dialogue," Peters and Sklar's (the authors of *Stevedore*) "fine sense of what movement on the stage can be made to signify," and Albert Maltz's "rich and warm feeling for personality in moments of crisis" (13).

Turning to the fiction, he lists among the "sound and affecting pieces of writing" the excerpts from *Jews Without Money, The Disinherited, The Executioner Awaits,* and *To Make My Bread* (13). At the same time, he sees "a serious limitation of some proletarian writers of fiction" in their failure "to let all the beauty or humor or cruelty of their human materials come out as freely and unreflectingly as they certainly might and should. . . . " He continues: " . . . they have been afraid of tenderness, or expansiveness, or the appropriate vehemence; and a good deal of proletarian fiction has been meager, dry and toneless as a result" (13). As an example he mentions James T. Farrell's short story "The Buddies," while indicating that "Michael Gold, Robert Cantwell and Albert Maltz have shown that a proletarian writer can be free, warm, precise, and natural at once . . . " (13).

Arvin finds the poetry less successful than the fiction and drama: "It is . . . an endlessly difficult job for a revolutionary poet to avoid bareness, prosaic literalness and even doggerel, and at the same time to break away from the excessive indirectness and allusiveness of the poets who have just preceded him in American poetry" (13). Michael Gold's "Worker Correspondence" and Stanley Burnshaw's "I, Jim Rogers" do not succeed, he explains, "in steering off the first rock," while Robert Gessner's "Cross of Flame" does not wholly avoid the second. He reserves favorable comment for Gold's "Strange Funeral," Horace Gregory's "Dempsey, Dempsey," Richard Wright's "Between the World and Me," and Isidore Schneider's "To the Museums" (13).

Leftism in Literary Criticism

In two long essays in 1934 and 1935 Phillips and Rahv turned their attention to certain features of literary criticism they found to be widespread. In connection with these essays Terry Cooney writes: "The editors of *Partisan Review* were not yet ready . . . to proclaim that the most prominent leaders of proletarian literature, the editors of the *New Masses*, were 'leftists' and thus subject to all their strictures . . . " (78). Referring to the 1935 essay, Alan Wald simply states that Phillips and Rahv "took issue with a long list of Stalinist literary shibboleths" ("Revolutionary Intellectuals" 190). In reality, they summarized views that had a long history within the movement and had been formulated by some of the same *New Masses* editors Cooney refers to. Like Freeman in 1928 and 1929 and Hicks in his 1932 *Modern Quarterly* article, the two *Partisan Review* editors insisted that the "Marxian method in criticism cannot be considered a purely sociological one" ("Criticism" 22). They characterized as "mechanical materialism" the assumption of "a direct determinism of the whole superstructure by the economic foundation, ignoring the dialectical interaction between consciousness and environment, and the reciprocal influence of the parts of the superstructure on each other and on the economic determinants" ("Problems and Perspectives" 6).

Mechanical materialism, they explained, manifested itself in the "vulgar utilitarian attitude" that literature should be directly agitational. Many essays and reviews, they asserted:

> ... distort the function of criticism by isolating the political equivalents of books from their total contexts, and by judging these equivalents chiefly on the basis of immediate tactics. ...
>
> One common assumption is that literature, in its normative character, is as direct a weapon as political and economic writing. By this we mean that literature is assumed to be capable of presenting as explicit a program of political action as, for example, newspaper articles or pamphlets. ("Criticism" 16, 18)

Probably referring to the agitprop theater and reportage, they allow that some literary forms "may approach this type of directness" ("Criticism" 18), but insist that agitational value cannot be generally applied in criticism. Like Hicks, they base their definition of the nature of art as a weapon on the idea of the unity of reflection and praxis, which in the Soviet Union had culminated in the description of the writer as "engineer of the human soul." Literature, they explain, "is not a system of signposts, but an instrument of reorienting social values, attitudes and sympathies" ("Criticism" 18–19).

As had been the case in the Soviet Union and Germany, Phillips and Rahv connect their criticism of utilitarianism with the call for a great proletarian epic. In keeping with the development away from agitprop, they reject the limitation of proletarian literature to the direct confrontation of workers and capitalists in strikes and demonstrations. In this connection they write: " ... it is the combing of the vast and complex background behind these overt acts that would give us epics of working class experience. ... What Balzac did for many strata of the bourgeoisie ... still awaits the genius of proletarian artists." They see in *Land of Plenty* and *The Disinherited* two novels that pointed in the right direction ("Criticism" 22–23).

Just as the criticism of tendentiousness was not an attack on proletarian literature in general, neither were any of these remarks directed against American Marxist literary critics as such. Writing in mid-1935, Phillips and Rahv attributed the prevalence of utilitarianism to the fact that "a good deal of what is presented as Marxian criticism is not being written by recognized Marxian critics but by people who lack both the critical temperament and a knowledge of Marxism. Yet all the weaknesses of our criticism are ascribed to the handful of 'critics.' There is too little recognition of what has been achieved . . . " ("Criticism" 16). Referring to Hicks's series, "Revolution and the Novel," in their first long essay on leftism they acknowledged that he had "probed these problems in fiction" and had "helped to clarify" their approach, although they doubted the usefulness of the series for writers ("Problems and Perspectives" 7).

In the second issue of the *Partisan Review* Rahv connected the high artistic level of recent proletarian novels to the quality of Marxist literary criticism in the United States:

> For some years Marxist critics in America have busied themselves with the building of a theoretical scaffolding for a partisan literature expressing the revolutionary reconstruction of society. Their efforts have not been in vain; in fact they could not have been in vain. But now there can no longer be any doubt about it. The new class novels coming off the press month after month, the new literary magazines springing up all over the country—all these are signs of a promise fulfilled. They prove the fusion of theory and practice in American revolutionary literature and its leaving behind the incipient phase of creative helplessness. ("The Novelist as Partisan" 50)

Nevertheless, in discussing utilitarianism a year later Phillips and Rahv did direct criticism at Hicks. In connection with the need to broaden the movement, they turned to the question of the heritage and modernism. Now, in 1935, there was no trace of the attitude toward non-Communist experimental writers that Magil had categorized as leftist in 1932. In that year Rahv had stated in the *New Masses:* " . . . the novels of a writer like William Faulkner leave the reader with nothing; it is merely stylized photography, the same old treadmill of naturalism . . . " ("The Literary Class War" 7). Having influenced Rahv's change in position was Engels's letter to Margaret Harkness, which he and Phillips quote at length to counter the facile class categorization of writers. Commenting on Faulkner's novel *Sanctuary,* they note that it presents "not ideology directly, but *specific content* in the shape of attitudes toward character, painting of moods, patterns of action, and a variety of sensory and psychological insights." They continue: " . . . we are judging a novel only when we are judging its specific content, and not when we judge the general ideology to which it may, by implication, be most closely linked" ("Criticism" 20).

Having a year before castigated other Marxist critics for not helping "fellow-travelers" to overcome their "backwardness," they now write:

> Many errors in evaluating fellow-travelers can be traced to this confusing of their ideology as public men . . . with what they actually write. It is conceivable that a writer taken in by the NRA may support it politically, but in writing a novel about a factory, his specific content about the lives of factory workers, if he has observed them accurately, may belie the political views he is upholding. . . . A writer's ideology and his specific content do not always dovetail as neatly as it is commonly assumed. While a general relation between the two . . . doubtless exists, the critic cannot assume a uniform relation applying to all writers. His job is to examine this relation anew when judging individual creations and creators. ("Criticism" 21)

The change in approach to non-Communist writers was also evident in remarks on T. S. Eliot. In 1932 Rahv had observed that, while Eliot's early poetry contained "masterly metric and superlative technical virtuosity" ("T. S. Eliot" 18), by the time he wrote "Waste Land" he had "slipped already and fallen into the swamp of mysticism and scholasticism, a double damnation" ("T. S. Eliot" 19). He criticized the latter poem for not pointing to the "way out": "Essentially this poem represents a flight from reality, not a solution or even an authentic examination of contemporary time, but an obfuscation. The modern world is bankrupt, but nevertheless a way out exists; a way out that requires a transference of allegiance from the idealist to the materialist world-view" ("T. S. Eliot" 19). He concluded: " . . . at the present time Eliot must be discounted as a positive force in literature. His place is definitely with the retarders of the revolutionary urge towards the creation of a new *human* humanity" ("T. S. Eliot" 19).

As an example of the leftist approach to the heritage, Phillips and Rahv now cite, not Rahv's own earlier statements, but rather Hicks's remarks on Eliot, which he had made in *International Literature* a year before they themselves attacked young proletarian poets for borrowing from the "bourgeois-esthetic little magazines" ("Problems and Perspectives" 6). Expounding on the question of the heritage in a condescendingly didactic manner, they write:

> Revolutionary literature is not the literature of a sect, like surrealism or objectivism; it is the product of an emerging civilization, and will

contain the wealth and diversity which any cultural range offers. In this sense, we shall have poets who will have learned much from Eliot and Crane.... There is a variety of fruitful influence in world literature, past and present, which revolutionary writers may select for their individual purposes. Some critics have denied, directly or indirectly, a usable tradition in post-war poetry. ("Criticism" 23)

Without mentioning Hicks they quote the article in *International Literature* in which he had maintained that Eliot's technical devices were of no use to proletarian poets. Commenting on this, they write:

> This approach to the literary heritage of American revolutionary poets is more like a search for *Marxian* ancestors than a sound orientation toward the critical reworking of the past. The very fact that most of our poets have been influenced by the so-called "experimental reactionary poets" shows either that most revolutionary verse is quite useless or that the conception of this influence is incorrect....
>
> There is no use whatsoever in talking about the usable past if we assume beforehand that nothing is usable save that which is near-Marxian. ("Criticism" 24)

Generalizing from Hicks's remarks on postwar American poetry, Phillips and Rahv suggest that this was typical of his approach to the heritage. However, as his statements on Proust demonstrated, it was not as simple as this. In fact his position on this writer, like their own observations on Faulkner, were based on Marx's and Engels's views on Balzac. While the *Partisan Review*'s editors now placed themselves unequivocally among those who included modernist writers in the heritage, Hicks was by no means on the opposite side in this question, as his position on Dos Passos's use of montage and stream-of-consciousness indicated. If American Marxist critics had not always paid enough attention to "specific content," Phillips and Rahv might just as well have presented their remarks in the form of general self-criticism, providing examples from their own writing.

Hicks's reaction was predictable. Replying in the same issue of the *Partisan Review,* he stated that there was a general consensus on theoretical questions, while on the problem of tradition there was "much less agreement": "That proletarian authors can learn something from bourgeois authors presumably all Marxist critics would affirm, but what it is they can learn is a question to which there are many answers. I cannot feel that Rahv and Phelps have helped to clear away the confusions and misunderstandings that sorround this problem, but at least they have called attention to its importance and its difficulty."[1] In regard to the quality of American Marxist literary criticism, he concedes that he is "conscious of innumerable defects" which he "should like to see remedied."[2] Having stated this, he observes: "We . . . have carried over into the proletarian literary movement some of the worst habits of the bourgeois literary world. . . . There is a distressing amount of the most uncomradely sniping and backbiting. We want self-criticism, of course, and our criticism of each other should be frank and full, but I think we need to ask ourselves whether, in criticizing one another, we are entirely free from personal rancor and petty jealousy."[3]

That there was little disagreement on theoretical questions was confirmed in 1936 by Alan Calmer in an article describing what he perceived as the consensus among "the more or less recognized left-wing critics" ("All Quiet" 13). He indicates that the principles he defines are based upon "answers abstracted largely from Hicks's 'Literature and Revolution,' Freeman's introduction to *Proletarian Literature,* Phillips's and Rahv's editorials in *Partisan Review,* and Edwin Seaver's article, 'Caesar or Nothing' " ("All Quiet" 13). In regard to the definition of proletarian literature and to the question of the heritage, he states: " . . . Marxians point out that it is the present outlook of the author and not his subject-matter, characters or class origin which determines whether his work is proletarian or not. . . . Proletarian literature is not something new springing out of the heavens, but a continuation of past literature" ("All Quiet" 13). Turning to the propaganda question, he indicates: "Marxians do not condone writing in which a political 'message' is *grafted* upon a literary work. . . . The effects of literature are not ordinarily the same as the effects of a direct appeal to action like a newspaper editorial or a soapbox speech—" ("All Quiet" 13) As for Marxist literary criticism, he states that whatever opponents may claim, it "is not a sociology but a literary criticism" requiring "the full tasks of interpretation and evaluation." In connection with this point he adds that, in actual practice, "many of the recognized Marxian critics—Hicks, in particular—have failed so far to fulfill these aims." He does not, however, mention any particular reviews. Finally, he asserts, "there is no official party line in literature, and numerous disagreements do exist among recognized Marxian authors" ("All Quiet" 13). Commenting in the *Daily Worker* on his article, Calmer explained: " ... I assaulted the enemy for misrepresenting the ABCs of our literary position. ... To a number of sincere writers 'leftism' is still synonymous with Marxism, and this keeps them away from us; they think we believe in many of the principles which, according to my article, Marxists repudiate."[4]

James T. Farrell's *A Note on Literary Criticism*

In his book *A Note on Literary Criticism,* which appeared a few months after Calmer's article, James T. Farrell employed a considerably less diplomatic tone in discussing the quality of criticism in the movement. The influence of this book on subsequent interpretations of the discussion over leftism cannot be overestimated. While most of the actual literary criticism within the proletarian-literature movement remains scattered in publications that are available only on microfilm and have no annual index of articles, such as the *Daily Worker* and the weekly *New Masses, A Note on Literary Criticism* offers a brief summary of what the author claimed were the main weaknesses of contemporary American Marxist literary criticism. The latest in the long list of literary historians who assign Farrell's book a central role is Terry Cooney. In his 1986 book he writes:

> Launching his own barrage against "leftism," Farrell combined the arguments of Phillips and Rahv, the complaints of other writers, and his own perceptions in a sustained assault on the leading lights of the *New Masses:* they had confused literature with propaganda; they had failed to understand the importance of the literary heritage; they had ridden roughshod over the qualities of uniqueness in individual writers and individual works; and they had introduced political standards into their criticism that produced vulgar, oversimplified, and irrelevant judgements. (83)

Thus Cooney takes Farrell's description of *New Masses* literary criticism at face value and describes his book as "the most substantial consideration of Marxist aesthetics by an American Marxist written during the thirties" (83). In reality, Farrell largely repeats points that were truisms in the movement by this time and, through omitting important information that runs counter to his allegations, presents a seriously distorted picture of the approach to literature and criticism in the *New Masses.*

While the *Partisan Review*'s editors had, up to this time, concentrated most of their fire on Hicks, Farrell takes to task a long list of critics, including Rahv. Arguing that art and literature have both a "pleasure-value" and a "use-value," he claims that overemphasis on the latter has led to "functional extremism," a term he uses interchangeably with leftism. Among its manifestations are an extreme proletcult attitude toward bourgeois literature of the past and present, oversimplification of the relation between base and superstructure, and the demand for narrow, agitational literature. In attacking the first tendency, he states:

> It [proletarian literature] will grow and develop as part of the development of literature in general. . . . In its growth it will—for some time to come—be constantly influenced by "bourgeois" literature" (86).

> Within the category bourgeois, there will be found both progressive and regressive elements. (93)

The critic's task is "understanding, assimilating, evaluating, interpreting the literature of the present in a manner analogous to that in which he treats the literature of the past" (94). Farrell bases these observations on Marx's and Engels's remarks on Balzac, and Lenin's views on Tolstoy.

Transgressions against these principles, Farrell contends, have taken two forms. One he calls "mechanically deterministic 'Marxism,'" which assumes "that literature follows economics obediently and directly" (31). He sees Granville Hicks as the most prominent offender here. The second form that leftism takes is "revolutionary sentimentalism," which includes an extreme proletcult approach toward literature and the heritage. Defining this tendency, he states: " . . . it seems to assume that revolutionary and proletarian literature will develop in pristine glory, beauty, and simplicity without benefit of antecedent influences" (30). "Perhaps the most famous representative of this tendency in America," he asserts, "is Michael Gold" (30). In this connection, he presents, in a footnote, a quote from a talk Gold had given at the American Writers Congress, where he had warned of the danger that the literary movement might become a "petty-bourgeois movement," and called on the participants to "stimulate and encourage and help the growth of proletarian literature which is written by workers" (qtd. in *A Note* 30).

Elaborating on what he regards as the correct approach to the heritage, Farrell implies that Hicks and Gold evaluated literature solely according to ideology and rejected all nonproletarian literature. As a result of functional extremism, he notes, the "proper duties of criticism are ignored, and the carry-over value of literature is almost completely disregarded" (85). Whatever definition of proletarian literature one accepts, he argues, it does not "constitute an *a priori* fiat for the critical destruction of works that will not slide into such a category" (87)

Meanwhile the two writers he discusses in explaining his own approach to the literature of the past—Shakespeare and Dickens—had already in 1926 been included by Gold in the heritage of proletarian writers. In the same year Gold saw permanent value in humanist writers who shared the "ideas and life of mankind" ("American Jungle Notes" 9). Now, ten years later, Farrell writes: "Certain works of literature possess a human worth and a carry-over power which endow them with a relatively inherent persistence-value..." (46). As an example of a contemporary writer whose work was "unqualifiedly non-proletarian," but who might nevertheless influence proletarian-revolutionary writers he cites Proust, without mentioning that Hicks had held up this very author as a model for revolutionary writers (88). In the *Daily Worker* in 1935, Gold had also praised the "perfect prose" of the French novelist and described him as "a great writer of our epoch."[5]

Turning to the propaganda question, Farrell criticizes the tendency to mix up "the tactics required for the role of agitator, strike leader, political leader, Marxian theoretician, and novelist" (147). This time he sees the early Philip Rahv as a prime offender. Citing his 1932 *New Masses* article, he states that the view that proletarian literature must be "a literature of action" had been "expressed by Philip Rahv, one of the present editors of *The Partisan Review and Anvil*, as consistently as by anyone in America" (33). However, in a footnote he adds: "... Rahv in his subsequent critical pieces has not followed the 'line' laid down by such a thesis. To the contrary, he has increasingly been developing an anti-'leftist' point of view" (33).

Farrell is probably a main source of the contention of Walter Rideout, James Gilbert and other literary historians that *New Masses* critics actively promoted tendentiousness. While Rahv in 1934 had attributed the lack of tendentiousness in recent proletarian novels to the work of Marxist critics ("The Novelist as Partisan" 50), Farrell asserts:

The mechanistic methods of "leftism" have been damaging in two important ways. First, writers have been led to create characters out of concepts—"the general"—instead of from life with the clarifying assistance that concepts provide. The result of this has been obvious-

ness. The characters often illustrate concepts that have not been
soundly applied. Second, such work has been unduly encouraged
and praised, so that it has been tacitly set up as a literary model to be
followed. (129–30)

> When literature has been urged to meet the requirements of limited
> conceptions of propaganda, the result has most often been the pro-
> duction of ineptitudes. The field of poetry, for instance, has been
> glutted with inept efforts during the last three or four years. (150)

As an example Farrell cites Robert Gessner's book of poetry, *Upsurge,*
which he describes thus: " . . . an empty, windy exhibition of generalized
feeling . . . a graceless editorial chopped up into lines to give it the typo-
graphical appearance of a poem" (152). Without mentioning which critics
had praised the book, he writes: "It is the mistaken approval of such work
as Gessner's that distorts any sense of values in the judgment of poetry.
The specious emphasis on activism . . . creates a confusion between verbal and actual direct action" (152).

Farrell sees a corollary to the promotion of such works in the panning
of books whose political standpoint was not considered satisfactory. Pointing to the discussion surrounding Malraux's novel *Man's Fate,* he explains:
" . . . whether its political interpretation and its direct political implica-
tions be *politically* sound or unsound, it retains its powerful emotional
drive; it conveys a sense of the Chinese revolution and of characters
participating in it; achieving this, it intensifies our awareness. . . . *Man's
Fate* remains a moving and powerful work of literature, regardless of the
soundness or unsoundness of its politics. In other words, political propaganda and creative are not *precisely* the same" (142–43). As in the case of
Proust, nowhere does Farrell indicate that this was the very position that
Hicks had taken in the controversy two years before.

In attempting to introduce clarity into the discussion over the relation
between literature and propaganda, Farrell confines the latter term to what
was commonly referred to as agitprop. Attacking the restriction of proletarian literature to this function he repeats the position that Hicks had
presented in 1932:

> Literature . . . is not so directly concerned with finding answers to
> social problems that will be immediately embodied in action. . . . (148)

> . . . the effect of living literature on its reader is not the same as the
> effect of an advertising slogan upon a prospective customer. (215)

Instead it furnishes "the material from which extended feelings and added thought are developed" (215). The reason he gives why literature cannot be limited to agitprop is practical rather than theoretical. "Works of literature," he points out, "are, generally, not quickly enough assimilated to become instruments of propaganda leading to the choice of immediate courses of action" (148). He does not, however, exclude the possibility of literature performing this function. Defining the "slogan" as "one of the instruments of propaganda," he repeats Franc Schiller's stricture against the "subjective preaching of a line not arising out of the action" ("Friedrich Engels" 126), as well as Freeman's and Rolfe's observations on poetry three years before in the *Daily Worker*. Farrell writes: " . . . if he [the writer] is to write poetry or any other so-called creative literature, he must give his political slogans internal relationship with other features of his work; his writing as a whole must be marked by intrinsic rather than extrinsic conviction" (155).

Farrell does not go beyond these remarks to develop the concepts of partisanship and tendentiousness that were basic to the *Partisan Review*'s approach to the propaganda question. Nor does he make the distinction Gold and others had made between the purposes and methods of agitprop, on the one hand, and the novel and full-length drama, on the other. Furthermore, while he criticizes the dualism of Calverton as un-Marxist, he reveals the same tendency here and elsewhere in his book. Failing to establish any link between pleasure and use, he ultimately abandons the idea of the unity of the good, the true and the beautiful, that had formed the basis of Hegel's and later Marx's aesthetics.

Although Farrell himself does not advance the discussion on any of the points he deals with, he becomes strongly polemical when evaluating the critical and theoretical writings of others in the movement. Referring to an article by Malcolm Cowley, in which he rejected the separation of art and propaganda into rigid, mutually-exclusive categories, he comments: "Mr. Cowley here suggests that he is doing road work to become a dialectician . . . " (158). He chides Hicks for "cooking up recipes for tomorrow's 'great' literature" (82) and refers at one point to Gold's "Marxmanship" (78).

While most of the points that Farrell makes in attacking leftism were truisms by this time, one misses in his book any sense of the development that had taken place in the American movement since the twenties. Taking Joseph Freeman to task for not coming down hard enough on leftism in the introduction he wrote for the book *Proletarian Literature in the United States,* he does not mention that Freeman rejected the simplistic sociological approach to criticism already in 1928 and 1929 in the *New Masses.* Although Farrell was theater critic for the *Partisan Review* at the time he wrote his book, he gives no indication of the long campaign in the theater movement for expansion beyond agitprop, and the accompanying criticism of abstractness and tendentiousness. In associating Hicks with a proletcult rejection of the heritage, he seems at times to overlook the fact that the whole purpose of *The Great Tradition,* whatever its shortcomings, was to establish the heritage of proletarian writers among novelists and poets of the past.

The failure to explain Hicks's position on Proust and Malraux are not the only instances where Farrell omits information that runs counter to his allegations. He mentions Phillip Rahv's 1932 article in the *New Masses* as an example of leftism, but does not discuss A. B. Magil's extensive criticism of Rahv some months later in the same magazine, in which he formulated many of the very positions that Farrell now puts forth four years later. Selecting a quote from Gold's speech at the first American Writers Congress, he suggests that Gold insisted on worker-authorship and demanded that proletarian literature deal exclusively with working-class life. In actuality he rejected this position at the Congress. When Edwin Seaver defined proletarian literature according to viewpoint, rather than the subject matter or the class origin of the writer, Martin Russak, a worker-writer, disagreed. As Walter Rideout indicates: "Thereupon, an extensive rebuttal was made by Michael Gold. . . . He opposed the "primitivism" of the attitude for which Russak was a spokesman and upheld Seaver's emphasis on political orientation . . . " (168).

The most glaring omission in Farrell's book, however, involves the contention that tendentiousness was encouraged and aesthetics disregarded by critics in the movement. While discussing Robert Gessner in this connection, he says nothing of the actual reception of his book of poetry, *Upsurge,* in the *New Masses* and *Daily Worker.* In the July 1934 issue of the *New Masses,* writers were invited to give their opinion of the magazine's literary criticism. While there were some, such as Farrell, who felt that it was too political, there were others who complained that too much emphasis was placed on aesthetics. Gessner was among the latter. Referring to the reception of his book, he wrote:

What kind of criticism then should a revolutionary writer expect from a revolutionary magazine? His work should be given the closest scrutiny from the point of view of Marxism-Leninism as to its value for the proletariat in formulating and intensifying their movement toward rebellion. What criticism did my poem *Upsurge* get from one of the editors of the New Masses? Simply an aesthetic analysis. This revolutionary critic concerned himself solely with image and diction, complaining that "the imagery lacks inevitability; some times it is frankly questionable . . . occasionally . . . unpleasantly superfluous . . . overlong stretches of violent language." Such phrases are more at home in a Village sheet, or in company with the aesthetic critic of the Nation. . . . Aesthetics may be important, but the editor of the revolutionary New Masses should not give only aesthetic criticism. . . . The same holds for Alfred Hayes' review in the Daily Worker. . . . No so-called revolutionary critic has yet criticized Upsurge as to its revolutionary intent.

Consequently I can't say that the criticism to date of my work in the New Masses has helped me (letters from un-aesthetic, class-conscious workers have), because it has not been revolutionary criticism based on Marxism-Leninism. Instead it has been superficial aestheticism derived from bourgeois hangovers. ("Authors' Field Day" 29)

In reply to this, Stanley Burnshaw, the reviewer of the book, stated: "The denigration of aesthetic analysis as 'superficial aestheticism derived from bourgeois hang-overs' and the implication that aesthetic analysis contradicts the growth of revolutionary literature are not merely absurdities but dangers. Fortunately most American revolutionary writers appreciate the importance of aesthetic problems. . . . The movement has a right to demand the highest standards of art" ("In Reply" 32). Having contributed to the same symposium in which Gessner and Burnshaw made these remarks, Farrell was undoubtedly aware of the actual criticism of *Upsurge* in the *Daily Worker* and *New Masses,* and deliberately created a false impression of the poem's reception.

It might be noted that, although Farrell had little good to say about American Marxist literary criticism, he concurred with Moissaye Olgin and others in associating the theory of socialist realism with various aspects of the campaign against leftism. In a long footnote, he observed:

I understand Socialist realism to be a reaction against leftist tendencies such as those sponsored some years back by the now-dissolved RAPP. Those who argue for a "line" of "Socialist realism" do not bar the assimilation of past cultural values, and therefore cannot be said to treat the categories *bourgeois* and *proletarian* as categories of value alone. . . .

Besides being an attack on leftism, socialist realism represents a vital and healthy tendency. (104)

Nevertheless he sees an example of "functional extremism" in Radek's criticism of Joyce, and argues against the exclusion of modernists from the heritage. Like the Soviet writer Leo Nikulin, whom Gold had quoted in 1933 on the danger of applying the slogan of socialist realism "abstractly" and "mechanically,"[6] Farrell anticipates the possibility of the theory being misused to impose new restrictions on writers (106–8).

Reactions to Farrell's book varied. Alan Calmer characterized it as "the first lengthy statement of a critical stand that must . . . become the dominant emphasis of Marxian criticism if proletarian literature in the United States is to grow instead of stagnate" ("Down with Leftism" 8). He found "a sense of direct and clear thinking" in Farrell's analyses, and saw the "numerous footnotes and parenthetical remarks" as indications of his "ability to handle intellectual concepts" ("Down with Leftism" 8).

In contrast to Calmer, Granville Hicks, writing in the *New Masses,* found Farrell's theoretical analyses to be a combination of truism and confusion, and maintained that the book failed "to deal incisively with a single one" of the problems it raised. In addition he criticized the author's unfairness: "In the course of his book he misrepresents the opinions of half a dozen revolutionary critics. . . . Not only does he wrench his quotations from the surroundings that explain them; he performs obvious feats of distortion . . . " ("In Defense" 109). Isidore Schneider perceived behind Farrell's vitriolic attacks on American Marxist literary criticism the danger of "a swing to the right" and "a distortion of revolutionary principles" as a result of the adoption of the Popular Front ("Sectarianism" 25).

In the *Daily Worker* Edwin Seaver agreed with Hicks that the book contained little that was new: " . . . the charges which Mr. Farrell levels against our Marxist literary criticism now, presumably for the first time in history, were already considered within the body of that criticism at least a year ago." Here Seaver is referring to his own article, "Caesar or Nothing," from which he presents some quotes. He continues:

Of course it is better to be late than never, but it is a bit foolish to discover that in getting there everybody has been out of step but yourself. And if I offer quotations from an essay of mine written more than a year ago, it is not because Mr. Farrell does not give me credit for covering the same ground before that he has attempted to cover now, but because he does not give such credit to the body of our Marxist literary criticism, which is constantly correcting its shortcomings and was by no means up a blind alley waiting for the word from Lonigan in Olympus to liberate it.[7]

If there were no fundamental theoretical differences between the staff of the *Partisan Review* and the other major critics in the movement, the question remains of the actual literary criticism that appeared in the *Partisan Review, New Masses,* and *Daily Worker.* Here again there was no marked difference in approach, which should not be surprising since many of the same people wrote for all three publications. Farrell himself contributed five critical reviews to the *New Masses* in 1935 alone, three of which occupied an entire page.[8] In the same year the magazine published one of his short stories, a very favorable review of his novel *Judgement Day* and a quarter-page ad for *Studs Lonigan.* Alan Calmer's most extensive analyses of leftism in proletarian literature appeared, not in the *Partisan Review,* but in the *New Masses.*

Discussing the reception of Henry Roth's novel, *Call It Sleep,* Walter Rideout implies that the short, negative review in the *New Masses* was indicative of the editors' disregard for aesthetic values, as opposed to the *Partisan Review*'s approach (238). Actually Joseph Wolf's commentary on this novel in the *Partisan Review* did not appear until after Seaver's article "Caesar or Nothing" in the *New Masses* and the *Daily Worker* review. Wolf's article is, in fact, almost a paraphrase of the latter. Thus he praises Roth's psychological insight and his handling of the dialect of the ghetto. His reservations are also similar. He complains of Roth's occasional "overwriting" (95), and finds that "the conception of the author remains partially obscure . . ." (95). Finally, he makes the same comparison as the *Daily Worker* reviewer, stating that "*Call It Sleep* is the most promising first novel since Joyce's *Portrait of the Artist as a Young Man*" (96).

Where opinions differed, the roles that literary historians have established—with *New Masses* critics applauding inept, politically "correct" works, while the *Partisan Review* staff insisted on aesthetic values—as often as not were reversed. While Hicks and Gold were rather critical of Jack Conroy's novel *The Disinherited,* Rahv saw it "setting new standards for the army of proletarian art" (" 'Land of Plenty' " 5). Commenting on Arnold B. Armstrong's *Parched Earth,* Hicks perceived "a certain dispar-

ity between Armstrong's knowledge of social tendencies and his understanding of human beings," with the result that the novel was "at times
schematic" ("The Novel and the Middle Class" 279). Rahv, in contrast,
held it up in his article "The Novelist as Partisan" as an example of a novel
that, despite its shortcomings, avoided blatant tendentiousness (50).

A disagreement arose between Farrell and Gold in 1935 over the play
Let Freedom Ring, a dramatization of Grace Lumpkin's novel *To Make My
Bread.* In keeping with the high standards he demanded of the professional revolutionary theater, Gold agreed with critics outside the movement who had pointed to aesthetic shortcomings in the play. Writing in
the *Daily Worker,* he stated: "*Let Freedom Ring* is not a great play. Judged
by the standards of our own emerging left-wing theatre in New York, it is
not even as good a play as *Stevedore* or *Waiting for Lefty.* It has technical
faults which the professional critics were quick to point out."[9] James T.
Farrell, in contrast, saw in the strike play "one of the most truthful,
moving and stirring plays seen on an American stage in recent years." *Let
Freedom Ring,* he finds, "dramatizes, with thoroughness, a true pattern of
experience of workers in a capitalistic system." Soon to lash out in his
book at a long list of fellow critics on the left, he now directs his fire at
critics outside the movement. He continues:

> The strike here grows naturally and unforced out of the trend and
> theme of the play. And since it does, it is impossible to conceive of
> the strike being presented on the stage without the characters discussing
> what it means and involves. And so the critics describe the play as a
> plaintive pleading for the downtrodden, as an argument justifying the
> organization of labor unions, and as . . . propaganda. The conclusion
> implicit in such criticism is that in a play describing industrial
> conditions, the characters must not talk about the industrial condi-
> tions which furnish the very theme itself. . . . One stands appalled
> before these five or six gentlemen who seem to be major stock-
> holders controlling the American drama.[10]

There was also divergence of opinion over the play *The Mother.*
Discussing the Brecht-Lukacs controversy in his book *The Revolutionary
Imagination,* Alan Wald places Farrell in the Brecht camp: "Any student
of the literary left in the 1930s can see at once that what existed between
the Communist party and its most talented literary allies was a state of
internecine warfare on the issues of style and technique. The public
manifestations of this controversy are most famously represented by the

debate between George Lukács and Bertolt Brecht in Europe and that between James T. Farrell and the Communist *New Masses* magazine in the United States" (14). As a matter of fact, their positions were reversed. As has been seen, the *New Masses* and *Daily Worker* were undogmatic in their approach to Brecht's innovations. In the *New Masses* the effort was made to understand and explain Brecht's concept of the epic theater before drawing conclusions. Critics such as Gold and Olgin were discerning enough to distinguish between the Theatre Union's production and Brecht's intentions. James T. Farrell in his theater column in the *Partisan Review* failed to make this distinction. In a manner that was becoming characteristic, he dismissed the epic theater in a few sentences and attacked Brecht personally. Summarizing the dramatist's approach, he wrote: "In brief, his theory is that the theatre is a kind of school, where people are taught. His conception, then, is of drama as education. *Mother,* the story of a working-class mother in the class struggle and the revolutionary movement, can thus be accepted as a kind of walking school-house."[11] After describing the mechanics of the stage, he continues: "*Mother,* it seems to me, might have been a satisfactory play to present to an audience which has not yet emerged from illiteracy. . . . It is fair to assume that Brecht, in insisting on this kind of an adaption of his play for an American audience, was simply indulging himself. Such an effort is unnecessary revolutionary snobbery. *Mother* was an illustrated lecture which assumed that audiences in New York . . . were capable of understanding very little."[12] He compares it with *Let Freedom Ring,* which he considers the better of the two plays.

While Moissaye Olgin in the *Daily Worker* recognized the importance of Brecht's concept of the epic theater to the discussion over Marxist aesthetics, Farrell did not even mention the German playwright in the long section on literature and propaganda in his book *A Note on Literary Criticism.*

The Response in the *New Masses* and *Daily Worker* to the *Partisan Review's* Attack on Leftism

What literary historians have described as a fundamental theoretical dispute between the *New Masses* and the *Partisan Review* probably appeared as nothing more than personal squabbling to those in the movement who were not directly involved. In any event, there was little in the *Daily Worker* between 1934 and 1936 to suggest that the Party was disgruntled with the *Partisan Review*'s stand on leftism. On the contrary, the magazine was commended on this very point, and was promoted throughout the two years of its existence. The issue containing the symposium on criticism, in which Phillips and Rahv attacked Hicks's position on postwar poetry, was described by Robert Adler as "splendid." The *Partisan Review,* he noted, "has distinguished itself by the consistently high standard of work. . . . " The writing of Phillips and Rahv, he continued, "has always been characterized by the probing of basic philosophic and esthetic concepts. . . . " He depicted the essay attacking Hicks as "an approach to a rigorous and definite statement on fundamentals for a Marxist science of esthetics." In only one sentence did he note that "Granville Hicks, participating in the symposium, takes issue with the authors" ("Partisan Review" 5).

The same tone was employed a few months later by the head of International Publishers, Alexander Trachtenberg, in what was essentially an advertisement for the *Partisan Review.* In the *Daily Worker* he stated: " . . . of all our literary publications, the one that has been most neglected is *Partisan Review.* Although it has published outstanding poetry, fiction and literary criticism, it is read by only a few thousand readers. . . . Both in its critical and creative work, *Partisan Review* has printed literature of a high quality, and from the very beginning it has fought against all attempts to reduce literature to sloganized, lifeless writing" ("Revolutionary Literature" 5).

The following year found Trachtenberg once again conducting publicity for the magazine, after it had combined with the *Anvil:* "*Partisan Review and Anvil* fill a long-felt need in the revolutionary movement, particularly since the *New Masses* has been expanded into a weekly journal of a basically political nature. As the only publication in the country devoted exclusively to literature, the magazine surely deserves and must have the support of the entire revolutionary movement" ("Revolutionary Literature: Partisan Review" 7).

Various *New Masses* editors also praised the magazine and lent it support. Commenting on the first issue, Isidore Schneider wrote: "By now the cultural front of the revolutionary movement has come to a stage where it can confidently face bourgeois culture. . . . The exciting thing is that proletarian culture is now adult; it has passed its childhood of revolutionary 'baby talk' " ("Partisan Review" 5). At the first American Writers Congress, in 1935, Granville Hicks acknowledged the *Partisan Review*'s contribution to the discussion over aesthetics and conceded the shortcomings of some of his literary criticism. Reviewing his work he finds a "lack of attention to technical problems of writers" and "insufficient study of the complex relationship between experience and creation" ("The Dialectics" 96). He commends the *Partisan Review* for placing emphasis on both of these issues. Commenting on the final issue of the magazine, Edwin Seaver wrote: "The *Partisan Review* has come to bat with the first number of the new season in excellent form. There is nothing in the issue which is not worth reading."[13] *New Masses* editors also lent material support. On April 12, 1936 the *Daily Worker* announced a lecture by Joseph Freeman and a talk by Isidore Schneider, the proceeds of which were to go to the *Partisan Review*.[14]

If the *Partisan Review*'s campaign against leftism was, from the beginning, in keeping with Party policy, the question remains of why the same *New Masses* editors were occasionally at odds with Phillips, Rahv, Calmer, and Farrell. In the first article in which Hicks criticized the *Partisan Review*, the issue was the distribution of resources in the movement and the function of the John Reed Club publications. Pointing to the difficulty of financing them—the *Partisan Review* accumulated heavy debts in the first two years of its existence—he finds their maintenance to be justified only if they make "some specific contribution." In this connection, he writes: "The usual purpose of such a magazine is to provide an outlet for the literary productions of the club's members. This is important. . . . The material they publish is often unsuitable for a magazine that reaches a large, varied, and partly hostile audience, but it has interest-value for readers in a particular area" ("Our Magazines" 22). Here he finds the *Partisan Review* lacking: "In each of the five issues that have appeared a large proportion of the contributions has come from writers who are not members of the club. Practically all the contributors, moreover, are well-established writers, who have no difficulty in publishing their work elsewhere" ("Our Magazines" 23).

James Gilbert sees Hicks's criticism as a reaction to the *Partisan Review*'s "attack on leftism and its roundabout jabs at leading proletarian theoreticians . . . " (130). There is little to support Gilbert's claim in regard to the first point. Up to this time the *Partisan Review*'s main statement on leftism had been the essay "Problems and Perspectives," in which they rejected abstractness and the distortion of character in proletarian literature, and mechanical materialism—the "direct determinism of the whole superstructure by the economic foundation" (6)—in literary criticism. As has been seen, there was nothing new in this, and Hicks himself had been among those who had criticized these same tendencies and practices. In the present article he couples his remarks on the *Partisan Review* with praise for the *New Theatre*, the current issue of which contained Herbert Kline's article attacking abstractness and stereotyping in the workers' theater:

> ... *New Theatre* has quickly and immediately made a place for itself. There is certainly no other journal that provides adequate space for the detailed discussion of the particular problems of the revolutionary drama and for the careful analysis in revolutionary terms of the bourgeois stage. The only questions are whether there is need for such analysis and discussion and whether there is an audience for them. The answer to the first question is obvious; the answer to the second has been triumphantly provided by the rapid growth in the circulation of *New Theatre*. ("Our Magazines" 22)

If there was anything in Phillips and Rahv's essay that aroused Hicks's hostility it was probably the second factor mentioned by Gilbert, including the attack on "some of our revolutionary editors and critics" ("Problems and Perspectives" 7), who were allegedly pandering to "fellow travellers" such as Dos Passos.

The other issue that elicited criticism from Hicks likewise involved his idea that the magazine should serve primarily as an organ of the local, amateur proletarian writer, rather than the middle-class professional. He objected to the abstruse, scholastic style of the long essays, which were probably difficult for the average intellectual, let alone nonacademic amateur writers looking for guidance in aesthetic matters. In the symposium on criticism in the July 1935 issue of the *Partisan Review* he warned: "The critic is always in peculiar danger of becoming doctrinaire, of losing touch not merely with writers but also with readers, of handing down from some mist-veiled mountaintop meaningless decalogs. For the revolutionary critic this is fatal" (29–30).

In his review of *Proletarian Literature in the United States* in *Partisan Review*, Newton Arvin also criticized this feature of Phillips and Rahv's writing. Commenting on their essay, as well as one by Hicks included in the anthology, he wrote:

> ... too few of the critical writers on the left have quite realized what a rich and interesting form of expression criticism can be, or how truly it can give voice to just as many kinds of thought and feeling as, in a wholly dissimilar vein, poetry and fiction do. There is no reason

under the sun why it has to be dryly expository or prosaically analytical, or why it can only be written from the eyebrows up. Yet that is what too much of it is like. One can agree wholeheartedly with the point that Phillips and Rahv are making in their essay, and still wish that they could make it in a less scholastic manner. One can feel that what Granville Hicks has done, in the essay here reprinted and in so many other places, is simply invaluable to the American movement; and still wish that when he writes criticism he would let himself give vent to more of the energies in a remarkable temperament than he often does. Imagination, anger, the subtle sense of form, the historical fancy and plenty of other things have as legitimate a role in criticism as the practical will or the discursive intelligence has. . . . (13–14)

In the *New Masses* Michael Gold expressed his endorsement of Arvin's observations. Criticizing both Hicks's piety as well as the abstruseness of Phillips and Rahv, he states: "One of the criticisms that needed to be made of our left-wing critics, however, has been on the score of their terrible mandarinism. . . . They perform academic autopsies on living books. They wax pious and often sectarian. Often they use a scholastic jargon no American could understand without a year or two of postgraduate study. Which of our critics shows his joy in battle and birth? Which of them breathes hard? They have squeezed most of the humanity out of the art of criticism" ("Papa Anvil" 22). Here he quotes Arvin's remarks on Hicks, Phillips, and Rahv, and describes his analysis as "the best critique I have seen in a long time . . . " ("Papa Anvil" 22).

Another source of irritation was the tone that was occasionally employed, particularly by Calmer and Farrell, in reviews of proletarian-revolutionary drama, fiction, and poetry. A year after his comments on amateur novelists, Calmer measured young revolutionary poets against the professional writer Archibald Macleish. Having been attacked in 1934 in the *New Masses* as "a kind of ur-Nazi" (Mather) because of disparaging remarks on Jews and revolutionaries in some of his writing, MacLeish had in the meantime explicitly come out against fascism. In 1936 Isidore Schneider reviewed his collection of poems *Public Speech* in the *New Masses*. Acknowledging the changes in MacLeish's political attitudes, he wrote a favorable review, describing him as "one of the most accomplished craftsmen in the whole range of English poetry" ("MacLeish" 21). While insisting on the essential correctness of much of the earlier political criticism of MacLeish, Schneider regretted its denunciatory tone.

Alan Calmer's review of *Public Speech,* which appeared two months later in the *Partisan Review,* differed from Schneider's in that it combined praise for MacLeish with criticism of proletarian poets. In the same supercilious manner that was evident in his earlier comments on amateur novelists he wrote: "Compared with MacLeish's new book most of the efforts of our younger proletarian poets loom rather small. . . . Anyone who has watched the emergence of the younger poets . . . must have noticed the lack of deep devotion to their craft, the absence of a profound sense of the integrity of their writing, which one finds in all of MacLeish's work. There are few evidences among them of a real determination to accept the discipline of their craft . . . " ("MacLeish" 20). He attributes this to the demands of the movement, as well as to "shortcomings in their own characters and abilities" ("MacLeish" 20).

In the article in the *Partisan Review and Anvil* in which Farrell accused Bertolt Brecht of "revolutionary snobbery," he also criticized Clifford Odets's play *Paradise Lost.* Odets had gained national attention with his one-act, agitprop piece *Waiting for Lefty,* which was initially produced under the auspices of the New Theatre League. The latter play was performed by workers theaters throughout the country, and was widely acclaimed by critics outside the movement. *Paradise Lost,* Odets's second attempt at a full-length drama after *Awake and Sing!,* dealt with the decline of a middle-class family, the members of which all suffer from one symbolic malady or another. The message of the play is that the declassed bourgeoisie, having been expelled from their former paradise, can only find redemption in a new social order.

As was the case with the Theatre Union's production of *The Mother,* the reception on the left was generally negative. In the *New Masses* Stanley Burnshaw found the characters unrepresentative and the conclusion contrived. Can the life of the middle class, he asked, "be truthfully conveyed by such symbols as sexual impotence, heart disease, sleeping sickness, barrenness and arson, larceny, racketeering, cuckoldry, feeble-mindedness, sex neurosis?" (" 'Paradise Lost' " 28). In addition, Burnshaw finds that "the final vision of a new social order is something tacked onto a structure where it does not belong, from which it has not organically developed." Nevertheless he praises the "stunning power and richness of the writing" as well as the "excitement" and "vitality" of individual scenes (" 'Paradise Lost' " 28).

There is little that Farrell says in his review that Burnshaw does not say. However, once again the tone of personal attack that marked his observations on *The Mother* emerges. In an ironical, introductory paragraph he notes: " . . . in a public speech Mr. Odets proved that Shakespeare, Bach, Beethoven, Walt Whitman, and Goethe were all propagandists, and that he himself was a propagandist; and he was hence able to draw the conclusion that he was in good company. I might, of course, compare Mr. Odets with Strindberg, but frankly I do not think that that would be an appropriate comparison, and I really do not think that there is a resemblance between Clifford Odets and Strindberg."[15] His evaluation of *Paradise Lost* is entirely negative, and ends with the remark: " . . . it is mistitled. It should be known to the world as *Lay Down and Die*."[16]

In the same article in which Michael Gold endorsed Newton Arvin's remarks on Phillips, Rahv, and Hicks, he responded to Farrell's review: "Mr. Farrell, in discussing *Paradise Lost,* the latest play by Clifford Odets, opens with a rather sour attack on Odets' personal character. He hints that Odets is vain and so forth. . . . Out of such prejudice . . . is it fair for a critic to say of another man's play, after he has attacked the man's character, that it was 'consistently, ferociously bad'?" ("Papa Anvil" 22). On the basis of this review and others by Farrell, Gold questions whether he has "the objectivity, fairness and generosity—let us add, common sense—to be a critic." It might be noted that Gold goes on to praise the rest of the issue in which Arvin's and Farrell's articles appeared, and declares that the *Partisan Review and Anvil* "deserves our interest and support" ("Papa Anvil" 22–23).

In regard to the *Partisan Review*'s attack on leftism in literary criticism, again it was less the editors' views that aroused hostility, than the manner in which they presented them. In discussing leftism they invariably pointed to others, when examples from their own writing would have served just as well. Their criticism of Hicks's remarks on the poets of the twenties, a year after they themselves had issued an editorial in which they came down on proletarian poets who were borrowing from the "bourgeois esthetic little magazines" ("Problems and Perspectives" 6), was only one instance. In the same editorial they mentioned Dos Passos and Horace Gregory as typical examples of wavering liberals friendly to the movement, and accused Marxist critics of opportunism for not helping them overcome their "backward views" ("Problems and Perspectives" 6).

Two years later in the *Partisan Review and Anvil,* Phillips included Dos Passos among "revolutionary novelists" whom he defended against unnamed "utilitarian" critics: " ... those revolutionary novelists ... who have been more faithful to the ethos of the American people than to the demands of the utilitarians on the 'left,' have often been criticized for not showing the 'way out.' Confusing political meanings with political pointers, these critics became the spokesmen for the most extreme literalisms. And it was not long before their formulas were in opposition to the more significant revolutionary novels." ("The Humanism" 18) At about the same time Phillips and Rahv published an article in which they described Gregory as a revolutionary writer whose work was free of leftism ("Private Experience" 104–5). In neither case was there any mention of their earlier criticism of these two writers or of their attack on other Marxist critics who, they had suggested, were pandering to Gregory and Dos Passos.

The lack of self-criticism among the editors of the *Partisan Review* was accompanied by the occasional tendency to attribute to themselves all advances in the campaign against leftism. Carried to an extreme in Farrell's book, *A Note on Literary Criticism,* it was also evident in an editorial on the Second National Conference of the John Reed Clubs, which was held in the Fall of 1934. At the first conference in 1932 leftism, in regard to relations with non-Communist, professional writers friendly to the movement, had been a major theme. In keeping with the principles formulated at Charkov, Freeman and Gold had attacked sectarianism and insisted that the clubs accomodate such writers. Among the younger participants in the movement who wanted to exclude them at that time was Philip Rahv. Some months after the First National Conference of the John Reed Clubs, A. B. Magil criticized Rahv's article, "The Literary Class War," as an example of the sectarianism that had to be overcome. In regard to leftism in proletarian literature and drama, criticism of tendentiousness and utilitarianism was widespread in the theater movement by the end of 1933. In the same year in the *New Masses,* Magil found fault with Grace Lumpkin's tendency toward "formal declarations" in her novel, *To Make My Bread* ("To Make My Bread" 20), while in the *Daily Worker* Joseph Freeman and Edwin Rolfe called on poets to avoid sloganizing. In his 1934 series, "Revolution and the Novel," Hicks also criticized tendentiousness, in the form of stereotyping and editorializing.

At the Second National Conference of the John Reed Clubs Magil again attacked "narrowness" and leftism, as did Alexander Trachtenberg and others (Johns 25). In the *Partisan Review* the editors' report on the conference related:

The other members of the writers' commission unanimously denounced the "leftist" character of some aspects of our young revolutionary literature. They condemned those practices in our work that lead fellow-travellers to think that they must become revolutionary-proletarian writers overnight. They directed a collective attack against writing which consists of unconvincing, sloganized tracts disguised as poetry and fiction. Together they showed that a living revolutionary literature could grow only out of genuine aesthetic recreation of the class struggle. ("National John Reed" 60)

Having criticized the liberalism of Dos Passos and Gregory just two issues before, the editors of the *Partisan Review* now describe the denunciation of leftism, not as the result of a long development within the whole international movement, but as evidence that "*Partisan Review* was exerting a wide influence among the young writers" ("National John Reed" 60).

The strong attack on leftism at the conference was accompanied by a proposal by Trachtenberg for an American Writers Congress and the establishment of a new type of writers organization. In fact in the two years that had elapsed since the First National Conference, the John Reed Clubs had failed to attract the increasing numbers of professional writers sympathetic to the Communist party. One of the most prominent of these, Malcolm Cowley, later described the atmosphere in the clubs that kept writers away. Every local branch, he related, had its "amateur politicians," some of whom "wanted to be young Robespierres intriguing for power and consigning their opponents to the scaffold" (*The Dream* 144). He quoted a memorandum that Joseph Freeman had written just before the first conference of the clubs: "Most of the people in the writers' group do not write and cannot write . . . ; they do not read; they do not know what is going on in the intellectual field and it is impossible to struggle with them on the basis of ideas. This is one of the reasons for the continual turmoil. The moment the struggle is settled on paper, it crops up again. . . ." (qtd. in *The Dream* 144)

By the time the American Writers Congress took place, in April 1935, the Party had withdrawn its support from the clubs, and most had already folded along with the magazines they had published. An exception was the *Partisan Review,* which combined with the *Anvil* and continued to appear until the end of 1936.

At the Congress the League of American Writers was set up, replacing the John Reed Clubs as the American section of the IURW. In contrast to the clubs the League was restricted to writers who had actually published, and was thus an organization of professionals. Those who supported this move no doubt felt that the Party was justified in diverting its resources from an organization in which sectarianism and leftism had seemed all but ineradicable. More often the transition to the League has been described as a high-handed abandonment of the rank and file of the proletarian literature movement. Terry Cooney, for example, writes that the "Party apparently intended to dump permanently those 'writers' who had not published" (80). Rideout conjectures that the "dissolution of the Clubs meant the destroying of part of the subliterary soil out of which future radical talent could have grown" (244).

However one evaluates the Communist party's cultural politics in the mid-thirties, the role played by the original *Partisan Review* is indisputable. While the editors did not originate the campaign against leftism, they did contribute significantly to it. With their increasingly harsh criticism of amateur proletarian writers between 1934 and 1936 and their unmistakable preference for the movement's more established writers, they did as much as anyone to provide ideological backing for the transition from the John Reed Clubs to the League of American Writers. In a long article in *International Literature* after the First American Writers Congress, Alan Calmer in fact specifically endorsed this move. Acknowledging the persistence of sectarianism within the clubs, he noted: " . . . the movement toward the left among American authors has proceeded so rapidly that all existing groups were found to be too narrow to encompass the varied activities of revolutionary culture in the U.S." ("A New Period" 75).

Considering the *Partisan Review*'s increasingly vehement antileftist stand, it was not surprising that the *Partisan Review*'s editors were approached in the Fall of 1936 with the proposal of making their magazine the organ of the League (Gilbert 153).

The New *Partisan Review* and the Reinterpretation of the Earlier Discussion over Leftism

The League's preconditions for affiliation were that the *Partisan Review* perform certain services for the organization and that two new members be added to the staff. At the same time, Rahv told Farrell, they were "vague about the immediate possibility of money" (qtd. in Cooney 98), so that Phillips and Rahv rejected the offer of making the *Partisan Review* the organ of the League.

By the time the new, revised *Partisan Review* went on the stands in December 1937, the political atmosphere had changed significantly since the early thirties, when Phillips and Rahv began their journalistic careers. New Deal reforms promised relief from the worst effects of the Depression, and revolution no longer seemed as imminent and inevitable as it had to some in the years immediately following the stockmarket crash. For many young, aspiring, socially critical writers, who might have turned to organizations such as the John Reed Clubs or the workers theaters a few years before, the Federal Writers and the Federal Theater Projects provided employment and the possible beginning of a career. Phillips and Rahv were themselves working for the Federal Writers Project in 1936 (Cooney 152).

Within the Communist party, cultural priorities had also shifted. While the emphasis at the First American Writers Congress had still been on revolution and proletarian literature, the Second Congress, in 1937, reflected the politics of the Popular Front, the focus being on the Spanish Civil War. In contrast to the first half of the thirties, when sympathetic non-Communist writers were approached for the purpose of drawing them into the proletarian literature movement, now the goal was mutual cooperation in a broad antifascist coalition. Thus, Archibald MacLeish was invited to the Second Congress as was Ernest Hemingway (Rideout 251).

The new political situation was also reflected in the *Daily Worker* and the *New Masses,* where more coverage was given to mainstream writers and popular culture. Nationalism having proven a powerful ideological weapon in the hands of the fascists, efforts concentrated on seeking out progressive trends in American history and culture and portraying Communism as their legitimate heir. In general there was more support for New Deal reform and less emphasis on revolution.

While the Popular Front succeeded for a time in uniting a wide spectrum of liberals and leftists, the process that would eventually lead to the almost complete isolation of the Communist party from American political and cultural life during the Cold War was already beginning. In 1938 the Dies Committee was formed—the predecessor of the House Un-American Activities Committee—and proceeded to investigate Communist influence in the Federal Theater Project. At the same time, signs of growing repression in the Soviet Union, as manifested in the Moscow trials, fostered an increasingly critical attitude toward the Soviet Union and the Communist party among many who had been sympathetic in the early thirties. By 1937 there was a sizeable number of left-wing intellectuals who had broken with the Communist party, but were not yet willing to disown their radical ideas. For many, Trotskyism became a halfway station on the way to reintegration into the mainstream of American political and cultural life, while the prospect of a slowly recovering economy offered hopes for renewed career possibilities.

It was against this background that Phillips and Rahv continued their search for financing, while pondering the direction that the revised *Partisan Review* would take. At the beginning of 1937 they considered an alliance with the Socialist party, which had merged with the Trotskyists in 1936 (Cooney 98–99). After they decided against this, money was finally provided by the artist George Morris, and a new editorial staff was formed. Its members included Dwight Macdonald, Mary McCarthy, former *New Masses* literary editor Frederick Dupee, as well as Phillips and Rahv (Cooney 106–107).

An editorial in the first issue of the new *Partisan Review* announced the magazine's intention to remain "revolutionary in tendency" but "unequivocally independent" ("Editorial Statement" 3). While there were no direct organizational ties to Trotskyism, the editors became increasingly supportive of Trotsky's ideas, and requested him to supply material for publication (Cooney 127). Over the following years, the Soviet Union, the Popular Front, and the cultural politics of the Communist party became frequent objects of the editors' ire, as polemics flew back and forth between themselves and the Communist press.

The tone of some of these exchanges is exemplified in an April 1938 essay, in which Phillips gave the following description of the earlier discussion over aesthetics in the proletarian literature movement:

> Up to about 1935, the communist literary movement, claiming to be the legitimate heir of every last nuance of Marx, sponsored two doctrines, under the slogans, "art is a weapon" and "build a proletarian literature." In fact it is these two notions, carried to their furthest implications, which most people thought to be Marxist criticism. And quite naturally so, for the Stalinist position in literature had all the militancy and subversiveness commonly identified with revolutionary thinking. Moreover it had the plausibility of baby-talk—was it not, therefore, a doctrine for the millions? The logic was simple. If society is divided into two principal classes, the bourgeoisie and the proletariat, argued the Stalinists, it follows that each class has its own art, and conversely, that art is so much advertising copy for the interests and the ideas of the class it serves. ("The Esthetic" 12)

The problem that now confronted the editors of the new magazine was how to reconcile this wholesale repudiation of the proletarian literature movement and the aesthetic theory that had developed around it, with the fact that the original *Partisan Review* had been one of the principal organs of the same movement. The solution was to construct a straw man—the orthodox, leftist *New Masses* approach to literature and aesthetics—and to portray their own role as a dissident one from the beginning. The opening editorial of the revised *Partisan Review* stated: "Formerly associated with the Communist Party, PARTISAN REVIEW strove from the first against its drive to equate the interests of literature with those of factional politics. ("Editorial Statement" 3)

The pattern had already been set in Farrell's *A Note on Literary Criticism*. In the months preceding the reissuing of the *Partisan Review* it emerged again in essays by Phillips, Rahv, and Calmer. In the *Saturday Review* Calmer claimed that *New Masses*' critics had promoted tendentiousness and utilitarianism and had disregarded native tradition. The development toward artistic quality and concreteness, he maintained, took place against their opposition. In the early thirties, he wrote, proletarian writers were encouraged to comprehend artistic values "chiefly in terms of immediate utility." In fiction the conversion ending was the rule, and much of the poetry consisted of "external, depersonalized composition." He describes the movement away from "wooden action," "platitudinous sermonizing" and "twisted wish-fulfillment" as a rebellion of young writers and critics against *New Masses* leftism:

> This new tendency, reflected in poetry, fiction, and criticism, constituted a reaction to what had become recognized as the official brand of proletarian literature. Soon the protest was directed not only against old practices but old practicioners. This revolt was inherent from the very start. The training of the hardy pioneers of revolutionary letters—Michael Gold, Joseph Freeman, and others—was opposed to the underlying literary aims of the young generation.... The young proletarian moved toward a discipline which endeavored to ... assert and deepen the native quality of modern American writing.... ("Portrait" 4)

In an essay published in Horace Gregory's anthology, *New Letters in America*, Phillips and Rahv made the same claims about *New Masses* criticism. Gold and Hicks, they stated, promoted utilitarianism and tendentiousness and disregarded the heritage. They were opposed by "the more conscious craftsmen in fiction and poetry," including Josephine Herbst and Henry Roth, and by "younger critics." In an obvious reference to themselves, they wrote: "As the novelty of this literature wore off, rifts and contradictions developed within Marxist criticism itself; and the younger critics stigmatized as 'Leftism' the passion for uniformity, the pious utilitarianism, and the contempt for tradition, that despite all protestations to the contrary, determined the mentality of the sectarian Marxists" ("Literature in" 172).

In 1939 in the *Southern Review,* Philip Rahv again addressed the question of leftism in the first half of the thirties. A large part of the article consists of criticism of the Communist party, which he claims was responsible for "the excesses and crudities" of proletarian literature:

> It is clear that proletarian literature is the literature of a party disguised as the literature of a class. This fact explains both the speed of its development and the speed of its disintegration. Its peculiar artificiality, the devious and volatile nature of its critical principles, its artistic chaos plus its political homogeneity and discipline, its uses as a cover for organizational activities—all these are explained by the periodic shifts and changes of the "party line." The growth of proletarian literature in this country between 1930 and 1935 is precisely coincident with the growth of the party during that period, when its policy was ultra-left and opposed to any united or people's fronts. At that time the party saw the revolution as an immediate possibility, and its literature was extreme in its leftism, aggressive, declamatory, prophetic. It was intolerant of all other schools of writing and proclaimed itself to be the sole heir of the literary creations of the ages. Its practicioners were persuaded by the party-critics to turn out sentimental idealizations of the worker-types they were describing in their stories and plays. These works, most of which were quite crude as literary art, presented a silly and distorted picture of America. ("Proletarian Literature" 623–24)

Rahv goes on to argue that, as a party literature, proletarian literature was necessarily utilitarian and devoid of artistic quality: "It is essential to understand the difference between the literature of a class and the literature of a party. Whereas the literature of a class represents an enormous diversity of levels, groupings, and interests, the literature of a party is in its very nature limited by utilitarian objectives. It cannot properly be called literature . . ." ("Proletarian Literature" 620). The final product of the movement was "an internationally uniform literature . . . whose main service was the carrying out of party assignments" ("Proletarian Literature" 620).

In his categorical dismissal of proletarian literature as party literature Rahv violated an important principle that the original *Partisan Review* had formulated in its remarks on Faulkner in 1935, namely that each work of literature had to be judged individually according to its "specific content," whatever the political affiliations of the author happened to be. Accusing Communist critics of tailoring their judgements to the current political situation, he himself now rejects a whole body of literature for which he still had much praise as late as 1936.[17]

Appearing in the *Southern Review,* Rahv's article, like Calmer's in the *Saturday Review,* was primarily addressed to largely uninformed outsiders for whom the credibility of the author rested on the fact that he had been an active participant in the movement he described. For Calmer and Rahv these articles served the purpose of scoring points against political opponents and creating the impression of continuity in their own position, whereas in fact they now repudiated much of what they had earlier stood for.

Whatever opinion one holds of the revised *Partisan Review*'s politics, the views expressed in the late thirties by Calmer, Phillips, and Rahv on proletarian literature and the discussion that had surrounded it bore little resemblance to positions they had propagated in the original *Partisan Review*. If there was one similarity between their later articles and the earlier ones on leftism, it was the tendency to point to others and to deny their own former involvement in what they later rejected.

Notes

1. Hicks's remarks appeared on page 28 in a subsection (entitled "Discussion") of Phillips and Rahv's article, "Criticism."
2. "Discussion" (see note 1) 30.
3. "Discussion" 29.
4. *Daily Worker Literary Supplement* 15 Mar. 1936: 10
5. *Daily Worker* 18 Apr. 1935: 5.
6. Nikulin was quoted in the *Daily Worker* 30 Oct. 1933: 5.
7. *Daily Worker Literary Supplement* 31 May 1936: 10.
8. Farrell's reviews appeared on March 19th, April 2nd, September 10th, November 5th and 10th.
9. *Daily Worker* 12 Nov. 1935: 5.

10. *New Masses* 19 Nov. 1935: 27–28.

11. "Theatre Chronicle," *Partisan Review & Anvil* Feb. 1936: 29.

12. Ibid.

13. *Daily Worker Literary Supplement* 18 Oct. 1936: 10.

14. Ibid. 12 Apr. 1936: 10.

15. "Theatre Chronicle," *Partisan Review & Anvil* Feb. 1936: 28.

16. "Theatre Chronicle," *Partisan Review & Anvil* Feb. 1936: 29.

17. See, for example, his and Phillips's favorable remarks on revolutionary poetry, p. 158.

Conclusion

CRITICISM of leftism in the proletarian literature movement in the mid-thirties was the culmination of a long process that began with the Proletcult controversy in the Soviet Union in the early twenties. At that time two principles were formulated that laid the groundwork for later developments. Rejecting Bogdanov's concept of proletarian culture as the spontaneous expression of a consciousness that could only be acquired through factory work, Lenin insisted on the importance of the bourgeois literary heritage and defined proletarian culture according to its Marxist orientation, rather than the subject matter or the class origin of the writer or artist.

In further defining the concept of proletarian literature the Central Committee of the Soviet Communist party in its 1925 statement, "On the Party's Policy in the Field of Literature," set the stage for later discussions over "utilitarianism." Describing worker-correspondence as an embryonic form, it called for a literature encompassing large forms, reflecting society in all its complexity from a Marxist viewpoint.

Pursuing this goal and formulating its aesthetic theory in conflict with rival groups such as the Proletcult and LEF, the RAPP developed the concepts of dialectical materialism and the living person. The groundwork was provided by Georg Plekhanov, whose writings on aesthetics had been influenced by Hegel's distinction between the methods of art and science, and by Marx and Engels's analysis of the relation between material base and ideological superstructure. Insisting on the unity of abstractness and concreteness, subjectivity and objectivity, reflection and praxis, the RAPP rejected most of what would later be defined as leftism in American proletarian literature: stereotyping, sloganizing and the conversion ending, as well as the demand that literature be narrowly agitational, addressing events of the moment. Again the importance of the heritage was emphasized, special value being placed on nineteenth-century realism. At the same time, leftism was evident in the group's politics. Tending to an all-or-nothing approach to proletarian literature, they engaged in vehement polemics against writers, including non-Communist "fellow travelers," who did not fulfill their aesthetic precepts.

As the proletarian literature movement spread to other countries, many of the same problems and issues arose elsewhere. In the *Linkskurve*—the organ of the German Bund proletarisch-revolutionärer Schriftsteller—positions similar to those of the Proletcult and LEF reemerged in 1929 and early 1930, as various contributors insisted that proletarian literature had to be by and about workers, elevated the agitational value to the sole criterion in judging individual works and blurred the distinction between imaginative literature and journalism, declaring worker-correspondence to be a form of proletarian literature. In addition, the attitude toward non-Communist writers was one of undifferentiated opposition.

Criticism of these positions and attitudes was initiated in March 1930 by the head of the agitprop department of the KPD's Central Committee, Joseph Winternitz, who insisted on the importance of the heritage and defined proletarian literature according to its ideological orientation, rather than the subject matter or the class origin of the writer. As in the 1925 statement of the Soviet Central Committee, he described worker-correspondence as an embryonic form, and called on proletarian writers to go beyond factory themes and to portray all of society from a Marxist viewpoint. Not only worker-writers, but also middle-class professionals, he insisted, were to be a source of the literature he envisioned.

Over the following months a BPRS member, Karl A. Wittvogel, presented a series of articles on aesthetics in which he closely approached the RAPP's theory of "dialectical materialism" and the "living person." The starting point in this case were writings of Franz Mehring, a contemporary of Plekhanov. At the Charkov Conference in November 1930 the sectarianism of the early *Linkskurve* was again criticized, while praise was expressed for the Wittvogel series. After the conference the central organization of the movement, the IURW, took an active part in the German discussion, supporting opponents of leftism. Georg Lukacs, an emissary of the IURW, summed up much of the discussion over aesthetics up to then in his article "Tendenz oder Parteilichkeit," which later appeared in English translation in the *Partisan Review*. His application of the results of that discussion in criticism of individual proletarian novels closely paralleled the criticism of leftism in American proletarian literature later on. Only on one issue did Lukacs differ from his counterparts in the United States: while he was emphatic in his rejection of modernism, a generally nondogmatic approach to this question persisted in the American movement throughout the thirties.

In confronting extreme antiliterary views within the Party, American Communist writers in the twenties first turned to writings of Upton Sinclair and V. F. Calverton in formulating their approach to proletarian literature and aesthetics. Rejection of one manifestation of leftism—the limitation of literary criticism to sociological analysis—began already in the mid-twenties. Going beyond sociology, writers such as Joseph Freeman, Moissaye Olgin and Michael Gold approached the RAPP's theory of dialectical materialism and the living person. At the same time, some of Gold's writings expressed views which were closer to those of the Proletcult and LEF. In general, far less attention was paid to aesthetic theory as such in the American movement than in the Soviet Union and Germany.

At the Charkov Conference leftist sectarianism in relations with sympathetic, non-Communist writers such as Upton Sinclair and John Dos Passos was criticized. After the conference Gold and Freeman worked toward the inclusion of such writers in the John Reed Clubs. Aesthetic theory, however, continued to be neglected in the *New Masses,* which eventually elicited criticism from the IURW.

Possibly in response to this, the *New Masses* published a long article by Anatole Lunacharsky on aesthetics in 1932, which contained positions that had been put forth in the magazine over the preceding years and anticipated the campaign against leftism. Thus he insisted on the importance of the heritage, in which he included modernists, and criticized excessive abstractness and mechanical materialism—the oversimplification of the connection between the socioeconomic base and the ideological superstructure.

Toward the end of the same year a major confrontation over leftism took place in the *New Masses.* On the one side was a member of the IURW executive council, A. B. Magil, while Philip Rahv was on the other. Quoting Lunacharsky's article as well as statements made at the Charkov Conference, Magil attacked Rahv's all-or-nothing attitude toward "fellow travelers" and his negative remarks on modernist writers.

The year 1932 witnessed a large-scale restructuring of cultural groups in the USSR. All the existing writers' organizations were dissolved, including the RAPP, and a proposal was made for the creation of a single organization of writers. These changes were accompanied by theoretical developments. Of particular importance were writings of Marx, Engels and Lenin on art and literature, some of which had been only recently discovered. On the basis of various of these writings the RAPP's sectarianism was attacked, with the argument that non-Communist, realistic writers were capable of grasping and portraying essential motive forces effecting social change and development, regardless of what their political sympathies might be. At the same time the RAPP's general approach to aesthetics was confirmed and eventually incorporated into the theory of socialist realism. The relevant writings of Marx, Engels, and Lenin were published in English in *International Literature* and played an important role in the American discussion over leftism.

By 1933 the growth of the American movement and the increasing participation of professionals provided the precondition for the fulfillment of the long-term goal of a broad proletarian literature and theater, encompassing large forms. At the same time the international rise of fascism made the demand for a quality literature and theater, addressing a large, varied audience, seem all the more imperative. The criteria that were applied in guiding the movement in this direction were derived from the distinction between art and science, which had formed the basis of the RAPP's theory and was likewise expressed in Marx's and Engels's writings on literature. In the workers-theater movement, critics like Nathaniel Buchwald and Harold Edgar criticized abstractness in characterization and dialogue, and called for living, believable persons. The same criteria were applied in criticism of proletarian literature in the *Daily Worker* and *New Masses*. Proceeding from the idea of reflection and praxis, Granville Hicks rejected a purely utilitarian approach to the proletarian novel. Like Lukacs in the *Linkskurve* he called for the great proletarian novel, reflecting all of society from a Marxist viewpoint, and urged writers to go beyond factory themes and avoid the tendentious distortion and coloring of reality.

Hicks's *New Masses* series, "Revolution and the Novel," was primarily intended, however, as an aid to writers rather than a theoretical treatise. After the establishment of the *Partisan Review* in early 1934, the magazine's editors addressed the question of aesthetics more systematically than the *New Masses*. Thus they succeeded in summarizing the results of the discussion up to then in a way that the other magazine had not, the most important influence being the letters of Marx and Engels which had been published in *International Literature* with commentaries by Franc Schiller. On the issue of modernism they remained within the spectrum of opinion that had been expressed in that magazine and in the American Communist press. The only new aspect of the *Partisan Review*'s attacks on leftism was the extension of the term to include tendentiousness and utilitarianism, the criticism of which had a long history in the proletarian literature movement by this time. It was not the content of their analyses that occasionally engendered hostility, but rather the manner in which they were presented: the tone of some of their criticism of proletarian writers, and the tendency to point to others when discussing the weaknesses of American Marxist literary criticism, while attributing to themselves all advances in the campaign against leftism.

When the *Partisan Review* was refounded in 1937, independent of the Communist party and sympathetic to Trotskyism, the former editors of the original *Partisan Review* assumed a generally hostile attitude toward the proletarian literature movement, eventually incorporating their criticism into a broad attack on Stalinism. Having to reconcile this with the fact that the original *Partisan Review* had been a principal organ of the same movement, they constructed a straw man—the leftist *New Masses*, Communist party approach to literature and aesthetics—and portrayed their own antileftist position as a dissident one from the beginning, which was only adopted opportunistically by the leadership of the movement in connection with the Popular Front.

Passed on from article to article and book to book since then, this description of the discussion over leftism in the proletarian literature movement in the United States in the mid-thirties has become widely accepted as established fact. It remains one of the most glaring misinterpretations in the writing of recent American literary history.

Bibliography

Aaron, Daniel. *Writers on the Left*. New York: Harcourt, 1961.

Abel, Lionel. *The Intellectual Follies: A Memoir of the Literary Venture in New York and Paris*. New York: Norton, 1984.

Adler, Robert. "Partisan Review Offers Splendid Congress Issue." *Daily Worker* 29 Apr. 1935: 5.

——. " 'The Shadow Before' Is Stirring Novel of Textile Mill Workers." Rev. of *The Shadow Before*, by William Rollins, Jr. *Daily Worker* 21 Apr. 1934: 7.

Albrecht, Friedrich, and Klaus Kändler. *Bund proletarisch-revolutionärer Schriftsteller Deutschlands 1928-1935*. Leipzig: VEB Bibliographisches Institut, 1978.

Alexandre, Laurie Ann. "The John Reed Clubs." MA-thesis. California University, 1977.

Anderson, Sherwood. *Beyond Desire* New York: Liveright, 1932.

Anisimov, Ivan. "The Films of Eisenstein." *Literature of the World Revolution* 1.3 (1931): 101-14.

Arbeitskollektiv "Proletarisch-revolutionäre Romane." Biographical information on Willi Bredel, appendixed to Bredel's novel *Rosenhofstrasse*. Berlin (West): Oberbaumverlag, 1974: 159-60.

Arvin, Newton. "A Letter on Proletarian Literature." *Partisan Review* Feb. 1936. 12-14.

Auerbach, Leopold. "The Speed of Self-disclosure." *Literature of the World Revolution* 1.2 (1931): 100-105.

——. "A Great Man and a Narrow Philistine." *Literature of the World Revolution* 2.2-3 (1932): 122-29.

"Authors' Field Day: a Symposium on Marxist Criticism." *New Masses* 3 July 1934: 27-32.

Barrett, William. *The Truants*. Garden City: Anchor, 1982.

Barth, Helmut, ed. *Zum Kulturprogramm des deutschen Proletariats im 19. Jahrhundert*. Dresden: VEB Verlag der Kunst, 1978.

Baxandall, Lee, comp. and ed. *Marxism and Aesthetics: A Selected Annotated Bibliography*. New York: Humanities, 1968.

——. "The Marxist Aesthetic Theory of Louis C. Fraina." *Proletarian Writers of the Thirties*. Ed. David Madden. London: Feffer, 1968. 194-221.

Becher, Johannes R. "Kühnheit und Begeisterung." *Linkskurve* May 1932: 1-11.

——. "Einen Schritt Weiter." *Linkskurve* Jan. 1930: 1-5.

Berman, Paul. "East Side Story: Mike Gold, the Communists and the Jews." *Radical America* 17.4 (1983): 39-53. Rpt. from March 1983 literary supplement of the *Village Voice*.

Bernstein, Irving. *The Lean Years.* Boston: Houghton, 1960.

Biha, Otto. "On the Question of Proletarian-revolutionary Literature in Germany." *Literature of the World Revolution* 1.4 (1931): 88–105.

——. "A Soldier and a Miner." *Literature of the World Revolution* 1.3 (1931): 135–38.

Blake, Ben. "The Drama of Scottsboro." Rev. of *They Shall Not Die,* by John Wexley. *New Masses* 26 June 1934: 26.

Blankfort, Michael, and Nathaniel Buchwald. "Social Trends in the Modern Drama." *American Writers Congress.* Ed. Henry Hart. New York: International, 1935. 128–34.

Bleiman, M. "Jules Romain and John Dos Passos." *International Literature* June 1934: 98–107.

Bloom, Alexander. *Prodigal Sons: The New York Intellectuals and Their World.* New York: Oxford, 1986.

Bodenheim, Maxwell. *Daily Worker* 3 July 1934: 5.

Bogardus, Ralph B., and Fred Hobson, eds. *Literature at the Barricades: The American Writer in the 1930s.* Tuscaloosa: University of Alabama Press, 1982.

Bonn, John [Bohn, Hans]. "Situation and Tasks of the Workers Theatres in the USA." *Workers Theatre* June–July 1932: 8.

Botka, Ferenc. "Der internationale Proletkult." *Internationale Literatur des sozialistischen Realismus 1917–1945.* Trans. Georg Lück. Eds. Klaus Kändler et al. Berlin DDR: Aufbau, 1978. 536–57.

Bredel, Willi. *Rosenhofstrasse.* 1931. Berlin (West): Oberbaumverlag, 1974.

Brown, Deming. *Soviet Attitudes Toward American Writers.* Princeton: Princeton University Press, 1962.

Brown, Edward J. *The Proletarian Episode in Russian Literature, 1928–32.* New York: Columbia University Press, 1953.

——. *Russian Literature Since the Revolution.* Cambridge: Harvard University Press, 1982.

Brüning, Eberhard. *Das amerikanische Drama der dreißiger Jahre.* Berlin DDR: Rütten, 1966.

Buchwald, Nathaniel. "The First International Olympiad of Revolutionary Theatres." *International Literature* Oct. 1933: 137–42.

——. "The Prize-Winners of the Spartakiade." *Workers Theatre* June–July 1932. Rpt. in Brooks McNamara and Mady Schuman, "Spartakiade." *Drama Review* Dec. 1973: 110–11.

——. "Workers' Theatre Movement Grows in Direction of More Popularity, Asserts Critic." *Daily Worker* 24 Jan. 1934: 5.

Bukharin [Bucharin], Nikolai. Excerpts from article in *Pravda* 12 Jan. 1927: n. pag. "Poetry and Common Sense." *New Masses* May 1927: 9–10. Trans. and Introduc. Joseph Freeman.

——. "Referat N. I. Bucharins über Dichtung, Poetik und die Aufgaben des dichterischen Schaffens in der UdSSR." Speech delivered on 28 Aug. 1934 at Soviet Writers Congress. Trans. Wenzel Götte. Rpt. in *Sozialistische Realismuskonzeptionen: Dokumente zum 1. Allunionskongreß der Sowjetschriftstel-*

ler. Eds. H. J. Schmitt and G. Schramm. Frankfurt am Main: Suhrkamp, 1974. 286–345.

Burke, Fielding [Dargan, Olive Tilford]. *Call Home the Heart.* New York: Longmans, 1932.

Burgum, Edwin Berry. "Faulkner's New Novel." Rev. of *The Wild Palms. New Masses* 7 Feb. 1939: 23.

Burnshaw, Stanley. " 'Paradise Lost': an Obituary." Rev. of *Paradise Lost,* by Clifford Odets. *New Masses* 11 Feb. 1936: 28.

——. Reply to Robert Gessner. "In Reply to Authors." *New Masses* 3 July 1934: 32.

——. "The Theatre Union Produces 'Mother.' " *New Masses* 3 Dec. 1935: 27–28.

Buttges, Dieter. *Der proletarische Roman in den Vereinigten Staaten von Amerika (1930–1935).* Meisenheim am Glan: Anton/Hain, 1977.

Caldwell, Erskine. Rev. of *Between the Hammer and Anvil,* by Edwin Seaver. *New Masses* 16 Mar. 1937: 20.

Calmer, Alan. "All Quiet on the Literary Front." *Partisan Review and Anvil* Mar. 1936: 12–13.

——. "Down with 'Leftism.' " *Partisan Review and Anvil* June 1936: 7–9.

——. "Early American Labor and Literature." *International Literature* Apr. 1934: 119–27.

——. "MacLeish and Proletarian Poetry." *Partisan Review and Anvil* May 1936: 19–21.

——. "A New Period in American Leftwing Literature." *International Literature* July 1935: 73–78.

——. "Portrait of the Artist as a Proletarian." *Saturday Review of Literature* July 1937: 3–4, 14.

——. "The Proletarian Short Story," *New Masses* 2 July 1935: 17–19.

——. "Reader's Report." *New Masses* 10 Sept. 1935: 23–24.

——. Reply to Edwin Seaver. *Daily Worker Literary Supplement* 15 Mar. 1936: 10.

Calverton, V. F. "The Need for Revolutionary Criticism." *Left* Spring 1931: 5–10.

——. *The Newer Spirit.* New York: Boni & Liveright, 1930.

Cantwell, Robert. "Outlook Book Choice of the Month" *New Outlook* Mar. 1934: 56–57.

Carter, Paul J. *Waldo Frank.* New York: Twayne, 1967.

"The Case of Clyde Griffiths." *Daily Worker* 7 Mar. 1936: 7.

Central Committee of the CPUSSR. "On the Party's Policy in the Field of Literature." Resolution of the Central Committee 18 June 1925. Trans. C. Vaughan James. Rpt. in *Soviet Socialist Realism: Origins and Theory.* C. Vaughan James. New York: St. Martin's, 1973. 116–19.

——. "On the Proletcults." Letter from the Central Committee *Pravda* 1 Dec. 1920: n. pag. Trans. C. Vaughan James. Rpt. in James. 113–15.

——. "On the Reformation of Literary-Artistic Organisations." Decision of the Central Committee 23 Apr. 1932. Trans. C. Vaughan James. Rpt. in James 120.

"The Charkov Conference of Revolutionary Writers." *New Masses* Feb. 1931: 6–8.

Christadler, Martin, and Olaf Hansen, eds. *Marxistische Literaturkritik in Amerika.* Darmstadt: Wissenschaftliche Buchgesellschaft, 1982.

Conroy, Jack. "A World Won." Rev. of *Seeds of Tomorrow,* by Mikhail Sholokov. *Partisan Review and Anvil* Mar. 1936: 30–31.

"Constitution of the League of Workers Theatres of USA." *Workers Theatre* June–July 1932: 14.

Cooney, Terry A. *The Rise of the New York Intellectuals: Partisan Review and Its Circle, 1934–1945* Madison: University of Wisconsin Press, 1986.

Cosgrave, Stuart. "Prolet-Bühne: Agit-prop in Amerika." *Performance and Politics in Popular Drama: Aspects of Popular Entertainment in Theatre, Film and Television 1800–1976.* Eds. David Bradby, Louis James, Bernard Sharrett. Cambridge: Cambridge University Press, 1980. 201–12.

Cowley, Malcolm. *The Dream of the Golden Mountains.* New York: Viking, 1964.

Dell, Floyd. Rev. of *Mammonart,* by Upton Sinclair. *Workers Monthly* May 1925: 326.

Dos Passos, John. "The Business of the Novelist." *New Republic* 4 Apr. 1934: 220.

——. Rev. of *Farewell to Arms,* by Ernest Hemingway. *New Masses* Dec. 1929: 16.

Dunbar, Robin. "Mammonart and Communist Art." *Daily Worker* 23 May 1925: n. pag.

——. "Maxim Gorky's Latest Thrill." Letter to the editor. *Daily Worker* 6 Sept. 1924: n. pag.

"Durchbruch der proletarischen Literatur." *Linkskurve* Feb. 1931: 1–4.

Eastman, Max. *Artists in Uniform.* 1934. New York: Farrar, 1972.

Editorial. *New Theatre.* Sept.–Oct. 1933: 3.

"Editorial Statement." *Partisan Review* Dec. 1937: 3–4.

Edgar, Harold. *Daily Worker* 25 Oct. 1933: 5.

——. *Daily Worker* 10 Nov. 1933: 5.

Eimermacher, Karl, comp. and ed. *Dokumente zur sowjetischen Literaturpolitik 1917–32.* Stuttgart: Kohlhammer, 1972.

Eisinger, Chester E. "Character and Self in Fiction on the Left." *Proletarian Writers of the Thirties.* Ed. David Madden. London: Feffer, 1968. 158–83.

Elias, Robert H. *Theodore Dreiser. Apostle of Nature.* Ithaca: Cornell University Press, 1948.

Elistratova, Anne. "New Masses." *Literature of the World Revolution* 2.1 (1932): 107–14.

Engels, Friedrich. Letter to W. Borgius. 25 Jan. 1894. Rpt. in *Marx/Engels/Lenin/über Kultur, Ästhetik, Literatur.* Ed. Hans Koch. Leipzig: Reclam, 1975. 31–34.

——. Letter to Paul Ernst. 5 June 1890. Trans. S. D. Kogan. *International Literature* Sept. 1934: 80–82.

——. Letter to Margaret Harkness. Apr. 1888. Rpt. in "Marx and Engels on Balzac." F. Schiller. *International Literature* July 1933: 113–14.

——. Letter to Minna Kautsky. 26 Nov. 1885. Trans. Jessie Lloyd. Rpt. (abridged) in "Friedrich Engels on Literature." F. Schiller. *International Literature* 3.2 (1933): 122–23.

——. Letter to Ferdinand Lasalle. 18 May 1859. Trans. S. D. Kogan. Rpt. in "Marx and Engels to Lasalle." *International Literature* Oct. 1933: 119–22.

Epstein. Speech delivered at Charkov Conference, Nov. 1930. Rpt. (abridged) in *Literatur der Weltrevolution* Sonderheft zur zweiten internationalen Konferenz revolutionärer Schriftsteller (1931): 181.

Ermolaev, Herman. *Soviet Literary Theories 1917–34.* Berkeley: University of California Press, 1963.

"Der erste Kongreß des IATB." *Arbeiterbühne und Film* [Berlin] July 1930: 15–17. Cologne: Gahme Henke, 1974.

Fadejew, Alexander. "Der Hauptweg der proletarischen Literatur." Speech delivered at All-Union Congress of Proletarian Writers, Moscow, 3 May 1928. Trans. Hannelore Freter. Rpt. in *Über Literatur.* Alexander Fadejew. Berlin DDR: Volk und Welt, 1973. 7–44.

——. "Über sozialistischen Realismus." *Literaturnaja Gazeta* 29 Oct., 11 Nov. 1932. Trans. H. Freter. Rpt. in *Über Literatur.* 45–57.

Fähnders, Walter, and Martin Rector. *Linksradikalismus und Literatur. Untersuchungen zur Geschichte der sozialistischen Literatur in der Weimarer Republik.* 2 vols. Reinbek bei Hamburg: Rowohlt, 1974.

Farrell, James T. *A Note on Literary Criticism.* New York: Vanguard, 1936.

——. Rev. of *Let Freedom Ring,* by Albert Bein. *New Masses* 19 Nov. 1935: 27–28.

——. "Theater Chronicle." *Partisan Review and Anvil* Feb. 1936: 28–30.

Fekete, Eva, and Eva Karádi, comps. and eds. *György Lukács: His Life in Pictures and Documents.* Trans. Péter Balabán. Budapest: Corvina Kiadó, 1981.

Fiedler, Leslie. "Henry Roth's Neglected Masterpiece." *Commentary* Aug. 1960. Rpt. in *The Collected Essays of Leslie Fiedler* Vol. 2. New York: Stein, 1971. 271–79.

Flury, Henry. Rev. of *Swann's Way,* by Marcel Proust. *New Masses* Mar. 1929: 16.

Folsom, Michael, ed. *Mike Gold: a Literary Anthology.* New York: International, 1972.

Fomina, W. A. *Die philosophischen Anschauungen G. W. Plechanows.* Trans. Nikolai Stscherbina. Berlin DDR· Dietz, 1977.

Freeman, Joseph. *An American Testament.* New York: Farrar, 1936.

——. "Bulgarian Literature or the Perfect Critical Method." *New Masses* Aug. 1927: 9–10.

——. *Daily Worker* 17 Nov. 1933: 5.

——. *Daily Worker* 20 Nov. 1933: 5.

——. *Daily Worker* 23 Nov. 1933: 5.

——. *Daily Worker* 27 Nov. 1933: 5.

——. "Letters from Sergei Dinamov." *Survey* Apr. 1965: 92–102.

——. "Literary Patterns." *New Masses* June 1929: 14–15.

——. "Notes on American Literature." *Workers' Monthly* Aug. 1928: 513–20.

——. "Poetry and Common Sense." *New Masses* May 1927: 9–10.

——. Rev. of *Chains,* by Henri Barbusse. *Workers' Monthly* Feb. 1926: 188–89.

——. "You Can Fight Here." Rev. of *You Can't Sleep Here,* by Edward Newhouse. *New Masses* 11 Dec. 1934: 25–26.

Friedrich, Gerhard. *Proletarische Literatur und politische Organisation: Die Litera-*

turpolitik der KPD in der Weimarer Republik und die proletarisch-revolutionäre Literatur. Frankfurt am Main: Peter D. Lang, 1981.

Gabor, Andor. "Über proletarisch-revolutionäre Literatur." *Linkskurve* Oct. 1929: 3–6.

——. "Zwei Bühnenereignisse." *Linkskurve* Nov.–Dec. 1932: 27–32.

Gallas, Helga. *Marxistische Literaturtheorie: Kontroversen im Bund proletarisch-revolutionärer Schriftsteller* Frankfurt am Main: Roter Stern, 1978.

Gassner, John. "Drama versus Melodrama." Rev. of *The Case of Clyde Griffiths,* by Erwin Piscator. *New Theatre* Apr. 1936: 8–10, 43.

Gelderman, Carol. *Mary McCarthy: a Life.* New York: St. Martin's, 1988.

Gessner, Robert. Statement in "Authors' Field Day." *New Masses* 3 July 1934: 29–30.

Gilbert, James Burkhardt. *Writers and Partisans: a History of Literary Radicalism in America.* New York: Wiley, 1968.

Gold, Michael [Granich, Irwin]. "America Needs a Critic." *New Masses* Oct. 1926: 7–9. Rpt. in *Mike Gold: a Literary Anthology.* Ed. Michael Folsom. New York: International, 1972. 129–139.

——. "American Intellectuals and Communism." *Daily Worker* 1 Dec. 1923: 5.

——. "American Jungle Notes." *New Masses* Dec. 1929: 8–10.

——. "A Barbaric Poem of New York." Rev. of *Manhattan Transfer,* by John Dos Passos. *New Masses* Aug. 1926: 25–26.

——. "O Californians, O Ladies and Gentlemen." *Gently Brother* Mar. 1924. Rpt. in *Mike Gold: a Literary Anthology.* 117–25.

——. *Change the World.* New York: International, 1937.

——. *Daily Worker* 30 Sept. 1933: 7.

——. *Daily Worker* 5 Oct. 1933: 5.

——. *Daily Worker* 12 Oct. 1933: 5.

——. *Daily Worker* 30 Oct. 1933: 5.

——. *Daily Worker* 29 Dec. 1933: 5.

——. *Daily Worker* 9 Feb. 1934: 5.

——. *Daily Worker* 11 June 1934: 5.

——. *Daily Worker* 14 June 1934: 5.

——. *Daily Worker* 18 Apr. 1935: 5.

——. *Daily Worker* 6 May 1935: 5.

——. *Daily Worker* 17 Oct. 1935: 5.

——. *Daily Worker* 5 Dec. 1935: 7.

——. *Daily Worker* 6 Dec. 1935: 9.

——. *Daily Worker* 10 Aug. 1937: 9.

——. Editorial. *New Masses* July 1928: 2.

——. "Go Left, Young Writers." *New Masses* Jan. 1929: 3–4. Rpt. in *Mike Gold: a Literary Anthology.* 186–89.

——. "Hemingway—the White-collar Poet." Rev. of *Men Without Women,* by Ernest Hemingway. *New Masses* Mar. 1928: 21. Rpt. in *Mike Gold: a Literary Anthology.* 157–61.

——. "In Foggy California." *New Masses* Nov. 1928: 10–12. Rpt. in *Mike Gold: a Literary Anthology.* 162–71.

——. *Jews Without Money.* New York: Liveright, 1930.

——. "Let It Be Really New!" *New Masses* June 1926: 20, 26.

——. Letter. *New Masses* Dec. 1929: 23.

——. "A Letter from a Clam Digger." *New Masses* Nov. 1929. Rpt. in *Mike Gold: A Literary Anthology.* 190–93.

——. "A Letter to the Author of a First Book." Rev. of *The Disinherited,* by Jack Conroy. *Daily Worker* 29 Jan. 1934: 7. Rpt. in *Change the World.* Michael Gold. New York: International, 1937. 215–20.

——. "Mr. Steffens Liked Everybody." *New Masses* June 1931: 5–6.

——. *New Masses* Dec. 1929: 6–8.

——. *New Masses* Apr. 1930: 3–4.

——. *New Masses* June 1930: 22.

——. "A New Program for Writers." *New Masses* Jan. 1930: 21.

——. "Notes of the Month." *New Masses* Sept. 1930: 4–5.

——. "Notes from Charkov." *New Masses* Mar. 1931: 4–6.

——. "Papa Anvil and Mother Partisan." *New Masses* 18 Feb. 1936: 22–23.

——. "The Stage No 'Critic' Knows." *New Masses* 27 Mar. 1934: 29.

——. "Stevedore." Rev. of *Stevedore,* by Paul Peters and George Sklar. *New Masses* 1 May 1934: 28–29.

——. "Three Schools of U.S. Writing." *New Masses* Sept. 1928: 13–14.

——. "Towards Proletarian Art." *Liberator* Feb. 1921: 20–24. Rpt. in *Mike Gold: A Literary Anthology.* 62–70.

——. "Wilder—Prophet of the Genteel Christ." *New Republic* 22 Oct. 1930: 266–67. Rpt. in *Mike Gold: a Literary Anthology.* 197–202.

Gopner, Serafina. "Speech of the Representative of the E.C.C.I." *Literature of the World Revolution* special Charkov issue (unnumbered) 1931: 85–93.

Gorbunow, Wladimir. *Lenin und der Proletkult.* Trans. Ruth Czichon and Ullrich Kuhirt. Berlin DDR: Dietz, 1979.

Goriely, Benjamin. *Les Poètes dans la Révolution Russe.* N.p.: Librairie Gallimard, 1934.

Gorsen, Peter, Eberhard Knödler-Bunte, and Bion Steinborn. Comps. and eds. "Proletkult: eine Dokumentation zur proletarischen Kulturrevolution in Rußland." *Ästhetik und Kommunikation* Reinbek bei Hamburg: Rowohlt Verlag, Feb. 1972: 63–201.

Gorzka, Gabriele. *A. Bogdanov und der russische Proletkult: Theorie und Praxis einer sozialistischen Kulturrevolution.* Frankfurt am Main: Campus, 1980.

Gregory, Horace, ed. *New Letters in America.* New York: Norton, 1937.

Günther, Hans. *Die Verstaatlichung der Literatur.* Stuttgart: J. B. Metzler, 1984.

Günther, Hans, and Karla Hielscher. *Marxismus und Formalismus.* Munich: Carl Hanser Verlag, 1973.

Gurko, Leo. *The Angry Decade.* New York: Dodd, 1947.

——. "John Dos Passos' USA." *Proletarian Writers of the Thirties.* Ed. David Madden. London: Feffer, 1968.

Hansen, Olaf. *Bewußtseinsformen literarischer Intelligenz.* Stuttgart: J. B. Metzler, 1977.

Hart, Henry, ed. *American Writers Congress.* New York: International, 1935.

Hayes, Alfred. "Fine Recreation of Immigrant Boy's Childhood." Rev. of *Call It Sleep,* by Henry Roth. *Daily Worker* 5 Mar. 1935: 5.

Hicks, Granville. "Characters and Classes" (Revolution and the Novel 4). *New Masses* 24 Apr. 1934: 23–25. Rpt. in *Granville Hicks in the New Masses.* Ed. Jack Alan Robbins. Port Wash.: Kennikat, 1974. 38–45.

——. Commentary on Dispute over *Man's Fate,* by Andre Malraux. *New Masses* 4 Sept. 1934: 28–30.

——. "The Crisis in American Criticism." *New Masses* Feb. 1933: 3–5. Rpt. in *Granville Hicks in the New Masses.* 5–14.

——. "The Dialectics of the Development of Marxist Criticism." Speech delivered at First American Writers Congress. Rpt. in *American Writers Congress.* Ed. Henry Hart. New York: International, 1935. 94–98.

——. "Drama and Biography as Models" (Revolution and the Novel 3). *New Masses* 17 Apr. 1934: 24–25. Rpt. in *Granville Hicks in the New Masses.* 33–45.

——. "The Future of Proletarian Literature" (Revolution and the Novel 7). *New Masses* 22 May 1934: 23–25. Rpt. in *Granville Hicks in the New Masses.* 59–66.

——. *The Great Tradition: an Interpretation of American Literature Since the Civil War.* New York: Macmillan, 1935.

——. "In Defense of James Farrell." *New Masses.* 14 July 1936: 23. Rpt. in *Granville Hicks in the New Masses* 106–9.

——. Letter to editor. *International Literature* 3.2 (1933): 129.

——. "Literary Criticism and the Marxian Method." *Modern Quarterly* Summer 1932: 44–47.

——. "The Novel and the Middle Class." *New Masses* 1 Jan. 1935: 41–42. Rpt. in *Granville Hicks in the New Masses.* 277–81.

——. "Of the World Revolution." *New Masses* 9 Jan. 1934: 26. Rpt. in *Granville Hicks in the New Masses.* 219–21.

——. "Our Magazines and Their Function." *New Masses* 18 Dec. 1934: 22–23.

——. *Partisan Review* Apr.–May 1935: 28–30.

——. "The Past and Future as Themes." (Revolution and the Novel 1). *New Masses* 3 Apr. 1934: 29–31.

——. "The Problem of Documentation" (Revolution and the Novel 6). *New Masses* 15 May 1934: 23–25. Rpt. in *Granville Hicks in the New Masses.* 53–59.

——. "Problems of American Fellow Travellers." *International Literature* 3.3 (1933): 106–109.

——. "Proust and the Proletariat." *New Masses* 20 Nov. 1934: 21–22. Rpt. in *Granville Hicks in the New Masses.* 206–9.

Homberger, Eric. *American Writers and Radical Politics, 1900–39: Equivocal Commitments.* London: Macmillan, 1986.

Howe, Irving. *A Margin of Hope: An Intellectual Autobiography.* San Diego: Harcourt, 1982.

Illes, Bela. "Report of the Secretariat of the I.B.R.L." *Literature of the World Revolution* special Charkov issue (unnumbered) 1931: 14–23.

———. "Vor dem Plenum der internationalen proletarischen Schriftsteller." *Linkskurve* Sept. 1930: 15–16.

James, C. Vaughan. *Soviet Socialist Realism: Origins and Theory.* New York: St. Martin's, 1973.

Jegorow, Oleg. "Die sozialistische Revolution und die internationalen proletarischen Literaturvereinigungen." *Literatur der Arbeiterklasse.* Berlin DDR: Aufbau, 1974. 204–37.

Johns, Orrick. "The John Reed Clubs Meet." *New Masses* 30 Oct. 1934: 25–26.

Johnson, Oakley. "The John Reed Club Convention." *New Masses* July 1932: 14–15.

Kändler, Klaus. *Drama und Klassenkampf.* Berlin DDR: Aufbau, 1967.

Kazin, Alfred. *On Native Grounds.* New York: Reynal, 1942.

Kempton, Murray. *Part of Our Time.* New York: Simon, 1955.

Kirpotin, V. "Fifteen Years of Soviet Literature." Report delivered on 29 Oct. 1932 at the Conference of the Organizational Committee of the All-Russian Union of Soviet Writers. Rpt. in *International Literature* 3.1 (1933): 141–46.

Kläber, Kurt. "An die Leser der 'Literarischen Welt.'" *Linkskurve* Aug. 1929: 24–28.

Klehr, Harvey. *The Heyday of American Communism.* New York: Basic, 1984.

Klein, Alfred. *Im Auftrag ihrer Klasse.* Berlin DDR: Aufbau, 1976.

Klein, Wolfgang. *Schriftsteller in der französischen Volksfront: Die Zeitschrift "Commune".* Berlin DDR: Aufbau, 1967.

Kline, Herbert. "Writing for Workers Theatre." *New Theatre* Dec. 1934: 22–23.

Knilli, Friedrich, and Ursula Munchow. *Frühes deutsches Arbeitertheater 1847–1918.* Munich: Hanser, 1970.

Koch, Hans. *Franz Mehrings Beitrag zur marxistischen Literaturtheorie.* Berlin DDR: Dietz, 1959.

Kraus, N. [Winternitz, Josef]. "Gegen den Ökonomismus in der Literaturfrage." *Linkskurve* Mar. 1930: 10–12. Rpt. in *Im Auftrag ihrer Klasse.* Alfred Klein. Berlin DDR; Aufbau, 1976. 652–655.

Krupnick, Mark. *Lionel Trilling: the Fate of Cultural Criticism.* Evanston: Northwestern University Press, 1986.

"Die Kulturrevolution und die zeitgenössische Literatur." Resolution des ersten Allunionskongreßes der proletarischen Schriftsteller im Anschluß an den Vortrag von L. Auerbach." *Na literaturnom Postu* July 1928: 1–11. Rpt. in *Dokumente zur sowjetischen Literaturpolitik 1917–32.* Ed. Karl Eimermacher. Stuttgart: Kohlhammer, 1972. 362–71.

Kurella, Alfred. Speech at Charkov Conference. Rpt. in *Zur Tradition der sozialistischen Literatur in Deutschland.* 261–63.

Landsberg, Melvin. *Dos Passos' Path to USA.* Boulder: Colorado Associated University Press, 1972.

Lasch, Christopher. *The Agony of the American Left.* New York: Knopf, 1969.

Leab, Daniel J. "'United We Eat': the Creation and Organization of the Unemployed Councils in 1930." *Labor History* 8.3 (1967): 300–15.

Lefèvre, Manfred. *Von der proletarisch-revolutionären zur sozialistisch-realistischen Literatur.* Stuttgart: Akademischer Verlag Hans-Dieter Heinz, 1980.

Leites, A. Excerpt from speech delivered at the Organization Committee of Soviet Writers in Spring 1933. *International Literature* Jan. 1934: 103–106.

Lenin, V. I. "Die Aufgaben der Jugendverbände." Address to Communist Youth League, 2 Oct. 1920. Rpt. in *Marx/Engels/Lenin: über Kultur, Ästhetik, Literatur.* Ed. Hans Koch. Leipzig: Reclam, 1975. 336–43.

———. "On Proletarian Culture." Resolution drafted on 8 Oct. 1920. Trans. from *Lenin on Art and Literature.* Moscow: Progress, 1970. Rpt. in *Soviet Socialist Realism: Origins and Theory.* C. Vaughan James. New York: St. Martin's, 1973. 112–13.

———. "Party Organisation and Party Literature." *Nóvaya zhizn'* 13 Nov. 1905. Trans. from *Lenin on Art and Literature.* Rpt. in *Soviet Socialist Realism . . .* 103–6.

"Lenin on Tolstoi." *International Literature* Dec. 1934: 85–92.

Lenzer, Rosemarie. "Abbild oder Bau des Lebens. Eine Debatte zur Literaturprogrammatik in der Sowjetunion der zwanziger Jahre." *Literarische Widerspiegelung: Geschichtliche und theoretische Dimensionen eines Problems.* Ed. Dieter Schlenstedt. Berlin DDR: Aufbau, 1981. 359–402.

Levine, Ira. *Left-Wing Dramatic Theory in the American Theatre.* Ann Arbor: UMI, 1985.

Lomidse, Georgi, and Leonid Timofejew. "Multinationale Sowjetliteratur. Literatur einer sozialistischen Gesellschaft." Trans. Anneliese Globig. Ed. Peter Kirchner. *Internationale Literatur des sozialistischen Realismus.* Ed. Klaus Kändler. Berlin DDR: Aufbau, 1978. 107–65.

Long, Terry. *Granville Hicks.* Boston: Twayne, 1981.

Lorenz, Richard, ed. *Proletarische Kulturrevolution in Sowjetrussland (1917–21): Dokumente des "Proletkult."* Trans. Uwe Brügmann and Gert Meyer. Munich: Deutscher Taschenbuch Verlag, 1969.

Ludington, Townsend. "Friendship That Won't Stand." *Literature at the Barricades.* Eds. Ralph Bogardus and Fred Hobson. Tuscaloosa: University of Alabama Press, 1982. 46–66.

Lukacs, Georg. "Aus der Not eine Tugend." *Linkskurve* Nov.–Dec. 1932: 15–24.

———. "On Socialist Realism." *International Literature* 9.4–5 (1938): 88–90.

———. "Reportage oder Gestaltung?" 1. *Linkskurve* July 1932: 23–30.

———. "Reportage oder Gestaltung?" 2. *Linkskurve* Aug. 1932: 26–31.

———. "Tendenz oder Parteilichkeit?" *Linkskurve* June 1932: 13–21. Published in abridged form as "Propaganda or Partisanship?" Trans. Leonard Mins. *Partisan Review* Apr.–May 1934: 36–46.

———. "Willi Bredels Romane." *Linkskurve* Nov. 1931: 23–27. Rpt. in *Im Auftrag ihrer Klasse.* Alfred Klein. Berlin DDR: Aufbau, 1976. 719–27.

Lumpkin, Grace. *To Make My Bread.* New York: Macaulay, 1932.

Lunacharsky, Anatole. "Lenin und die Kunst." *Chudoshnik i Sritel* No. 2/3 (1924). Trans. Leon Nebenzahl. Rpt. in *Vom Proletkult zum sozialistischen Realismus.* Anatoli Lunatscharski. Berlin DDR: Dietz, 1981. 142–47.

———. "Marxism and Art." Original title and date not given. Trans. Joseph Freeman. *New Masses* Nov. 1932: 14–16.

———. "Problems of the Soviet Theatre." Speech delivered at the second plenary session of the Organization Committee of the All-Russian Union of Soviet Writers. Trans. S. D. Kogan. *International Literature* 3.3 (1933): 88–96.

——. *Die Revolution und die Kunst: Essays, Reden, Notizen*. Trans. Franz Leschnitzer. Dresden: VEB Verlag der Kunst, 1974.

——. "Thesen über die Aufgaben der marxistischen Kritik." *Na literaturnom Postu* No. 11/12 (1928). Trans. Franz Leschnitzer. Rpt. in *Vom Proletkult zum sozialistischen Realismus*. 165–78.

——. "Unsere Aufgaben im Bereich der schönen Literatur." Stenogramm des Vortrags im Verlagsaktiv vom *Zemlja i fabrika* 28 Oct. 1929. *Dokumente zur sowjetischen Literaturpolitik 1917–32*. Ed. Karl Eimermacher. Stuttgart: Kohlhammer, 1972. 391–92.

——. *Vom Proletkult zum sozialistischen Realismus: Aufsätze zur Kunst der Zeit*. Ed. A. Jermakowa. Trans. Franz Leschnitzer et al. Berlin DDR: Dietz, 1981.

Madden, David, ed. *Proletarian Writers of the Thirties*. London: Feffer, 1968.

Magil, A. B. "Pity and Terror." *New Masses* Dec. 1932: 16–18.

——. "Red Front, Comrade Renn!" *New Masses* 13 Feb. 1934: 16–17.

——. "To Make My Bread." Rev. of *To Make My Bread*, by Grace Lumpkin. *New Masses* Feb. 1933: 19–20.

Marx, Karl. Letter to Ferdinand Lasalle. 19 Apr. 1859. Trans. S. D. Kogan. *International Literature* Oct. 1933: 117–19.

Marx/Engels/Lenin über Kultur, Ästhetik, Literatur. Ed. Hans Koch. Leipzig: Reclam, 1975.

Mather, Margaret Wright. "Der Schöne Archibald." Rev of *Poems 1924–1933*, by Archibald MacLeish. *New Masses* 16 Jan. 1934: 26.

McNamara, Brooks, and Mady Schuman "Spartakiade." *Drama Review* Dec. 1973: 99–112.

Mehring, Franz. "Ästhetische Streifzüge." *Neue Zeit* 1898. Rpt. in *Franz Mehring Werkauswahl*. Ed. Fritz Raddatz. Darmstadt: Luchterhand, 1975: 30–140.

——. "Kunst und Proletariat." 1. 1896. Rpt. in Raddatz: 16–23.

——. "Kunst und Proletariat." 2. 1898. Rpt. in Raddatz: 24–29.

——. "Der heutige Naturalismus." *Volksbühne* Jan. 1893: 9–12. Rpt. in Raddatz: 12–15.

Mirsky, D. S. "James Joyce." Trans. S. D. Kogan. *International Literature* Apr. 1934: 92–102.

Mittenzwei, Werner. *Brechts Verhältnis zur Tradition*. Berlin DDR: Akademie, 1976.

——. *Der Realismus-Streit um Brecht*. Berlin DDR: Aufbau, 1978.

"National John Reed Club Convention." *Partisan Review* Nov.–Dec. 1934: 60–61.

Neets, J. Q. [Kunitz, Joshua]. "Upton Sinclair and Thornton Wilder." *New Masses* May 1930: 18.

Nössig, Manfred, Johanna Rosenberg, and Bärbel Schrader. *Literaturdebatten in der Weimarer Republik*. Berlin DDR: Aufbau, 1980.

North, Joseph. "Theatre Union's 'Black Pit.'" Rev. of *Black Pit*, by Albert Maltz. *New Masses* 2 Apr. 1935: 42–43.

Ol'chovyj, B. "Für eine klare Parteilinie im Bezug auf die Führung der proletarischen Literatur." *Pravda* 20 Oct. 1929. Rpt. in *Dokumente und Analysen zur sowjetischen Literaturpolitik 1917–1932.* Ed. Karl Eimermacher. Stuttgart: Kohlhammer, 1972. 389–91.

Olgin, Moissaye. "First Choice of New Book Union Is a Comprehensive Anthology of Proletarian Literature of High Order." Rev. of *Proletarian Literature in the United States. Daily Worker* 10 Oct. 1935: 5.

——. "For a Workers' Theatre" 1. *Daily Worker Supplement* 2 Apr. 1927: 4.

——. "For a Workers' Theatre" 2. *Daily Worker Supplement* 9 Apr. 1927: 4.

——. " 'Mother': the Theatre Union's New Play." Rev. of *The Mother*, by Bertold Brecht. *Daily Worker* 22 Nov. 1935: 5.

Pells, Richard. *Radical Visions and American Dreams: Culture and Social Thought in the Depression Years.* New York: Harper, 1973.

Phelps, Wallace [Phillips, William]. "The Methods of Joyce." *New Masses* 20 Feb. 1934: 26.

——. "Poetry Journal Maintains High Selective Level." *Daily Worker* 28 May 1935: 5.

Phelps, Wallace, and Philip Rahv. "Criticism." *Partisan Review* Apr.–May 1935: 16–25.

——. "Problems and Perspectives in Revolutionary Literature." *Partisan Review* June–July 1934: 3–10.

Phillips, Robert, ed. *The Letters of Delmore Schwartz.* Princeton: Ontario, 1984.

Phillips, William. "The Esthetic of the Founding Fathers." *Partisan Review* Mar. 1938: 11–21.

——. "The Humanism of Andre Malraux." *Partisan Review and Anvil* June 1936: 16–19.

——. *A Partisan View.* New York: Stein and Day, 1983.

——. "Stalinism of the Right." *Partisan Review* 52.3 (1985): 167–71.

Phillips, William, and Philip Rahv. "Literature in a Political Decade." *New Letters in America.* Ed. Horace Gregory. New York: Norton, 1937. 170–80.

——. "Private Experience and Public Philosophy." *Poetry* May 1936: 98–105.

Pike, David. *German Writers in Soviet Exile, 1933–1945.* Chapel Hill: University of North Carolina Press, 1982.

——. *Lukacs and Brecht.* Chapel Hill: University of North Carolina Press, 1985.

Piscator, Erwin. "Piscator Describes Combination of Cinema and Stage Technique." *Daily Worker* 8 Mar. 1936: 6.

Pizer, Donald. "James T. Farrell and the 1930s." *Literature at the Barricades.* Eds. Ralph Bogardus and Fred Hobson. Tuscaloosa: University of Alabama Press, 1982. 187–203.

Plechanow [Plekhanov], Georgi W. "Die französische dramatische Literatur und die französische Malerei des 18. Jahrhunderts vom Standpunkt der Soziologie." *Pravda* Sept.–Oct. 1905: 49–70. Trans. Joseph Harhammer. Rpt. in *Kunst und Literatur.* G. W. Plechanow. Berlin DDR: Dietz, 1955. 172–197.

——. "Die Kunst und das gesellschaftliche Leben." *Sowremennik* Nov. 1912: 290–304, Dec. 1912: 108–22, Jan. 1913: 130–61. Trans. Joseph Harhammer. Rpt. in *Kunst und Literatur.* 230–96.

——. "Vorwort zur dritten Auflage des Sammelbandes 'Zwanzig Jahre.' " 1908. Rpt. in *Kunst und Literatur* 219–229.

Poore, Carole Jean. *German-American Socialist Literature in the Late Nineteenth Century.* Diss. University of Wisconsin, 1979. Ann Arbor: Xerox Microfilms, 1980.

Proletarian Literature in the United States. Eds. Granville Hicks et al. New York: International, 1935.

"Proletarian Poetry and Music in the Soviet Union." *Literature of the World Revolution* 1.2 (1931): 107–108.

Raddatz, Fritz, ed. *Franz Mehring Werkauswahl.* Darmstadt: Luchterhand, 1975.

Radek, Karl. Speech delivered on 24 Aug. 1934 at First Soviet Writers Congress. Trans. Rudolf Hermstein. *Sozialistische Realismuskonzeptionen: Dokumente zum 1. Allunionskongreß der Sowjetschriftsteller.* Eds. H. J. Schmitt and G. Schramm. Frankfurt am Main: Suhrkamp, 1974. 140–213.

Rahv, Philip. "'International Literature' Grows in Popularity among American Workers, Writers." *Daily Worker* 22 Jan. 1934: 5.

——. "'Land of Plenty' Sets New Standards for Revolutionary Novel." Rev. of *Land of Plenty,* by Robert Cantwell. *Daily Worker* 14 May 1934: 5.

——. "The Literary Class War." *New Masses* Aug. 1932: 7–10.

——. "Marxist Criticism and Henry Hazlitt." *International Literature* June 1934: 112–16.

——. "New Standards for Short Story Form Set by Caldwell." Rev. of "Kneel to the Rising Sun," by Erskine Caldwell. *Daily Worker* 19 June 1935: 5.

——. "The Novelist as Partisan." *Partisan Review* Apr.–May 1934: 50–53.

——. "An Open Letter to Young Writers." *Rebel Poet* Sept. 1932: 3–4.

——. "Proletarian Literature: a Political Autopsy." *Southern Review* Spring 1939: 616–28.

——. Rev. of *Scottsboro Limited,* by Langston Hughes. *Rebel Poet* Aug. 1932. 7.

——. "T. S. Eliot." *Fantasy* Winter 1932: 17–20.

——. "Valedictory on the Propaganda Issue." *Little Magazine* Sept.–Oct. 1934. 1–2.

Die Redaktion der *Linkskurve.* Reply to Maxim Vallentin. *Linkskurve* Apr. 1930: 16–17.

"Resolution on Political and Creative Questions." *Literature of the World Revolution* special Charkov issue (unnumbered) 1931: 85–92.

Rev. of *Call It Sleep,* by Henry Roth. *New Masses* 12 Feb. 1935: 27.

Rhodes, Peter C. "Modern Goya." *Daily Worker Supplement* 22 Aug. 1937: 10.

Richter, Trude. Letter. *Linkskurve* Mar. 1932: 27–29.

Rideout, Walter. *The Radical Novel in the United States 1900–1954.* Cambridge: Harvard University Press, 1956.

Robbins, Jack Alan, ed. *Granville Hicks in the New Masses.* Port Washington: Kennikat, 1974.

Rolfe, Edwin. *Daily Worker* 13 Oct. 1933: 5.

Rollins, William, Jr. "The Collective Novel." Rev. of *And Quiet Flows the Don,* by Mikhail Sholokov. *Partisan Review* Sept.–Oct. 1934: 59–61.

——. "The Gastonia Trial." *New Masses* Oct. 1929: 3–4.

——. *The Shadow Before.* New York: McBride, 1934.

——. "What Is a Proletarian Writer?" *New Masses* 29 Jan. 1935: 22–23.

Salzman, Jack. "Hoover, Maltz and the Literary Left." *Journal of Human Relations.* Fall 1967: 37–50.

Schevill, James. *Sherwood Anderson: His Life and Work.* Denver: University of Denver Press, 1951.

Schiller, Franc. "Engels against Mechanicism and Vulgarization of Marxism in Literary Criticism." Trans. S. D. Kogan *International Literature* Sept. 1934: 80–89.

——. "Friedrich Engels on Literature." Trans. Jessie Lloyd. *International Literature* 3.2 (1933): 122–28.

——. "Marx and Engels on Balzac." Trans. H. Scott. *International Literature* 3.3 (1933): 113–24.

Schmitt, Hans-Jürgen, and Godehard Schramm, eds. *Sozialistische Realismuskonzeptionen: Dokumente zum 1. Allunionskongreß der Sowjetschriftsteller.* Trans. Wenzel M. Götte et al. Frankfurt am Main: Suhrkamp, 1974.

Schneider, Isidore. "MacLeish and the Critics." Rev. of *Public Speech,* by Archibald MacLeish. *New Masses* 24 Mar. 1936: 21–22.

——. " 'Partisan Review,' New John Reed Club Organ, Hailed as Achievement." *Daily Worker* 8 Feb. 1934: 5.

——. "Sectarianism on the Right." Rev. of *A Note on Literary Criticism,* by James T. Farrell. *New Masses* 23 June 1936: 23–25.

Schrader, Bärbel. "Aufbruch in ein neues Zeitalter." *Literaturdebatten in der Weimarer Republik.* Eds. Manfred Nössig et al. Berlin DDR: Aufbau, 1980. 9–220.

Schwartz, Lawrence. *Marxism and Culture: the CPUSA and Aesthetics in the 1930s.* Port Washington: Kennikat, 1980.

Seaver, Edwin. "Caesar or Nothing." *New Masses* 5 Mar. 1935: 21.

——. *Daily Worker Sunday Supplement* 31 May 1936: 10.

——. *Daily Worker Sunday Supplement* 18 Oct. 1936: 10.

——. "Realism and Abstraction in Contemporary Art." *Daily Worker* 15 July 1937: 7.

——. Rev. of *The Trial,* by Franz Kafka. *Daily Worker* 25 Oct. 1937: 7.

——. "Socialist Realism." Rev. of *Problems of Soviet Literature: Reports and Speeches at the First Soviet Writers' Congress. New Masses* 22 Oct. 1935: 23–25.

Sebastian, John. "Charles Ives at Last." *New Masses* 7 Feb. 1934: 30–31.

Sekretariat des IVRS. *Literatur der Weltrevolution* special Charkov issue (unnumbered) 1931: 15–26.

Shukotoff, Arnold. "Proletarian Short Stories." *New Masses* 3 Jan. 1939: 22–23.

Siegel, Holger. *Sowjetische Literaturtheorie (1917–1940).* Stuttgart: Metzler, 1981.

Simons, Elisabeth. "Der Bund proletarisch-revolutionärer Schriftsteller Deutschlands und sein Verhältnis zur Kommunistischen Partei Deutschlands." *Literatur der Arbeiterklasse.* Berlin DDR: Aufbau, 1974. 118–90.

Sinclair, Upton. *Mammonart.* Westport, Conn.: Hyperion, 1925.

Slonim, Marc. *Soviet Russian Literature: Writers and Problems 1917–77.* New York: Oxford University Press, 1977.

Smiley, Sam. *The Drama of Attack: Didactic Plays of the American Depression.* Columbia: University of Missouri Press, 1972.

Smith, Vern. "Soviet Authors in 'Daily' Interview Tell What Writers' Congress Achieved." *Daily Worker* 24 Sept. 1934: 5.

"Soviet Literature and Dos Passos." *International Literature* 3.5 (1933-34): 103-112.

Starr, Alvin. "Richard Wright and the Communist Party: the James T. Farrell Factor." *CLA Journal* Sept. 1977: 44-47.

"Statutes of the Union of Soviet Writers of the USSR." *International Literature* July 1934: 166-68.

Steffen, Erich. "Die Urzelle proletarischer Literatur." *Linkskurve* Feb. 1930: 8-9. Rpt. in *Im Auftrag ihrer Klasse*. Alfred Klein. Berlin DDR: Aufbau, 1976. 649-52.

Stieg, Gerald, and Bernd Witte. *Abriß einer Geschichte der deutschen Arbeiterliteratur*. Stuttgart: Klett, 1973.

Strachey, John. "Fascism and Culture." *International Literature* Sept. 1934: 90-110.

Swanberg, W. A. *Dreiser*. New York: Scribner, 1965.

Taylor, Karen Malpede. *People's Theatre in Amerika*. New York: Drama Book Specialists, 1972.

"To Depict a New Kind of Man is the Rare Destiny of Soviet Writers, Says Ilya Ehrenbourg Addressing Writers Congress." *Daily Worker* 27 Sept. 1934: 5.

Trachtenberg, Alexander. "Revolutionary Literature." *Daily Worker* 1 July 1935: 5.

——. "Revolutionary Literature: Partisan Review and Proletarian Literature." *Daily Worker* 11 Mar. 1936: 7.

Troschenko, E. "Marx on Literature." Trans. S. D. Kogan *International Literature* Mar. 1934: 138-48.

Trotski, Leon. *Literatur und Revolution*. Trans. Frida Rubiner. Vienna: Verlag für Literatur und Politik, 1924.

Vallentin, Maxim. "Agitpropspiel und Kampfwert." *Linkskurve* Apr. 1930: 15-16.

Vishnevsky, A. Excerpt from speech delivered at the Organization Committee of Soviet Writers, Spring 1933. *International Literature* 3.5 (1933-34): 106-110.

Vorse, Mary Heaton. "The Feeling of a Strike." Rev. of *The Shadow Before*, by William Rollins, Jr. *New Masses* 17 Apr. 1934: 26.

Wald, Alan. *James T. Farrell: The Revolutionary Socialist Years*. New York: New York University Press, 1978.

——. *The New York Intellectuals: The Rise and Decline of the Anti-Stalinist Left from the 1930s to the 1980s*. Chapel Hill: University of North Carolina Press, 1987.

——. *The Revolutionary Imagination: The Poetry and Politics of John Wheelwright and Sherry Mangan*. Chapel Hill: University of North Carolina Press, 1983.

——. "Revolutionary Intellectuals: *Partisan Review* in the 1930s." *Literature at the Barricades*. Eds. Ralph Bogardus and Fred Hobson. Tuscaloosa: University of Alabama press, 1982. 187-203.

Webster, Grant. *The Republic of Letters*. Baltimore: Johns Hopkins University Press, 1979.

"Wege und Formen der Entwicklung des Arbeitertheaters in den kapitalistischen Ländern." *Arbeiterbühne und Film* [Berlin] Nov. 1930: 8-11. Cologne: Gaehme, Henke, 1974.

Weiss, Edgar. "Die sozialistischen deutschen Schriftsteller in ihrem Verhältnis zur sowjetischen Literaturentwicklung in der Periode 1917–1933." *Literatur der Arbeiterklasse.* Berlin DDR: Aufbau, 1974. 291–311.

Whitfield, Stephen J. *A Critical American: The Politics of Dwight Macdonald.* Hamden, Conn.: Archon, 1984.

Wicks, M. "Bourgeois Intellectuals and Communism." *Daily Worker* 12 Jan. 1924: 5.

Wilson, Edmund. *The Shores of Light.* New York: Farrar, 1952.

Wittvogel, Karl A. "Zur Frage einer marxistischen Ästhetik." 7 pts. *Linkskurve* May–Nov. 1930. Rpt. *Zur Frage einer marxistischen Ästhetik.* K. A. Wittvogel. Cologne: Kölnkalkverlag, 1973.

Wolf, Joseph. "Portrait of the Artist as a Child." Rev. of *Call It Sleep,* by Henry Roth. *Partisan Review* Apr.–May 1935: 95–96.

Zetkin, Clara. "Erinnerungen an Lenin." *Arbeiterliteratur* [Vienna] 1.1–2 (1924): 69–81. Berlin (West): LitPol, 1977.

Zur Theorie des sozialistischen Realismus. Eds. Hans Koch et al. Berlin DDR: Dietz, 1974.

Zur Tradition der sozialistischen Literatur in Deutschland: eine Auswahl von Dokumenten. Berlin DDR: Aufbau, 1962.

Index

A Note on the Author

JAMES MURPHY teaches English at the Freie Universität in Berlin. His articles have appeared in the journals *Gulliver, Dollars & Träume,* and *The Nation.*